T0355201

Democracy

Democracy

A Guided Tour

JASON BRENNAN

OXFORD
UNIVERSITY PRESS

OXFORD
UNIVERSITY PRESS

Oxford University Press is a department of the University of Oxford. It furthers
the University's objective of excellence in research, scholarship, and education
by publishing worldwide. Oxford is a registered trade mark of Oxford University
Press in the UK and certain other countries.

Published in the United States of America by Oxford University Press
198 Madison Avenue, New York, NY 10016, United States of America.

Library of Congress Cataloging-in-Publication Data
Names: Brennan, Jason, 1979– author.
Title: Democracy : a guided tour / Jason Brennan.
Description: New York : Oxford University Press, [2023] |
Includes bibliographical references and index.
Identifiers: LCCN 2022045722 (print) | LCCN 2022045723 (ebook) |
ISBN 9780197558812 (hardback) | ISBN 9780197558836 (epub) |
ISBN 9780197558843 (ebook) | ISBN 9780197558829
Subjects: LCSH: Democracy—Philosophy. | Democracy—Moral and ethical aspects. |
Political science—Philosophy. | Democracy—History.
Classification: LCC JC423 .B7836 2023 (print) | LCC JC423 (ebook) |
DDC 321.801—dc23/eng/20221117
LC record available at https://lccn.loc.gov/2022045722
LC ebook record available at https://lccn.loc.gov/2022045723

DOI: 10.1093/oso/9780197558812.001.0001

1 3 5 7 9 8 6 4 2

Printed by Sheridan Books, Inc., United States of America

Contents

Preface and Acknowledgments

This book provides a guided, curated tour of the major arguments in philosophy, political science, and economics for and against democracy over the past 2,500 years.

I'm not a neutral observer. But I got where I am by considering the options and the arguments for and against those options.

I've written at great deal about the various pathologies and shortcomings of democracy. At the same time, I'm in a way a fan of democracy. (I often joke I'm its truest fan, because a true fan admits when a band has a bad album or an institution has flaws.) Democracy is perhaps the best political system we've tried so far, but it has serious issues. I hope that readers can come away from this book understanding the promises and perils of democracy. I especially hope that they can see that the issues are not simple. Too often, democracy's defenders ignore its problems or evade them by mouthing platitudes about how the problems of democracy can be solved with more democracy, or that any dysfunctional real-world democracy is not true democracy anyway.

Instead, I hope readers see that institutional design is difficult. In the real world, we cannot rely on our good intentions. Translating abstract principles of justice into functional institutions means understanding how real-world actors will respond to the often perverse incentives our institutions create. If we care about justice, we don't throw up our hands and say, "That's not real democracy!" We acknowledge the problems and look for feasible solutions.

This is a history of thought book written for the kinds of people who are not interested in the history of thought for the sake of the history of thought. For historians of philosophy, the action is often

viii   PREFACE AND ACKNOWLEDGMENTS

in clarifying the most obscure passages from long-dead theorists, drawing out their implicit but unstated views on topics, or puzzling over whether translating a word this way or that way affects our understanding of the theorists' views. Sometimes, historians are tempted to argue that philosophers famous for arguing X really mean not X.

That's not my interest here. (Indeed, that's one reason I mostly stick to public domain, open-access translations of philosophers when quoting them.) I want readers to examine arguments from the past that are interesting not because they are from the past, but because they continue to shine light on democracy today. In this case, we should read what Plato and Aristotle said not because Plato and Aristotle said it, but because we should be concerned with the issues they raised.

At the same time, we live in a golden age of democratic theory. We have better data and better research methods than those that came before us. We can see farther not merely because we stand on their shoulders, but because we have better eyes and a bigger world to look at. For that reason, every chapter will bring readers up to current work. Debates about democracy did not end in, say, 1848 when there were hardly any democracies. Much of the best work in the history of thought appeared in the last seventy or even twenty years.

Writing a book like this is a bit like trying to curate a "best of" album for the Beatles. Sure, there are some things that absolutely must be included—such as "Yesterday" or Plato's *Republic*—but then after getting the obvious hits, we have lots of options for filling out the rest. I *must* discuss Plato, Aristotle, Rousseau, de Tocqueville, and John Stuart Mill, but it's largely optional whether and how much I cover, say, Diderot, Montesquieu, Schmitt, or Nietzsche. Of course, just as with compiling a best-of album for the Beatles, reasonable people will disagree about which songs are "necessary" and "optional." Even if this book were three times the length, I would have to make choices.

I want to thank Lucy Randall, my editor at Oxford University Press, for suggesting I write this book. Thanks to Jessica Flanagan and Christopher Freiman for their continued help as I sounded off various ideas about what to say, how to cover it, and how to frame issues. This was especially valuable as I wrote this book during the isolation of the COVID-19 pandemic. Thanks to multiple referees for their assistance. Thanks also to the countless philosophers, political scientists, and economists whom I've learned from over the years, many of whom are cited and discussed throughout the text.

1

Democracy

Why or Why Not?

For and Against

Democracy is both an obvious and dubious idea.

Here's why democracy is an obvious idea: for most of history, most governments divided people into the few who rule and the many who obey. The few then used the state to advance their own private interests at the expense of the many. Rulers were less like noble protectors appointed by God and more like intestinal parasites. The obvious solution is to eliminate the distinction between those who rule and those who obey. Make every citizen *both* a ruler and a subject of that rule. This ensures government promotes everyone's interests.

Thus, democracy is the best form of government. It's too bad it took most of civilized history to realize this—and too bad that the world isn't more democratic than it is.

Here's why democracy is a dubious idea. Government decisions are high stakes. It decides matters of war and peace, prosperity and poverty, freedom or oppression. Yet we let incompetent people steer the ship of state. Most voters are ignorant and process what little information they have in biased and irrational ways. They fall prey to propaganda and demagogues. They are conformists and don't even try to vote their interests. Democracy is the political equivalent of drunk driving.

Thus, democracy is a defective form of government. Democracy is a method by which the masses shoot themselves in their feet.

Democracy. Jason Brennan, Oxford University Press. © Oxford University Press 2023.
DOI: 10.1093/oso/9780197558812.003.0001

Philosophy students often start essays by writing, "Since the dawn of time, humanity has pondered. . . ." In this case, these arguments and concerns are old, if not dawn-of-time old. We find laypeople, pundits, social scientists, and philosophers making these two arguments today. But in ancient Athens, Socrates, Plato, and Aristotle said similar things.

Today, many Westerners assume that democracy is not only the best form of government, but also the *only* legitimate form. Yet, at the same time, most admit that democracy as we find it has serious problems. (Most of these problems, they'll add, could be fixed if only their favorite party had uncontested power.)

For most of Western history, the word "democracy" was pejorative. Aristotle used the term "democracy" to refer to the degenerate or deviant form of the rule of the many. Today, you can still find smug AP US history students saying, "The United States is a *republic*, not a democracy." Here, speakers insist on using the word as it was used in the 1700s, where "democracy" connoted something like the unconstrained tyranny of the majority.

But today in the West the word "democracy" also often connotes an unassailable ideal. People tend to presume that *of course* we ought to have democracy. The only interesting questions are which *form* of democracy is best or how much of life should be subject to democratic control.

Democracy is so ascendant an ideal that non-democratic countries pretend to be democratic. In 1936, Hitler held a sham referendum asking citizens whether they favor the German occupation of the Rhineland and Nazi rule. On paper, the 1936 Soviet Constitution vested the supreme power of the state in a national legislature elected through "universal, direct, and equal suffrage by secret ballot," with voting rights extended to all women and ethnic minorities.[1] But the USSR was not democratic in 1986 under Gorbachev, let alone under Stalin. Today dictators or semi-dictators—such as Indonesia's Suharto, Egypt's Mubarak, or Russia's Putin—host rigged elections. In the countries where the people have little power, the people with power nevertheless proclaim that the people empowered them.

How things have changed! Back in the day, Louis XIV, Genghis Khan, Darius and Xerxes, and Muhammed felt no compunction to pretend that they derived their authority *from* their subjects. Their right to rule came from God, from birth, or from the sword.

Despite democracy's ascendant status, many scholars believe democracy is in decline. The Economist Intelligence Unit, the research division of the group that publishes the *Economist* magazine, produces an annual Democracy Index that rates countries on a 1–10 scale from least to most democratic. Freedom House, a US government–funded research organization, produces a similar ranking. Both hold that the total number of democracies dropped over the past twenty years. In 2020, about 70 percent of the countries in the Democracy Index received a lower overall score.[2] In 2017, the *Economist* downgraded the United States from a "full democracy" to a "flawed democracy," though you might wonder whether this reflects partisan disdain for Trump.[3]

Political theorists call this phenomenon "democratic backsliding." Around the world, large populist movements are unhappy with democracy. People believe that their democratic governments are too slow and inefficient. They believe their democracies are captured by insiders and bureaucrats who promote elite interests but ignore the masses. The people's response to these perceived problems is surprising: to ensure the system represents the people better, they should install a strongman and remove constraints on his power. In practice, populism leads to authoritarianism, not democracy.[4]

Why do people think all these ways? Why do such contradictory ideas appeal to so many, and often to the same people? This book offers part of the answer. My goal is to give you a guided tour of the best and most important arguments for and against democracy over time. I want you to understand why a reasonable person might think democracy is the ideal form of government and that all the problems of democracy can be fixed with more democracy. I also want you to understand why a reasonable person might think democracy has built-in flaws that must be contained, or why democracy is simply bad. I want you to see why a reasonable person might think democracy is the end of history, and why a reasonable person might think the era of democracy should give way to something better.

How to Value Democracy

We value different things in different ways.

Consider how we value hammers. We regard hammers as tools. We don't value them for their own sake, but because they help us accomplish our goals. The point of a claw hammer is to pound in or remove nails. A good hammer must be good for us as we are. A hammer fit for a giant or superhero might be a bad hammer for people like us. No one would insist on using a hammer when a different tool, like a wrench, is more effective. No one would insist on using a poor-quality hammer when a better-quality hammer is easily available.

Consider how we value paintings. A painting might be useful the way a hammer is. For instance, you could swat flies with a Matisse, or you could sell it. But we also typically care about *who* made the painting. If Picasso scribbles on a napkin, the napkin is worth $50,000; if I make identical scribbles on a napkin, the napkin is ruined. We also care about what the painting symbolizes or expresses, or how it makes us feel. Paintings are valuable because of their genesis and because of what they express.

Consider how we value people. Like hammers, people can be useful. Like paintings, we care about who made them or what they express. But we also tend to say that people are ends or values in themselves.

When it comes to democracy, the debate is not merely over what value democracy has, but how democracy should be valued. Perhaps democracy is instrumentally valuable, the way hammers are. That is, maybe one way to judge democracy (and its competitors) is by asking whether democracy is useful, for real people like us, as a mechanism for delivering independent values. Maybe democracy is good because it tends to make wise decisions that track the independent truth about what justice requires. Maybe it tends to promote freedom, equal outcomes, the rule of law, general economic prosperity, good culture, tolerance, or some other values. Maybe it is good not because it makes smart decisions, but because it tends to avoid terrible decisions. Or maybe not. As we will see, many of the arguments about the value or disvalue of democracy concern things like this.

Perhaps democracy is valuable the way the paintings are. For instance, many people think that democratic decisions are rendered good and just because of who made them; democratic decisions are right because *we* decided them. In their view, if we the people vote to cut taxes, that makes it right to do so, but if a benevolent dictator had imposed that very same tax cut upon us for the same reasons, it would not be just or right. Or, many people think that what makes democracy good is not that it *produces* equal outcomes, but that it *expresses* the idea that we are all equal. On this view, having a democracy is like having a banner declaring "All people matter the same!" As we will see, many of the arguments about the value or disvalue of democracy concern issues like these.

Perhaps democracy is valuable as an end in itself, just as people are. Still, if people are ends in themselves, there must be *something* about people that makes them ends in themselves, some feature that people have that makes their lives have inherent value. (For what it's worth, philosophers have surprising difficulty explaining what this feature or set of features might be.)[5] Perhaps it is because human beings are moral agents, or can reason, or have free will, or whatnot. (If so, the philosopher Peter Singer asks, what about the human beings—such as the severely disabled, infirm, or very young—who aren't moral agents, cannot reason, or who lack free will?)[6] Similarly, if democracy is an end in itself, or if it is inherently just and good, there must be some feature of democracy that makes it so. Perhaps it is because it is fair, equal, or free. (But what if it's not?)

As we will see, philosophical disagreements about the value of democracy are often about *how* to value democracy. Is it instrumentally useful, symbolically valuable, an end in itself, and/or are democratic decisions good simply because the right people made them the right way?

The Sixth Grade Model of Democracy

Disagreements about the value of democracy often rest not disagreements about moral principles but on empirical disputes about how democracy functions. In my experience, most citizens, journalists, college students, and so on in the United States and Western Europe tend to share the same basic model of how democracy works. They share this model because they learned it in civics courses around sixth grade. Thus, let's call this the sixth-grade model.

First, the sixth-grade model holds that citizens know their own interests, values, and concerns. The model doesn't posit that everyone is selfish. People might care about the local or distant poor, about the future or past, about high-level values like tradition or low-level values like the price of milk. But the important starting point is that people care about things and understand their own values.

Second, the model holds that because citizens want to promote their values through politics (and other means), they learn how the world works. They discover what politics can and can't accomplish, and how. They learn how the economy functions, what the government can do, what sorts of laws could be implemented, and what sorts of results those laws might have. They learn the relevant facts and some of the social scientific knowledge needed to understand those facts or predict what causes what. Citizens thus adopt what we might call, non-pejoratively, an "ideology," by which I mean an organized and largely coherent set of political principles. At the very least, they form somewhat stable preferences about what policies they want to see implemented. These ideologies result from a combination of citizens' values plus their beliefs about how the world works. Some citizens become conservative, some left-wing, some authoritarian, some centrist, some libertarian, and so on.

Third, citizens use elections and other occasions for participation as means to implement their preferred types of policies. They thus examine the different political parties and candidates on the menu. They support the candidates and parties they think will best realize their values. Sometimes this means voting for a candidate who shares their ideology, but sometimes—if that candidate has no chance of winning—they vote for the second- or third-best option with a better shot.

At the same time, political parties and politicians want to win. They recognize that to win, they need votes, and to get votes, they need to push the policies the people want.

Political parties compete for votes the way tech companies compete for dollars. Thus, what voters want determines what the parties offer and try to do.

Because of this, after an election takes place, the winning candidates tend to share, and try to implement the values, policy preferences, and ideologies of their supporters. Lawmakers pass new laws, regulations, and policies that reflect citizens' overall ideological preferences, or at least reflect a kind of compromise among their disparate preferences. Lawmakers will respond to the goals and preferences of the many, if not literally all.

According to the sixth-grade model, democracy disciplines winning lawmakers because they know the next election is coming. Just as Apple wants you to be a repeat customer, so do the Social Democrats or Nationalists. Politicians know that come the next election, citizens will evaluate how well they performed. If candidates failed to keep their promises, did a bad job, were corrupt and unethical, or if the policies they implemented (even if the people wanted them) produced bad results, citizens will vote them out. (The technical term for this behavior is "retrospective voting.")

This is perhaps the most common and widely shared empirical model of how democracy works today. It models democracy as a kind of market, so this model makes democracy seem appealing the way that markets seem appealing. Democracy is a form of trade and exchange by other means. People know their interests, and democracy enables people to get what they want.

Over the course of this book, we will examine how this kind of model arose. Some philosophers and social scientists think it is more or less correct, while others think nearly every piece of it is mistaken. But perhaps more interesting and surprising is that many of the arguments for and against democracy have nothing to do with this model at all.

Five Big Values

When people advocate democracy—even if they think democracy is an end in itself—they value it for a reason. There must be some underlying value that democracy promotes, realizes, or instantiates that explains why democracy is good or just. In this book, I will focus on five values that figure most prominently in the most important historical texts. These five values get the most discussion and seem to be something that everybody—not just professional theorists—cares about. These values are stability, virtue, wisdom, liberty, and equality.

Regarding *stability*, I have in mind questions and concerns like this: Will the government collapse into civil war? How can we give people enough stake in their government to ensure that they get along with each other and go along with the rules? Will there be constant factionalism and internal conflict? Will our governments go to war with other governments, or will we have peace? Will people be willing to follow and respect the law, or will they resist it because they see it as an imposition?

Regarding *virtue*, I have in mind questions like these: Does democracy tend to make people morally better or worse? Does it encourage them to become active, intelligent, benevolent, and upright, or to become passive, stupid, selfish, or venal? Will it enhance or demote their character?

Regarding *wisdom*, I have in mind questions like these: Does democracy make smart or good choices? Does democratic decision-making tend to track objective or procedure-independent facts about which policies are efficient, effective, just, or good? What counts as a smart choice? Are there any external standards by which to judge the quality of democratic decisions, or are democratic decisions good simply because they are democratic? Can democracy make smart choices even if most citizens are badly informed, tribalistic, and/or irrational? Does democracy tend to promote prosperity or demote it? If we want to produce good outcomes, how much democracy is optimal, and can too much democracy be a bad thing?

Regarding *liberty*, I have in mind questions like these: What is freedom, and will democracy promote or demote it? Does democracy increase or reduce citizens' ability to lead the lives they want to lead? Will government be a mechanism by which dominate others, or can democracy instead prevent such domination? Is participating in government itself a way of being autonomous or free? Does democracy merely promote freedom or is democracy itself a form of freedom? In democracy, am I forced to obey rules set by others, or does democracy somehow ensure I am bound only by laws I set for myself?

Regarding *equality*, I have in mind questions like these: Is democracy good because it is fair, or because it makes people equal in some important way? Is it right that there should be no division between who rules and who obeys, even if some people are smarter, more competent, or more virtuous than others? Should democracy produce equal outcomes, or is it sufficient that it has equal inputs? How should democracy cope with actual inequalities that grant some people more de facto power than others? What should democracy do about persistent minorities who, while nominally equal, have no real power?

Over the next ten chapters, I will present the best or most important historical arguments for and against democracy in terms of these ten values. Each value will get a pair of chapters. The first chapter will be a guided tour of arguments holding that democracy realizes or enhances that value, the second will examine skeptical and critical arguments to the contrary.

You might notice these values and concerns are interrelated. For instance, the chapters on virtue will focus on how democracy affects the virtue of its citizens, including their intellectual virtue. But immediately afterward, we will examine the question of whether democratic institutions as a whole tend to make wise decisions. This is different question from—but closely related to—the question of whether democracy makes individual citizens more or less wise. Does the wisdom of the crowd depend upon the wisdom of the individual members of that crowd, or might democracy be wise even if most individual citizens are not wise? Similarly, concerns about freedom and equality are closely related. If some people oppress other people, that evinces a lack of freedom. But perhaps political inequality is the mechanism behind such oppression—people oppress others *because* they have differential levels of power. The solution, some say, is equal power.

This book is a historical guided tour of arguments for and against democracy. Thus, in each chapter, I begin somewhere in the West's intellectual past and move toward the present day. Further, one reason I start with values like stability and virtue but end with freedom and equality is that people in the past tended to be more concerned with the former, while people today tend to be more concerned with the latter. Indeed, today you see few philosophers writing about stability, but earlier theorists who had lived through civil wars, world wars, bloody revolutions, and conquests were deeply concerned about it.[7] Intellectual historians get something right: what we consider important often depends on our historical contexts.

What Is Democracy?

Political theorists fight about what counts as "real democracy." These debates about "real democracy"—about the best way to define the word "democracy"—are often ways of masking a normative disagreement about which form of democracy is best.

Definitions should facilitate discussion, not inhibit it. For the purposes of this book, I will work with a wide concept of "democracy," as many political philosophers, economists, and political scientists now do. Consider this basic definition from philosopher Thomas Christiano: a democratic society is "a society in which all or most of the population has the opportunity jointly to play an essential if not always very formative role in the determination of legislation and policy."[8] Elsewhere, Christiano elaborates more:

> To fix ideas, the term "democracy" . . . refers very generally to a method of group decision making characterized by a kind of equality among the participants at an essential stage of the collective decision making. Four aspects of this definition should be noted. First, democracy concerns collective decision making, by which I mean decisions that are made for groups and that are binding on all the members of the group. Second, this definition means to cover a lot of different kinds of groups that may be called democratic. So there can be democracy in families,

voluntary organizations, economic firms, as well as states and transnational and global organizations. Third, the definition is not intended to carry any normative weight to it. It is quite compatible with this definition of democracy that it is not desirable to have democracy in some particular context. So the definition of democracy does not settle any normative questions. Fourth, the equality required by the definition of democracy may be more or less deep. It may be the mere formal equality of one-person one-vote in an election for representatives to an assembly where there is competition among candidates for the position. Or it may be more robust, including equality in the processes of deliberation and coalition building. "Democracy" may refer to any of these political arrangements. It may involve direct participation of the members of a society in deciding on the laws and policies of the society or it may involve the participation of those members in selecting representatives to make the decisions.[9]

Some things to note here. We can talk intelligently about "democracy" in the workplace, among friends making decisions about what to eat, about decisions for where the family will take their next vacation, and so on. However, this book will focus on *political democracy*, that is, democracy in *government*.

Following the philosopher Gregory Kavka, let's define a "government" as the subset of a society that claims a monopoly on the legitimate use of coercion, and that has coercive power sufficient to maintain that monopoly.[10] Governments are entities that claim the right to make rules, to enforce those rules with coercion and threats of violence, and to stop others from making similar rules. They also claim that when they make rules, other people are supposed to obey them.

Political democracy, then, means that at certain essential and important stages of government decision-making, (almost) all the people subject to those decisions have a right and a real opportunity to participate in some way as equals, with no distinctions or ranking among them.

Christiano also notes that on this definition, democracy is not stipulated to be good. By analogy, consider the difference between "murder" and "killing." It makes sense to ask whether a particular instance of killing was wrongful, but not whether murder is. Murder is by definition wrongful killing. Thus, on Christiano's definition, it is an open question whether democracy is good or bad, functional or dysfunctional, just or unjust.

Further, Christiano intentionally uses a broad definition that leaves open when and how the people participate in democracy, and that leaves open how the democratic government is structured. A democracy might be big or small. It might meet frequently or infrequently. It might have separated powers with checks or balances, or it might not. The people might decide some issues themselves, some decisions might be made by their representatives, some decisions might be made by people appointed by their representatives, and so on. Representatives or decision makers might be chosen by votes or through sortition (random lotteries). Votes or decisions might involve structured deliberation or not. Elections might be more or less frequent. There could be a bicameral, unicameral, or some other kind of legislature. Maybe laws are written the way Wikipedia is written. There could be unitary executive with lots of power or not. There might be judicial review of legislation or independent bureaucracies, or not. They might have first-past-the-fence voting, Condorcet voting, proportional representation, or some other voting mechanism. There might be constitutional bills of rights or strong constitutional restrictions on the scope of government power, or not. Political participation might be optional or compulsory.

Like Christiano, I define "democracy" broadly such that all these variations count as different *kinds* of democracy. That way, instead of having sneaky arguments about whether, say, judicial review is democratic, we can focus on the real issue, which is whether judicial review is just and good. What makes a polity democratic or undemocratic is determined fundamentally by *who* rules, but this leaves open *how* or *what* they rule.

Still, as Christiano himself admits, the problem with his definition is that as a matter of fact, no actual government has full equality in any decision-making stage. Some countries succeed more than others. But none is fully equal.

Part of the problem is that every government of the people must decide who counts as "the people." As the philosopher Claudio López-Guerra notes, most contemporary democratic countries exclude children (even if they are informed and capable of voting well), the mentally impaired, convicted felons, and long-term resident aliens.[11] We like to say that in democracies, all people subject to a political decision should have an equal say in it, but it's not true. Democracies do not allow foreigners greatly affected by their decisions to vote. The 2003–2011 Iraq War affects Iraqis more than Americans, but Iraqis had no vote on whether or how the US would conduct the war or who US leaders will be. Australia's immigration restrictions affect anyone who might want to move there, but foreigners have no say. And so on.

Relatedly, most countries divide citizens into congressional or parliamentary voting districts, but this usually means that some citizens' votes count more than others. A Wyomingite has greater representation in Congress and a more powerful vote for president than I do as a Virginian.

Even when by law certain people are supposed to have equal power, in practice, they almost never do. In most democracies, rich, attractive, well-connected, intelligent, and well-spoken people born to prestigious families have a much better chance of winning and holding power than others. Your chances of being elected or holding power are higher if you are a member of the ethnic and religious majority. Privileged people generally find it easier to vote, advocate for their interests, acquire the information needed to vote well, form political coalitions, and so on.[12]

So, Christiano's definition is a broad umbrella meant to cover all sorts of possible variations of democracy. At the same time, we recognize that actual democracies are never fully equal. This is one reason why theorists are so tempted to say, "That's not *real* democracy" whenever something goes wrong in a real democracy.

Words Change Meaning over Time

"Democracy" was a pejorative term throughout most of Western history. To call a political system democratic was to call it disorganized, unstable, and unchecked. Before the mid-1800s, people who defended widespread suffrage and contested elections—people we would call democrats today—would instead say they advocate a "republic," a "polity," or a "constitutional government," or that they favor "liberal republican democracy" rather than "pure democracy." (Here, a "liberal republic" is supposed to signify a government in which the people have voting rights, but their own and government officials' powers are constrained by constitutional measures that are meant to ensure the government recognizes and protects people's freedom of religion, speech, lifestyle, and economic choices.) Today, though, to call a government democratic is to praise it. Indeed, political theorists love to say that "democracy is an essentially contested concept"; that is, what counts as democracy is itself a political debate that can never be settled.[13]

Words change meaning over time. For instance, the philosopher David Hume wanted to introduce the "experimental" method into philosophy. What he meant by "experimental" back then is what we mean by "observational" today; he was not referring to what we would now call "experiments."[14] It's interesting that the word "experiment" meant something different in 1740 than it does today, but if we want to understand Hume's arguments, the important issue is to note the change in meaning and move on.

Similarly, Alexander Hamilton, James Madison, and Aristotle used the word "democracy" to mean a degenerate, unconstrained form of the rule of the many. If you had a political system with universal suffrage, but in which there were checks and balances on majority rule, they would label that a "republic" instead. The important thing is to note they used the word differently from how we do now, and then move on.

Today, philosophers, political scientists, and economists tend to use the word "democracy" as an umbrella term to refer to all the various forms of government in which, in one way or another, fundamental political power is spread (nearly) equally among (nearly) all the people subject to it. It's interesting that people use the same word in different ways at different times, but if we care about understanding arguments, the important thing is to note the change and to be clear about what we mean when we talk.

What Kind of Guided Tour?

This is (mostly) a philosophical investigation of democracy. As the philosopher Robert Nozick says, philosophers love arguments more than they love wisdom per se. Indeed, he jokes that philosophers seem to want to produce "arguments so powerful they set up reverberations in the brain: if a person refused to accept the conclusion, he *dies*."[15] (Nozick himself practices a gentler mode of philosophy.)

Arguments are series of statements that attempt to establish a conclusion. To offer an argument is offer reasons to believe or disbelieve a conclusion. Good arguments generally start with relatively uncontroversial premises that the audience already believes, and then show that these premises suggest more controversial, interesting, or surprising conclusions that the audience did not already believe. For example, this chapter's starting arguments offer you reasons to approve or disapprove of democracy. One provides reason to think democracy tends to promote the interests of all; the other provides reasons to the contrary.

Nozick says that the other thing philosophers do is to explain complex ideas. We are confused and our concepts are unclear; philosophers illuminate the darkness and render ideas coherent. For instance, people tend to use the word "democracy" in thinner or thicker ways, in purely descriptive or normatively loaded ways, in pejorative or laudatory ways. This makes talking about democracy difficult, because often we often talk past each other. Philosophy can help us to talk to each other. It can help us understand why we think what we think.

This book offers a guided tour of *whys* and *why nots*, as seen in the history of philosophical arguments for and against democracy. It examines related concepts, such as liberty, freedom, equality, power, authority, and virtue. I want readers to walk away with a good sense of why smart, well-meaning, truth-seeking, justice-loving people have so often defended democracy, as well as why smart, well-meaning, truth-seeking, justice-loving people have so often rejected it or found it troubling.

This book focuses on examining how Western philosophers and political theorists have defended or critiqued democracy over the past 2,500 years. My emphasis will be more on the arguments than on the people themselves. I will focus on the biggest, most important, or best arguments. Further, in the West, both democracy and democratic theory take a long hiatus after the fall of the Roman Republic. While the ancient Greeks and Romans debated and sometimes practiced partly democratic forms of government, both democracy and theorizing about democracy largely disappear from the West from the end of the Roman Republic until the Renaissance.

This book also covers a large amount of *recent* intellectual history, in particular, work produced by political scientists, economists, and philosophers after World War II. One reason to do so is that widespread democracy with nearly universal suffrage among adults is a relatively recent phenomenon. For most of history, most countries were not democratic, and the few that were had greatly limited suffrage. Even in ancient Athens, only about 10–20 percent of the population—usually adult male citizens who had completed military training—were allowed to participate in government. Women, children, slaves, free slaves, and long-term "foreign" residents (residents whose families had lived in Athens for generations) were ineligible to vote. Until quite recently, there were few experiments in democracy and few theorists writing about it. However, after World War II, we have far more democracy and thus far more sources of data and evidence.

Further, after World War II, social scientific and philosophical methods became more rigorous and sophisticated. Thus, much of the *best* work on democracy is recent work. Recent authors have better data, better evidence, and better methods. We see farther today not merely because we stand on the shoulders of giants, but because we have better eyesight and there's more to see.

2

For Stability

Stability through Shared Power

Philosopher John Rawls declares, "Justice is the first virtue of institutions, as truth is to systems of thought."[1] He says coordination, efficiency, and stability are secondary concerns.

Rawls published this statement in 1971 as a citizen of a rich democracy that mostly respected the civil rights of people like him. It's a privileged manner of thought. I doubt people living through revolutions, civil war, foreign occupation, or war would agree. When the social order around you has collapsed or the rival ethnic group roams the streets with machetes, peace and stability probably seem more important than the ratio of income between local workers and managers.

You might be familiar with psychologist Abraham Maslow's hierarchy of needs. Maslow illustrates needs as a kind of pyramid. At the bottom are the most urgent matters, such as maintaining proper air pressure on one's body, getting adequate oxygen, and experiencing proper temperatures. Moving up, we get to food, water, shelter, and then to social values like friendship and love. At the top are higher-order values such as self-transcendence and self-realization. Maslow claims that the needs at the bottom are the most urgent. People tend to pursue higher needs only once the lower needs are met. The needs at the top are perhaps what constitutes the good life, but people do not focus on achieving self-realization when they are starving or in physical danger.

If we constructed an equivalent "hierarchy of institutional needs," what Rawls calls "justice" is probably near the top of the

Democracy. Jason Brennan, Oxford University Press. © Oxford University Press 2023.
DOI: 10.1093/oso/9780197558812.003.0002

pyramid, while peace and stability are at the very bottom. Peace and stability are the most urgent values, if not the most important. They are not what makes a society *good*; they are what makes a society a society at all. They are the branches from which other values can grow or the fabric upon which other values could be sewn. Justice is the first virtue of institutions the way candles are the first virtue of birthday cakes. Peace and stability are the cake.

This chapter discusses how philosophers and others have argued that some form of democracy is good because it promotes stability and peace. The next chapter examines historical skepticism about these arguments, including those who think democracy is comparatively unstable and those who think democracy is stable only when tightly constrained.

The Problems of Peace and Stability

I suggested that what Rawls calls "justice" is a higher-level value on par with love or self-transcendence, while peace and stability are lower-level values equivalent to, well, literally not being on fire. The analogy holds quite well. Rome was sacked—with large portions burned or destroyed—in AD 390, 410, 455, and 546. If, as Rawls thinks, justice is about setting the fair terms of cooperation, a precondition of justice is that we are even cooperating.

The problem of social stability, then, encompasses each of these problems: Are people working together enough to even constitute, in some way, something we can reasonably call a society? To what degree is human interaction ordered or chaotic? Are there known and widely recognized rules of interaction? Do these rules change slowly in predictable ways, change constantly in unpredictable ways, or do they frequently collapse and disappear? Do people sufficiently agree on what the rules are so that they get along? Do they agree on who oversees creating, enforcing, and interpreting the rules? Do people generally resist or obey these rules? Do they fight among themselves for power, and if so, in what ways? Is there literally civil war, are political conflicts seen as means to seize power to exploit others, or are disputes nevertheless peaceful? Is there war against others seen as outside the polity, and how extensive? Do people generally trust each other, or not?

Consider the main question of Adam Smith's *Wealth of Nations*: why are some countries rich and others poor? Smith argues—and contemporary economists, armed with better data and more rigorous research methods agree—that the answer is not better resources, better geography, or larger empires, but instead better *institutions*.[2] Institutions are the rules that structure social life and cooperation. A good one-sentence summary of economics would thus go as follows: constraints shape institutions that determine incentives that affect and determine human behavior, which in turn leads to outcomes. Smith's big idea is that changing the rules of the game changes how people behave. In some societies, the rules encourage people to put down their weapons, to truck and barter, and to resolve disputes through peaceful political compromise. In other societies, the rules (or lack thereof) encourage mutual predation—a kill-first-lest-you-be-killed mentality.

We need institutional frameworks that encourage people to trust each other, to make trades with one another, and to safely experiment with new ideas. We want people to feel confident in investing in themselves, in property, and in others with an eye to the future, rather than feeling that they must consume all they have immediately or that any such investment is a waste. We want them to have an incentive to work for their own and for others' benefit, rather than an incentive to do nothing, or worse, to prey upon and exploit one another. We want them to have a good understanding of what is allowed and what is not, so that they do not spend their time disputing the rules with one another.

Capricious rulers, war, and general instability make all this impossible. Consider: a college student invests time and money into acquiring a degree and developing her human capital. A responsible worker saves money for her retirement, money that is invested in other productive outcomes. Homeowners maintain their property rather than let it rot. Now imagine that you live under a ruler who changes the laws and might seize your property at whim. Or imagine that at any moment, the prevailing government might collapse in civil war. Or imagine that foreign powers stand ready to invade. Or imagine that things are so chaotic that you have no idea who will rule, if anyone, and in what form, a few years from now. In a world like that, long-term planning is neither possible nor rational; it makes sense instead to think and act short-term. Stability does not guarantee prosperity, and sometimes stability leads to complacency. But chaos creates deprivation.

Aristotle on the Stability of Constitutional Government

In Aristotle's (384–322 BC) time, there was no hard distinction between philosophy and the natural or social sciences. We remember Aristotle chiefly as a philosopher, but he wrote extensively on physics, biology, geology, astronomy, and other sciences. Aristotle's most famous work of political philosophy, *The Politics*, mixes normative philosophical theorizing with the empirical approach we would today identify as political science.

For Aristotle, stability was a fundamental concern. He claims that the goodness of government consists both of the quality of the laws themselves (including whether they are just, help citizens flourish, or encourage virtue), and also of whether the citizens are inclined to obey the laws.[3] If the laws or institutions look good on paper but the citizens do not follow them, there is bad governance.

Aristotle regards the fundamental way to distinguish different forms of government is to ask, *who rules?* He claims there are three basic answers to this question: the one, the few, or the many.

Aristotle further divides forms of government into two sub-forms based on *how* the people in power rule, in particular, whether the rulers pursue the common good in a virtuous fashion, or whether they instead pursue their own self-interest. He says:

> Of the forms of government in which one rules, we call that which regards the common interest kingship; that in which there are more than one, but not many, rule, aristocracy; and it is so called because the rulers are the best men, or because they have at heart the best interests of the state and of the citizens. But when the many administer the state for the common interest, the government is called by a generic name—a constitution. . . .
>
> Of the above-mentioned forms, the perversions are as follows—of kingship, tyranny; of aristocracy, oligarchy; of constitutional government, democracy. For tyranny is a kind of monarchy which has in view the interest of the monarchy only; oligarchy has in view the interest of the wealthy; democracy, of the needy; none of them the common good of all.[4]

Figure 2.1 places these categories into a table. Note that for Aristotle, the "many" does not signify universal participation or enfranchisement. Even the most egalitarian of Greek city-states excluded women, slaves, and resident foreigners from participating in power. When Aristotle considers city-states ruled by the "many,"

	The One	The Few	The Many
"True" Form: Government for the Common Good	Monarchy	Aristocracy	Polity/Constitutional Government
"Defective" Form: Government for the Interests of the Rulers	Dictatorship/Tyranny	Oligarchy	Democracy

Figure 2.1 Aristotle's Forms of Government

he means states in which only about 20 percent of the population have any share of political power.

Aristotle recognizes that merely living in a place long-term does not make one a citizen. There are different degrees of membership within a political community. Aristotle himself lived in Athens for much of his life, but as a Macedonian, he was never a citizen with any right to vote.

He defines the citizen in the "strictest sense" as one who "shares in the administration of justice, and of offices."[5] On this strict definition, then, most long-term inhabitants in monarchies and aristocracies bearing the legal title of citizen are not true citizens; they have stronger legal rights than slaves or resident aliens, but little political power.

Aristotle's classification scheme in Figure 2.1 somewhat conflates institutional descriptions—that is, objective descriptions of the constitutions of different places—with normative assessments of how well the rulers rule or what the rulers' intentions are. A kingdom becomes a tyranny when the king becomes a jerk. Oligarchies apportion power to the rich while aristocracies apportion power to the noble and wise, but Aristotle also tends to think that the noble and wise tend also to be fairly rich. (In part, this is because Aristotle thinks that poverty impedes the development of virtue, though he thinks excessive wealth impedes virtue too.) Still, the constitutions of aristocracies and oligarchies look almost identical; an oligarchy is in effect a badly run aristocracy.

But this also partly explains why Aristotle worries that monarchy and aristocracy are unstable. Monarchies are one birth away from becoming tyrannies. Aristocracies often begin as the rule of the wisest, but over time, they become the rule of the rich, who run governments on their own behalf. Further, Aristotle worries that both systems exclude the great mass of citizens from holding power. This dishonors them and makes them worry they lack a proper stake in the government. It thus increases the likelihood they will disobey or rebel against the current order.

In contrast, Aristotle's distinction between a polity (or constitutional government) and a democracy is more substantive. If oligarchy is the rule of the rich, democracy is in effect the rule of the poor. In a democracy, all citizens possess an equal share of power, and, on Aristotle's definition, democracies have few institutional constraints on how they might exercise that power. Since the poor usually outnumber the middle class or the rich, the expected effect of instituting democracy is that the poor will use their political power to enrich themselves at the expense of others. The system will thus be unstable—as the middle class and rich will fight against it, or the poor fight for shares of the spoils. Aristotle further worries that democracies are unstable because the unwise masses are easily flattered by demagogues. Democracies can thus easily collapse into tyrannies when the people fall for demagogues' tricks.[6]

In contrast, Aristotle thinks constitutional governments are relatively stable because they combine different forms of government and divide power. Aristotle claims that "polity" or "constitutional government"—the good form of the rule of the many—is a fusion of oligarchy and democracy.[7] For instance, Aristotle claims that polities borrow from democracy a lack of property qualifications for having the right to vote or run for office, but they borrow from oligarchies the tendency to apportion and concentrate power in the hands of the few, who are elected by the many. They also divide different powers among different offices.[8] This tends to ensure that the people who wield the most power are of higher quality, while also preventing anyone (including the majority as a whole) from using all the state's power for their narrow self-interest.

Aristotle also claims that polities are stable because they mostly empower the middle class. The very rich tend to despise others as inferior; they learn how to command but never how to obey. The poor tend to be venal and servile; they learn how to obey but are unfit to rule. The middle class is rich enough not to be covetous but not so rich as to be corrupt. They have a long-term stake in the stability and prosperity of their city-state. Thus, Aristotle thinks, states will be stable and functional when the middle class is largest group and holds the most power.[9]

Aristotle dedicates a large portion of the *Politics* to assessing the historical causes of revolutions and rebellions. He sees many grounds: sometimes people simply want to usurp power, such as when a general kills the king and installs himself as tyrant. Other times, revolution occurs when the great mass of people, or a powerful group of people, feel disrespected and disregarded by the state. Sometimes it occurs when it becomes clear that those in power profit themselves at the expense of those without power. And so on. Aristotle's solution is largely institutional, and once again, constitutional government emerges as the best overall form. Constitutional governments ensure that no particular set of individuals can seize power and that there is sufficient overlap between the interests of the rulers and the interests of all.

Though Aristotle uses "democracy" as a pejorative term, what he calls "polity" or "constitutional government" corresponds roughly with what the American founders would have called "republican government" or what we might call "constitutional democracy" today. This is no accident. As we will see, modern constitutional democracies were designed in part because their founders took Aristotle's advice.

Republicanism and the Idea of Mixed Government

Niccolò Machiavelli (1469–1527) is best known for his work *The Prince*, which reads as an instruction manual for how a prince can retain power. How to interpret *The Prince* remains a subject of debate,[10] but scholars agree that *The Discourses on Livy* best represent Machiavelli's own views on proper governance.[11] Machiavelli takes his lead from Aristotle and other theorists of classical antiquity.

Like Aristotle and other older writers, Machiavelli was deeply concerned about how stable different forms of government were. Perhaps this was merely an intellectual concern, but he lived in a period of frequent war between city-states and emerging nation-states. He was forced to live in exile (after being tortured and interrogated for conspiracy) when the Florentine Republic was overthrown in 1530 by the Medici Pope Clement VII, Holy Roman Emperor Charles V, and the allied Spanish army.

Indeed, Machiavelli largely breaks from earlier writers because he sees the creation and preservation of order as the *primary* goal or point of politics. While ancient Greek or Roman political theorists, or medieval Christian theorists, of course agree that order is a pre-condition of achieving higher goals, they nevertheless tend to think that the function or goal of the state was to develop or protect some higher value, such as virtue.

In the *Discourses on Livy* (1531), Machiavelli copies Aristotle's division of forms of government. He claims that monarchy, aristocracy, and democracy are unstable:

I say, as has been said before by many who have written of Governments, that of these there are three forms, known by the names Monarchy, Aristocracy, and Democracy, and that those who give its institutions to a State have recourse to one or other of these three, according as it suits their purpose. Other, and, as many have thought, wiser teachers, will have it, that there are altogether six forms of government, three of them utterly bad, the other three good in themselves, but so readily corrupted that they too are apt to become hurtful. The good are the three above named; the bad, three others dependent upon these, and each so like that to which it is related, that it is easy to pass imperceptibly from the one to the other. For a Monarchy readily becomes a Tyranny, an Aristocracy an Oligarchy, while a Democracy tends to degenerate into Anarchy. So that if the founder of a State should establish any one of these three forms of Government, he establishes it for a short time only, since no precaution he may take can prevent it from sliding into its contrary, by reason of the close resemblance which, in this case, the virtue bears to the vice.[12]

Note that Machiavelli also uses "democracy" as a kind of pejorative term, even though today we would call him a kind of democrat. Machiavelli does not provide much direct evidence for the claims in the quotation above. We can charitably read him partly as making what he takes to be accurate generalizations of known European and Middle Eastern history, and partly as making a kind of rational-choice argument. He sees that different institutional arrangements create different sets of incentives, which he thinks have predictable long-term effects.

Machiavelli benefits from having thousands of years more history than Livy or Aristotle from which to draw his conclusions. For instance, Machiavelli notes that Solon's democratic reforms in Athens were unstable. Athenian democracy lasted forty years, then a despot ruled, then the democracy was restored for only a century, then it collapsed again.

Machiavelli had a pessimistic view of human nature. He regarded people as selfish, lazy, but predatory. Designing a good state thus meant trying to create political structures that incentivize flawed people to cooperate rather than fight. Or, to be more precise, for Machiavelli, constitutional design is about finding a way to arrange government such that people's natural rapaciousness and desire to dominate others are sublimated and kept in check through the political system. This is one reason why Machiavelli is quick to advocate things we would consider brutal or, well, Machiavellian by today's standards. For instance, he claims that when a new participatory republic is founded, it is wise to make a public example by killing the enemies of the regime that might wish to install themselves as rulers. He further claims that Gaul's sack of Rome

(c. 387 BC) was useful in forcing the Romans to reform their regime and return to their roots.

Indeed, Machiavelli frequently claims that external threats are *good* for a city or state. Of course, it's terrible to be invaded. But, Machiavelli argues, the threat of invasion forces states to organize properly and forces citizens to cooperate with one another to protect against a common empire. External threats create internal harmony, while the lack of external threats allows citizens to indulge their internal conflicts.

Machiavelli overall advocates a republican form of government, one that largely copies or mimics Rome's republican period. While he did not advocate universal participation, he thought rich and poor alike should be given some share of power.

For Machiavelli, though, the goal was not to find a way to make permanent peace, to make people equal, or to generate and civic friendship. Instead, Machiavelli thinks that people will always have separate interests, including the inherently conflict-generating desire to rule and control others. Allowing a wide range of people with varying interests to participate in politics will tend to ensure that whatever laws are passed will benefit all. He did not expect consensus, but rather mutually agreeably compromises. Machiavelli sees a participatory republic as a way not merely to contain conflict, but to use selfish attitudes to further the glory and power of the state.

The Federalist

After the American War of Independence, the United States' original constitution (the Articles of Confederation) created a weak federal government and left the individual states as the primary repositories of political power. The country suffered strife, with problems as far-ranging as individual states violating the 1783

Treaty of Paris, to internal conflicts between states over land and tariffs, to the inability of the government to suppress rebellions.

In the *Federalist Papers* (published as serials between 1787 and 1788), Alexander Hamilton (1757–1804), James Madison (1751–1836), and John Jay (1745–1829) defend a stronger central state with the powers enumerated in the drafted US Constitution. (They succeeded; it was adopted in 1789). Hamilton, Madison, and Jay were well educated and had studied the classics of political thought, including many of those we'll discuss in this very book. However, while Aristotle, Machiavelli, John Locke, Montesquieu, and Thomas Paine all *wrote* about high-stakes issues, Hamilton, Madison, and Jay were actually *making* high-stakes decisions. They were in fact designing government. As revolutionaries, they were running a political experiment with dire consequences if they were wrong. Any mistakes they made could directly result in chaos, poverty, oppression, or war. They knew that country they founded had deep divisions over slavery, commerce, and other matters.

Madison begins Federalist No. 10 by arguing his audience should be worried not merely about foreign wars, but by the even "more alarming" "dangers" that result from "dissensions between the States themselves and from domestic factions and convulsions."[13] He claims that one would "be far gone in Utopian speculations" to doubt that if the states are only partly united, that they would not fall into "violent contests with each other."[14]

Here, Madison grounds his argument for a strongly unified central government on a pessimistic account of human nature: people are "ambitious, vindictive, and rapacious."[15] Individual people who gain power are quick to sacrifice the public interest for "personal advantage or personal gratification." He believes political units behave much like ambitious, vindictive, and rapacious people. They love power and are jealous of the power of others; they want "pre-eminence and dominion."[16] Madison, like Machiavelli and many others before him, sees individual people and political bodies as not merely as tending toward selfishness, but as tending to desire power and dominion over others. Thus, the key task for constitutional design is to build something straight from the crooked timber of human nature. A proper constitutional design in part restrains these rapacious attitudes and in part puts them to good use.

Madison thus thinks civil war among the states is inevitable unless they are strongly unified. He opens Federalist No. 14 as follows:

> We have seen the necessity of the Union, as our bulwark against foreign danger, as the conservator of peace among ourselves, as the guardian of our commerce and other common interests, as the only substitute for those military establishments which have subverted the liberties of the Old World, and as the proper antidote for the diseases of faction, which have proved fatal to other popular governments, and of which alarming symptoms have been betrayed by our own.[17]

We know, though Madison did not, that his Constitution nevertheless failed to prevent a civil war seventy years later. We might wonder, though, if the United States would have fallen into civil war even earlier, or whether there would have been multiple and continual civil wars instead.

In Federalist No. 51, Madison argues that the US Constitution is designed to contain these failings of human nature:

> Ambition must be made to counteract ambition. The interest of the man must be connected with the constitutional rights of the place. It may be a reflection on human nature, that such devices should be necessary to control the abuses of government. But what is government itself, but the greatest of all reflections on human nature? If men were angels, no government would be necessary. If angels were to govern men, neither external nor internal controls on government would be necessary. In framing a government which is to be administered by men over men, the great difficulty lies in this: you must first enable the government

to control the governed; and in the next place oblige it to control itself.[18]

Madison borrows from the French philosopher Montesquieu, who defended the idea of the separation of powers. The key to reducing internal strife and to prevent a majoritarian faction from abusing everyone in the minority, Madison thinks, is to both to divide the powers of government among separate people in separate branches, while also giving each branch some sort of check or veto power over the other branches.

Thus, Madison advocates separating the three functions of government—legislative, executive, and judiciary—into three distinct branches—the Congress, the presidency (and what would later become the administrative bureaucracy), and the various courts. For checks and balances, he advocates allowing the president to veto legislation (but allowing Congress to override vetoes with enough votes), for allowing Congress to fire the president, and for the courts to review legislation. (While judicial review is not explicitly written into the Constitution, Hamilton defends judicial review in Federalist No. 78.)

Further, the Electoral College was intended to give the legislature a check on the presidency. The original expectation was not that the states would succeed in choosing a president. Instead, the drafters of the Constitution expected that in most cases, the states would forward candidates to the House of Representatives, who would choose a president. The Electoral College was intended to be a kind of search committee for the president. (They were wrong and the system never in fact functioned this way.) Still, Hamilton, Madison, and Jay intended the different branches of government to check one another by given each some say in who serves in each branch.

Notice the advance this represents over Machiavelli and other defenders of "mixed" constitutions. For Machiavelli and Aristotle, "mixed" constitutions meant allowing people of different classes to participate in politics and hold some degree of power. Mixing thus meant the mixing of classes and relevant interests. For the *Federalist* authors, mixing instead means something more profound. The US Constitution was meant to mix Aristotle's three kinds of government. The presidency is analogous to a monarchy, the judiciary to an aristocracy, and Congress to a democracy. The hope was that having all three kinds of government at once would increase stability and prevent the government from degenerating into a corrupt or deviant forms.

Kant and the Democratic Peace Theory

In 1795, the German philosopher Immanuel Kant (1724–1804) published *Perpetual Peace: A Philosophical Sketch*, which outlined what he believed were the political conditions under which nation-states could enter a condition of permanent and perpetual peace instead of internecine war. His first "definitive article for perpetual peace" held that "the civil constitution of every state should be republican."[19] That is, Kant holds that a world full of republics would be a world at peace.

Kant's main argument appeals to citizens' self-interest:

> [I]f the consent of the citizens is required in order to decide that war should be declared (and in this [republican] constitution it cannot but be the case), nothing is more natural than that they would be very cautious in commencing such a poor game, decreeing for themselves all the calamities of war. Among the latter would be: having to fight, having to pay the costs of war from their own resources, having painfully to repair the devastation war leaves behind, and, to fill up the measure of evils, load themselves with a heavy national debt that would embitter peace itself and that can never be liquidated on account of constant wars in the future. But, on the other hand, in a constitution which is not republican, and under which the subjects are not citizens, a

declaration of war is the easiest thing in the world to decide upon, because war does not require of the ruler, who is the proprietor and not a member of the state, the least sacrifice of the pleasures of his table, the chase, his country houses, his court functions, and the like. He may, therefore, resolve on war as on a pleasure party for the most trivial reasons, and with perfect indifference leave the justification which decency requires to the diplomatic corps who are ever ready to provide it.[20]

In a republican form of government, citizens exercise fundamental power. The ability to declare war depends upon their consent. They would likely realize that the costs and dangers of war greatly exceed whatever benefits they might obtain. Thus they would want to avoid war.

Kant's argument here can be compared to Scottish economist Adam Smith's (1723–1790) *Wealth of Nations* (1776). Smith's book was, among many other things, the first sustained economic critique of war and imperialism. Smith amassed data about the value of the raw materials and other goods the European empires extracted from their colonies. He then compared this to the costs of empire, such as tax expenditures needed to maintain them or the economic distortions they created. He concluded that the European empires, far from being a sort of goldmine for the conquering countries, were each a net *loss*. It was as if a robber pilfers a bank, but spends twice as much money on guns and the getaway car than he makes from the robbery.

Why, then, would empires persist, if they harm rather than help the conquering country? Here, Smith explains that benefits of the empire-building were concentrated among the politically well-connected few, such as weapons makers, certain monopoly trade companies, the military, and the kings and queens. The costs—which exceeded the benefits—were in turn passed on to and spread among the helpless, hapless many, among the taxpayers forced to pay for the wars, the conscripts forced to fight and die, and the consumers forced to pay what were in many cases artificially high prices.[21] The empire is bad for the country as a whole and most people in it, but good for the king and a few others.

Kant hopes that republican forms of government eliminate this kind of dynamic. While a king can enjoy the benefits of empire but pass the costs on to subjects, a republic eliminates the distinction between rulers and ruled. Everyone pays. Thus, if the costs of war exceed the benefits, republican citizens pursuing their rational self-interest should avoid war.

It's worth noting a few key assumptions of Kant's argument. Kant assumes that voters in republican forms of government will vote in their rational self-interest. We will examine arguments for and against this position in chapters 6 and 7, which discuss the connection between democracy and wisdom. He also assumes that in republics, voters have enough of a check on their elected leaders that the kind of problem Smith identifies—where some people benefit from war but pass the costs on to others—does not emerge. However, in chapter 11, we will examine how realistically, in republican forms of government, special interest groups often exploit the public.

De Tocqueville on Stability

In 1831, the French aristocrat Alexis de Tocqueville (1805–1859) visited the United States at the request of the new French government to study the US prison system. (In July 1830, a revolution had overthrown the previous king in favor a new, more liberal one.) Instead, Tocqueville studied American culture and government. In 1835 and 1840, he published two volumes of his classic work *Democracy in America*, which includes his observations of American politics, economics, religion, government, and culture, and his speculations about how the Puritan religion in New England led to the United States' democratic culture, and how the

democratic republican government affects the character and behavior of the American people.

In particular, Tocqueville was curious why democratic government seemed so stable and functional in the United States when
it was unstable and tended to collapse elsewhere. After all, shortly
after the American Revolution, France had its own democratic revolution, which was a disaster. In the short term, it led to widespread
violence and state-sponsored killings, then to Napoleon's empire
and wars, then the restoration of the Bourbon monarchy, and then
to more constitutional and liberal Orleans monarchy under which
Tocqueville served. Even today, scholars debate why the same laws
or formal constitutions can work well in some polities and poorly
in others. Tocqueville argued that Americans, thanks to their religious history and other cultural factors, developed a mindset that
facilitated democratic self-rule.

At the time Tocqueville was writing, many liberal philosophers
argued that democracy would tend to make smart decisions *because* it enabled the people to rule themselves. Just as individual
people best know how to serve their own interests, the rule of
the people would ensure government responds to the people's
interests. We will examine arguments like this and objections to
it in chapters 6 and 7. Tocqueville thought these arguments were
absurd; on the contrary, he thought democracies (including
American democracy as he saw it) tended to make rash and stupid
decisions.

Instead, he claims that one of the major advantages of universal suffrage is that it produces stability and guards against
revolutions. Under anything less than universal suffrage, people
know that the government cannot claim to represent the majority.
But under universal suffrage, the majority rules. Further, while
the minority might resent the rule of the majority, they at least
have an outlet to express their discontent. They recognize that
they have a turn to speak in politics, and that they can petition
others to their side.

Tocqueville claims that in non-democratic governments, radical and revolutionary factions gain a kind of prestige, as they can say they are the oppressed fighting against their powerful oppressors. But in democracies with universal suffrage, this takes the hot air out of their balloons. Instead of being oppressed, minority ideological or interest-based factions are more often seen simply as the people who lost because they couldn't convince others to take their side in a fair contest.[22]

Tocqueville believed that non-democratic governments tended to devolve into strongman dictatorships. He said, "if the peaceful dominion of the majority is not established among us in good time, we will sooner or later full under the unlimited authority of a single man."[23] His argument seems to be that competition among elites in non-democratic governments leads over time to reductions in the number of elites who hold power, and thus increasing increased concentration of power in fewer and fewer hands. Further, in non-democratic countries, because the people do not have power or participate in politics, they do not resist and may even welcome a demagogic strongman who promises to fix things. In contrast, he claims that when everyone has power, citizens pay greater attention to politics and thus do not so easily allow strongmen to emerge.

Further, Tocqueville argues that democracy increases respect for the law and thus reduces chaos and social turbulence. In a true monarchy or aristocracy, the great mass of people recognize they are subjects. The laws are imposed upon them, without their say. They often infer that the laws serve the interests of rulers more than the ruled. But in democracies, people regard the laws as their own, and are thus more inclined to follow them.

While Tocqueville was a democrat, *Democracy in America* often reads as a highly anti-democratic book, for reasons we'll review in later chapters. However, for Tocqueville, one of democracy's main advantages, if not its greatest advantage, is that it tends to be stable. He thinks democracy is stable, though, only if accompanied by a culture that itself supports and stabilizes democracy.

The Democratic Peace Thesis

After Kant, many liberal theorists and political scientists defended the "democratic peace thesis," which holds more specifically that democratic countries tend not to go to war with other democratic countries. Notice that this a more limited and less interesting claim than Kant's. Kant argued that democratic countries (he, like others in his time, used "democracy" as a pejorative term) would not want to go to war, period.

Whether the democratic peace thesis is correct remains hotly disputed in contemporary political science. Many scholars claim that there is a clear empirical evidence that democracies do not make war on other democracies.[24] However, some political scientists claim that this is the correlation without causation fallacy, as what explains the observed lack of war between democracies is not that they are democracies, but some other factor.[25] For instance, perhaps US hegemony over other democratic states plus the alliance of interests during the Cold War prevented war among democracies.[26] Others claim that whether the thesis holds up depends upon how we define "democracy" or "war," or which countries count as democracies. It might be that researchers defending the thesis use narrow definitions to avoid counterexamples.[27] Or consider that democracies with nearly universal suffrage were exceedingly rare until after World War II. Perhaps we do not have enough of a time horizon to know whether democracies make war on each other. (In contrast, eighty years of democratic experience might be enough to make reliable conclusions about more frequent events, such as how democratic elections affect GDP growth.)

Consider, for instance, how to think about World War II. It is easy to see World War II as a battle between democratic countries (the United Kingdom and the United States) plus an authoritarian ally (the USSR) against authoritarian states (Germany, Italy, and

Japan). But Germany and Italy were democracies that became fascist states through democratic malfunction. Should World War II thus count as evidence for or against the democratic peace thesis?

One might also wonder how interesting the democratic peace thesis is. Kant thought democracies would not want to wage war, period. But the democratic peace thesis holds that democracies tend not to wage war on other democracies. Still, in 2021, more than a third of world's population was living under an authoritarian regime, with only about 8 percent living in a full democracy (as measured by the Democracy Index). The United States has been at war with various other non-democratic countries for something like thirty-four out of the forty-one years I'd been alive as of the time I wrote the first draft of this paragraph. By extension, NATO—the military alliance that represents most Northern Hemisphere democracies—has been involved in wars almost my entire life. If I care about peace, should I delighted to know all these wars, invasions, and attacks were against non-democratic regimes?

What We Should Learn

Throughout the history of political thought, theorists have argued that the main function of government is to reduce violence and keep the peace. It's a bit weird that philosophers today hardly talk about it.

Peace does not by itself make a life good, but it's hard to have a good life without peace. Similarly, peace and stability do not suffice to make a policy just or good, but it's hard to have a just or good polity without them. Peace and stability are the background conditions of good lives and just polities.

In this chapter, we saw that many theorists argue that democracy and divided governments are unusually peaceful and stable. The main mechanism seems to be that by giving everyone a stake and a say in government, this should reduce the degree to which people see government as an imposition to be overthrown, and instead give everyone a stake. On international relations, the hope is that democracy causes citizens to internalize the costs of their decision to go to war—and thus reject war.

3

Against Stability

Passion and Polarization

Chapter 2 examined some of the historically and philosophically important arguments that claimed democracy promotes peace and stability. In this chapter, we'll see that democracy's detractors instead thought it was unstable, would collapse, would produce chaos, or, more mildly, that it would induce tribalism and polarization.

Plato and the Problem of Factionalism

Most democratic theory is a footnote to Plato (428–348 BC), who was famously skeptical of democracy. We'll hear from Plato multiple times throughout this text. Plato thought democracy tended to make stupid decisions, tended to corrupt the youth and character of a society, and also tended to create factionalism that enabled powerful demagogues to seize power. For Plato, these worries are interconnected: democracy's inclusiveness encourages stupidity, which encourages vice, which increases factionalism, which leads to instability.

As we discussed in the last chapter, Machiavelli knew something Aristotle didn't: Athenian democracy was not particularly stable. It would rise, collapse into tyranny or oligarchy, rise again, and collapse again. It depended on slave labor and the exploitation of its empire, which it managed poorly. In the end, it was absorbed into and controlled by other empires.

Democracy. Jason Brennan, Oxford University Press. © Oxford University Press 2023.
DOI: 10.1093/oso/9780197558812.003.0003

Plato was well-educated. He probably traveled extensively throughout the Greek, Italian, and North African city-states. He knew Athens' own troubled history with democracy and saw his mentor and friend, Socrates, executed on absurd charges. In their writings, Plato tends to argue from philosophical principles, while Aristotle draws from observation. Still, both mixed normative philosophy with what they regarded as reliable empirical generalizations.

In Book VIII of the *Republic* (c. 375 BC), Plato offers an account of how governments might predictably change from one form to another. In previous sections of the *Republic*, Plato had defended what he regards as kind of idealized state, in which rulers are trained from a young age to possess wisdom and to be motivated to rule for the common good. (We will discuss this further in chapter 7.) In Book VIII, Plato wonders how such a state might collapse. He asks whether there is a "simply but unvarying rule, that in every form of government revolution takes the start from the ruling class itself."[1] While Plato had taken pains to describe how, in an ideal state, an aristocratic "guardian" ruling class could be selected and trained to rule for the good of the city, he then describes how over time, the rest of his ideal city would become further focused on money-making and self-interest. At the same time, the guardian class will become corrupted in part because it is selected from this increasing corrupted population. Over time, the ideal city state will degenerate into an oligarchy—the rule of the rich for the rich.

As the rich rule in their own interests, the gap in power and wealth between the rich and poor widens. Plato says:

> [S]uch negligence and encouragement of licentiousness in oligarchies not infrequently has reduced to poverty men of no ignoble quality. "It surely has." "And there they sit, I fancy, within the city, furnished with stings, that is, arms, some burdened with debt, others disfranchised, others both, hating and conspiring

against the acquirers of their estates and the rest of the citizens, and eager for revolution."[2]

Plato argues that over time the number of poor increases and the rich decreases. Further, when these different classes fight together on the battlefield against foreign enemies, the poor will witness how fat and sickly the rich have become. The poor will conclude that the rich are weak cowards.[3]

The poor will thus conspire with each other to overthrow the oligarchs and establish a democracy. Democracy, in principle, is the rule of all as equals. However, Plato, like Aristotle, claims that in effect democracy is the rule of the poor, since the poor form the majority.

Democracy, like the other systems, contains the seeds of its own undoing. Just as money-making and greed cause oligarchy to collapse, so liberty causes democracy to collapse. A self-serving culture of licentiousness causes democratic citizens to disregard education and refinement, and instead indulge their vices. Various factions arise. Since the masses are badly educated, reason poorly, and easily misled, a crafty demagogue can easily propel himself to power on the back of populist movements. A would-be tyrant can grab power by calling himself the spokesperson of the people.[4]

Indeed, if democracy leads to factionalism and chaos, as Plato thinks, people will become eager for a strongman to seize power and end the conflict. Each faction believes that social problems could be fixed if they could impose their will. They will of course disagree about *which* strongman should rule; each faction wants its own. But once a tyrant takes over, he can be expected to rule for his own interests rather than those of the faction that appointed him.

Plato in turn thinks tyranny is unstable. After all, tyrants tend to exploit everyone for their own sake, so most everyone has some stake in deposing the tyrant, even if the goal is merely to install themselves in his place.

So, to some degree, this might dampen Plato's criticism of democracy as unstable. Plato seems to think, in the *Republic*, that *every* form of government is unstable over the long run. The difference between Plato's favored form of government and democracy, then, when it comes to stability and factionalism, is one of degree rather than kind. Under Plato's favored aristocracy of the wise, there are perhaps two major factions, and it takes ages for the system to decay. In democracy, there are innumerable, ever-shifting factions, and the society is ever vulnerable.

Hobbes and Democracy as the War of All against All

The Republic is perhaps the most famous and foundational text in moral and political thought, period, but Thomas Hobbes's (1588–1679) *Leviathan* (1651) is probably the most important and foundational text in *modern* political thought. *Leviathian* was written during the English Civil War (1642–1651), which pitted parliamentarians and constitutional monarchists against absolute monarchists who supported King Charles I. Hobbes had seen political turmoil for most of his adult life. Like Aristotle, Hobbes was also a polymath who published in mathematics, the natural and social sciences, and philosophy.

Leviathan is striking compared to works that preceded it. For one, earlier political philosophers tended to take for granted that of course people will and should live together under some sort of government. The question for them was which kind of government is best and why. They also tended to assume that the purpose of government was in part to make people virtuous and to promote the common good. They tended to understand the common good as not merely being the conditions that improve the individual good of all citizens, but as rather as a higher value of the community as a whole somehow independent of the good of citizens. They further tended to think that selfishness and avarice were vices to be squashed or discouraged in favor of public-spiritedness.

In contrast, Hobbes starts, in effect, by treating anarchy as a baseline from which departures must be justified. Here, "anarchy" means not the absence of order or moral rules, but rather the absence of government per se, where government is understood as an institution that claims the monopoly right to make rules and enforce these rules with violence and coercion. Hobbes's main strategy to defend government is to try to show that the absence of government would be so bad that every rational person would agree to institute it. While ancient authors often focused on virtue, wisdom, or freedom as the main goal of government, Hobbes concluded that the fundamental purpose was stability: government should maintain law, peace, and order, and prevent internal conflict and war. Hobbes had a pessimistic view of human nature and did not much concern himself with cultivating higher virtues. Instead, he proceeds by imagining people to be rational egoists, but tries to explain why rational egoists should and would agree to abide by common rules.

What is perhaps most striking about Hobbes is the gap between his starting point and ending points. *Leviathan* is a thoroughly individualistic text, which tries to ground the justification of government on the rational and enlightened self-interest of the people subject to that government, in light of their actual (rather than idealized) values. For this reason, *Leviathan* is often treated as a kind of foundational text in liberal political theory.[5] Yet, surprisingly, while Hobbes begins with individualist premises, he concludes that something close to absolute monarchy is the best form of government.

In *Leviathan*, Hobbes defends the existence of government on the basis of a rational-choice, hypothetical consent model. He asks readers to imagine people living in anarchy, that is, in the absence of any kind of binding or recognized authority and in the absence of any power capable of forcing people to comply with valuable rules. He calls this the "state of nature."

He models people as rational agents, who have a "perpetual and restless desire for power after power that ceaseth only in death."[6] Note that Hobbes does not use the word "power" to mean power over others. Rather, he defines "the power *of a man* (to take it universally) is his present means to obtain some future apparent good."[7] So, "power" here means the capacity and ability to achieve one's goals. When Hobbes says that people have a restless desire for power after power, he does not mean that everyone necessarily wants to dominate others. Rather, he means that people, being rational, will always want to increase their ability to achieve their goals.

In the state of nature, everyone is approximately equal in ability, in the sense that everyone can benefit from others' help but everyone is also potential threat. We face scarcity; there is not enough to satisfy all of our desires and perhaps not even enough for everyone to get what they need, absent cooperation. There is danger in cultivating or developing anything because others might steal our crops or work.

Further, we face multiple sources of quarrel: for safety, gain, and reputation. If everyone preferred peace and only took up arms because they feared others, then achieving peace could be easy: one could signal peacefulness by putting down one's arms, assured that by proving one is not a threat, others will also put down their arms. But, Hobbes says, things are not that easy. We know some people want to prey upon us for personal gain or because they enjoy dominion over others.[8] So, people are rightly and rationally suspicious toward everyone else, because they cannot determine who the predators might be, and have no reliable means to stop them.

Hobbes famously thinks that the resulting mutual diffidence, in the absence of a common power to control everyone, would lead to a "war of all against all" in which life will be "solitary, poor, nasty, brutish, and short."[9] To solve this problem, he argues that everyone would recognize that they need a mechanism to keep the peace.[10] So, he thinks they would agree to create a sovereign who has power over all of them. They would agree to obey that sovereign's orders.

Note that in Hobbes's hypothetical social contract, people contract with each other to accept this sovereign. The contract is *not* between the people and the sovereign itself; indeed, Hobbes thinks that the idea of a contract with a sovereign is incoherent.[11] Instead, Hobbes thinks that the sovereign—to enhance its own glory and status—will have sufficient rational incentive to keep the peace and promote the welfare commonwealth. (Later in this chapter, we will see how contemporary economists argue something similar.)

So, for Hobbes, the main justification of government is to keep the peace and maintain order. Peace and order are necessary conditions for the other, higher-level values. People cannot invest in their human capital, in public works or private business, in art and music, in divine grace or self-transcendence, or in situations where no one can trust anyone else and in which there is a constant threat of external predation. Indeed, modern economists working on institutions largely agree with Hobbes on this point.[12]

Hobbes argues that the best, most stable sovereign is an absolute monarch. Ultimately, he thinks that any kind of divided sovereignty—such as a deliberative aristocracy or democracy—will inherit the same problems as the state of nature. In a democracy, everyone has the hope of realizing their private goals, but the reality is always that some people get their way and others do not. What democracy ends up doing is creating a continued competition to gain power so that people can achieve their ends. Rather than eliminating the destructive competition of the state of nature, democracy relocates that competition and makes it more polite. The same problems that plagued the state of nature—including mutual diffidence, the desire for glory, and the desire to dominate others—remain. Democracy officially gives every citizen equal right to rule, but in fact, the one who rules is that one who wins the competition and actually exercises power.[13]

Hobbes thinks that when *groups* rule, the multitude will be unstable, because they will have divided interests, goals, and designs. He expects that under democracy, one or two powerful orators will tend to win de facto control for short periods of time, only to be replaced by the next strong and persuasive person sometime later.[14]

Further, Hobbes thinks that the sovereign is, by definition, whoever exercises final authority and has the genuine power to rule. He argues that only in an absolute monarchy is the capacity to rule all the time actually realized. Deliberative bodies such as aristocratic councils or democratic legislatures only meet on occasion. In the interim, someone has to rule, and that usually ends up being the people appointed by that council to oversee the government when they are not meeting.[15]

Perhaps Hobbes is mistaken or exaggerating when he says that in democracy, power will at any time fall into just a few hands. Still, some of what he says seems prescient. Consider, for instance, that in modern democracies, legislatures delegate almost all of their power to bureaucratic bodies that take most of their orders from the chief executive. In fact, in modern democracies, the people—and even their elected representatives in parliament—do very little ruling.

To summarize, consider Hobbes's sources of conflict: competition for resources and power, glory, domination, and diffidence. Hobbes seems to admit that diffidence remains in every system. Even in his recommended absolute monarchy, people will rightly worry that the monarch cannot fully be trusted. However, he claims that in democracy, everyone will continually compete for power, while a minority will seek glory and domination over others for their own sake. The problem will be less severe than in the state of nature, but democracy will be a continued war of all against all by other means.

Edmund Burke and the Dangers
of Abstract Philosophy

Edmund Burke (1729–1797) was a protestant Irish philosopher, economist, and longtime member of British Parliament (in addition to holding other offices in the British government). While many of the theorists and authors discussed in this book were academics or theorists, Burke (like Hamilton, Madison, and Jay in the previous chapter) was a practicing member of government whose work was shaped by and often targeted toward immediate practical concerns.

For instance, he spent much of the mid-1770s unsuccessfully trying to craft a compromise with the American colonies to avoid war. In particular, while he seemed to think that in principle British Parliament should exercise supremacy over the local parliaments of its empire, in practice, how Parliament should behave depends upon the particular exigencies it faces. For instance, he advocated in 1774 and 1775 having the American colonies tax themselves rather than submit to British taxes, in large part because he thought that asserting the right to tax would fail. American colonists had adopted from England a preference for local rule and participation. Previous attempts to coerce them into compliance had backfired. It was unclear whether Britain could win a war without scorching the earth and rendering the colonies useless, or win in a stable way that didn't require continual and expensive military occupation afterward.

Burke did write abstract works of philosophy, but his most famous and important writings are often reflections or commentaries on particular matters of policy or recent historical events. The reason for this was not merely that MP Burke was dealing with practical matters that needed resolution. Rather, it reflected Burke's own skepticism about abstract reasoning in general. Burke worried that highly abstract ideas, concepts, and principles, unless attached to real historical examples, were largely devoid of content.[16]

His most famous work was *Reflections on the Revolution in France* (1790). Again, this work has both practical and academic goals. From an academic standpoint, Burke wanted to assess the causes and character of the French Revolution, to analyze whether it was working and by what standard, and to predict how the Revolution would end. From a practical standpoint, Burke wanted to persuade his fellow citizens not to support the Revolution (and probably not to wish for one of their own). *Reflections* was widely read at the time of publication, with some readers sympathetic and others, such as liberals Mary Wollstonecraft and Thomas Paine, highly critical. But a few years later, the book's stature greatly increased, as Burke correctly predicted that the new government would be chaotic and corrupt, that it would practice mass terrorism against its own people, and that its revolutionary democracy would eventually fall into military dictatorship.

In the *Reflections*, Burke expresses skepticism for the idea of philosophically determined government. For instance, earlier Enlightenment writers—including the French philosophes who provided intellectual firepower and support for the Revolution— often talked as if governments were consciously chosen or con- sciously agreed-upon artifacts designed, from first principles, for the purpose of securing people's rights. Enlightenment intellectuals often believed they could use philosophy to design better governments for whatever purpose they deemed fit.

Burke, in contrast, was skeptical that people really understood how societies or governments fit together, what makes them work, or what makes people cooperative or not. He thus was opposed to what the British conservative philosopher Michael Oakeshott (1901–1990) would later dub "rationalism." Rationalism, as used here, refers to the idea that people are smart enough, and under- stand society enough, to remake and rebuild society according to their own goals. In contrast, Burke worried that what makes society and government function well is highly complicated and poorly understood. In today's language, we might say that society is not like an engine designed by smart engineers for a purpose, an engine that can be improved and tinkered with by other engineers. It is more like an ecosystem that has a logic of its own, a logic we only partially understand. Today, we recognize that human beings have only a limited capacity to "manage" or "govern" ecosystems, and that our attempts to do so usually lead to dangerous unintended consequences. Burke, in effect, worried that the same applies to the ecosystem of human society and government. Philosophers and pundits impressed with their own wisdom convince themselves they can fix or replace institutions they barely understand.

Burke worried that other philosophers tended to have highly simplified conceptions of human nature (even if they disagreed with each other about what this nature was like). Philosophers might describe people as working together because, say, they understood that everyone's rational self-interest required agreement on common norms and restraint. On the contrary, Burke thought that cooperation and success might depend upon "prejudices,"[17] habits of mind, common religious beliefs, "untaught feelings" of morality,[18] and so on.

What Burke seems to have in mind is that codes of morality, principles of government, rules of chivalry and etiquette, norms of commerce, laws, and so on are for the most part the products of human action but not human design. That is, for the most part, these formal and informal institutions develop over time, in response to genuine problems. Whether they survive or die, expand or contract, flourish or languish depends on how well these norms function in the real world, in light of real-world stresses and trials. Over time, more functional norms tend to survive and poorly functioning norms tend to die. Just as today, it would be hubris for us to think we can engineer a better ecosystem—because we don't quite understand how ecosystems work—so it is hubris for utopian philosophers, poets, and politicians to think they can remake and engineer a better society. They understand only a small bit of what makes everything work together. Indeed, Burke claims that philosophers should spend more time investigating how various traditional norms function; they will often uncover hidden "sagacity" if they do.[19]

Regarding France's early revolutionary democracy, Burke said:

> I do not know under what description to class the present ruling authority in France. It affects to be a pure democracy, though I think it in a direct train of becoming shortly a mischievous and ignoble oligarchy. But for the present I admit it to be a contrivance of the nature and effect of what it pretends to. I reprobate no form of government merely upon abstract principles. There may be situations in which the purely democratic form will become necessary. There may be some (very few, and very particularly circumstanced) where it would be clearly desirable. This I do not take to be the case of France or of any other great country. Until now, we have seen no examples of considerable democracies. The ancients were better acquainted with them. Not being wholly unread in the authors who had seen the most of those constitutions, and who best understood them, I cannot help concurring with their opinion that an absolute democracy, no more than absolute monarchy, is to be reckoned among the legitimate forms of government. They think it rather the corruption and degeneracy than the sound constitution of a republic. If I recollect rightly, Aristotle observes that a democracy has many striking points of resemblance with a tyranny. Of this I am certain, that in a democracy the majority of the citizens is capable of exercising the most cruel oppressions upon the minority whenever strong divisions prevail in that kind of polity, as they often must; and that oppression of the minority will extend to far greater numbers and will be carried on with much greater fury than can almost ever be apprehended from the dominion of a single scepter. In such a popular persecution, individual sufferers are in a much more deplorable condition than in any other. Under a cruel prince they have the balmy compassion of mankind to assuage the smart of

their wounds; they have the plaudits of the people to animate their generous constancy under their sufferings; but those who are subjected to wrong under multitudes are deprived of all external consolation. They seem deserted by mankind, overpowered by a conspiracy of their whole species.[20]

Burke thus worries that an unconstrained democracy could be even more tyrannical and oppressive than an unconstrained monarch. Earlier, he says:

But where popular authority is absolute and unrestrained, the people have an infinitely greater, because a far better founded, confidence in their own power. They are themselves, in a great measure, their own instruments. They are nearer to their objects. Besides, they are less under responsibility to one of the greatest controlling powers on the earth, the sense of fame and estimation. The share of infamy that is likely to fall to the lot of each individual in public acts is small indeed, the operation of opinion being in the inverse ratio to the number of those who abuse power. Their own approbation of their own acts has to them the appearance of a public judgment in their favor. A perfect democracy is, therefore, the most shameless thing in the world. As it is the most shameless, it is also the most fearless.[21]

It's thus no surprise that Burke regards the French Revolution, as of 1790, as a "monstrous tragicomic scene," a "strange chaos of levity and ferocity."[22]

It's important to note, though, that Burke was not critical of democracy per se, in the sense that we use the modern term. Indeed, Burke supported British constitutional monarchy with its strong parliamentary government. Today, we would label Burke a liberal democrat, though he used the term "democracy" in the old-fashioned pejorative sense we discussed in chapter 1. However, Burke belongs here because of the way he critiques democracy.

Burke wasn't much interested in questions such as whether democracy is good or bad, *tout court*. On the contrary, he thinks it's a philosopher's caprice to think we can answer such a question in the abstract. The best form of government depends on the people, the time, and the place, and upon facts and truths to which we lack access.

Instead, Burke offered a theory of the limits of democracy's ability to produce positive, stable change. Democratic bodies—like philosophers and theorists—lack the understanding to produce their utopian visions. At best, Burke thought, social changes should come gradually and a few at a time, because this gives societies a chance to experiment and see, firsthand, what works and what doesn't. Thus, while Burke was a philosophical liberal—he agreed that protecting liberty was a vital goal of government—he was also a kind of conservative. He cautioned in favor of a limited style of politics that did not attempt to eradicate human imperfection. Indeed, he would caution us that the next time some mass movement promises to fix everything, we should first recognize that the proponents almost certainly don't understand social dynamics. Second, the greater this group's ambition, the more likely they will fail, and the more likely they will turn tyrannical in their desperation to succeed.

Marx on the "Internal Contradictions" of Liberal Capitalist Democracy

The German philosopher Karl Marx (1818–1883) was a relentless critic of liberal, capitalist democratic states. He was not a critic of democracy per se; he advocated various forms of worker democracy. However, just as Burke thought revolutionary democracy was unstable and would lead to terrorism and dictatorship, Marx thought that the liberal capitalist democratic states would eventually collapse under the weight of their own internal contradictions.

In contrast to mainstream economics, Marx and his frequent coauthor and patron, the wealthy capitalist Friedrich Engels, generally write from the perspective of methodological collectivism. While economists generally model individuals as individuals trying to achieve their own goals, Marx and Engels tend to model individuals as members of socially constructed teams whose behaviors and goals are shaped by history and their group membership. Marx and Engels modeled people as playing the role and having the goals associated with their socioeconomic class.

Marx and Engels argued that early humans lived in classless, egalitarian societies. But once agricultural-based civilization began, this created "social surpluses" (i.e., production above bare subsistence), which in turn incentivized and enabled class divisions to occur. Societies have since been divided into a productive class that creates value and an exploitative class that consumes the social surplus created by the productive class. Earlier, in feudal societies, the divide was between working peasants and exploitative lords, knights, kings, and priests. Under capitalism, the class divide is between working laborers (the "proletariat") and bourgeoisie or capitalists. (It's amusing to note here that Engels and Marx themselves were, by their own theory, bourgeois exploiters of the proletariat; nearly all of their work was funded by the Engels's family stocks and cotton mills, which may have used cotton obtained from literal slave labor.)

Marx and Engels believed that the capitalist class exploited the proletariat working class. The capitalists own the means of production, such as factories and machines. Workers owned nothing but their own labor. Workers thus had no choice but to work for the capitalists. The alternative was starvation. Thus, Marx and Engels claimed, workers did not genuinely consent to their employment.

Marx and Engels also thought that to make a profit, capitalists had to *underpay* the workers. The argument for this conclusion is technical, but it's worth pausing to understand. First, at the time Marx and Engels did most of their writing, modern economic price theory—which holds that prices are an emergent property of the forces of supply and demand—had not yet been developed. Marx and Engels subscribed instead to the now defunct "labor theory of value," which holds that the price of a good on the market is determined by the amount of labor that went into making it. (The theory is more sophisticated than that, but the specifics won't concern us here.) Marx and Engels discovered an interesting implication of this theory: if the labor theory of value is true, the only way a capitalist could make a profit is by underpaying workers.

Consider: imagine that the Engels's factories produce cotton shirts. Let's say they sell for $P on the market. By hypothesis, the price, $P, is determined by the amount of labor that went into making those shirts. The price of the shirts is determined by two inputs: $L, the value of workers at the factory, and $R, the value of the raw materials the laborers worked on. ($R is itself determined by the value of the labor it took to produce those raw materials.) So, in short, $P = $R + $L. In order for the Engels family to make a profit, their revenue must exceed his costs. But by hypothesis, according to the labor theory of value, when the Engels family buys raw materials on the market, they pay the full value of those materials. Thus, according to Engels' own economic theory, they cannot make a profit there. Thus, for them to make a profit, they must pay their workers a wage, $W, which is less than $L, the full value of their labor. Their workers accept this exploitative wage because they have no better choice. So, while cotton shirts sell for $P, where $P = $R + $L, the Engels family make the profit represented by $L − $W. In Engels's own language, they profit by capturing the "surplus value" of his workers' labor.

At the time Marx and Engels were writing, capitalist liberalism was on the ascent. More and more states were gradually developing liberal, republican governments with increasingly widespread suffrage. But Marx and Engels believed these new governments were unstable. On paper, the governments claimed to represent all voting individuals as equal participants, each with an equal claim to vote or run for office. But, Marx and Engels claimed, this equality was illusory. In reality, just as feudal monarchies reinforced the feudal class structure, capitalist democracies tend to reinforce the capitalist class structure. The state claims to be neutral, but in effect sides with capital against labor by defending the existence of private property in the means of production. (Marx thought such private property was inherently disadvantageous to the poor.)

Just as Plato speculated that every form of government contains the seeds of its own collapse, Marx held that class-based economic systems would over time collapse because of their internal problems. Marx and Engels say:

> The development of Modern Industry, therefore, cuts from under its feet the very foundation on which the bourgeoisie produces and appropriates products. What the bourgeoisie, therefore, produces, above all, are its own grave-diggers. Its fall and the victory of the proletariat are equally inevitable.[23]

But there are a few major differences between them. In the *Republic*, Plato seems to offer an almost cyclical view of government. Tyranny collapses into timocracy, which collapses into aristocracy, then democracy, then back to tyranny. Marx instead thought history had a direction. Pre-agricultural hunter-gatherer egalitarian societies became variations of feudal monarchies, which gave birth to the bourgeoisie class, which in turn displaced the lords in favor of liberal republicanism. But liberal republicanism would collapse as well, not because *democracy* is inherently unstable, but because *capitalism* is.

Marx predicted that capitalism would collapse. He offers various accounts in different writings about precisely why it would collapse, so there may not be one account that qualifies as *the* account. But throughout his writings we see common strands. For one, Marx thought that capitalism would face cyclical crises. Note that Marx was predicting particular kinds of crises with particular causes and particular results. Thus, pace what some internet Marxists seem to think, Marx is not vindicated by every recession.

In particular, Marx claimed that the emergence of new markets would lead to industrial expansion in the attempt to profit from those markets. This would lead to overproduction, which would in turn would lead to busts, which would in turn lead to contraction, which would in turn lead to fewer and fewer remaining capitalist businesses. The emergence of new markets would cause production, wages, and employment to rise, but this would lead to excess production, and in turn falling profits, falling wages, and the businesses failing.[24] Over time, these cycles would destroy more and more of the capitalists and force them into the proletariat class. Private property would increasingly be concentrated in the hands of fewer and fewer capitalists.

Note, here, that concentration is not simply measured in terms of *percentage* of wealth. Imagine, as a dummy example, that I have $900 and you have $100. Right now, then, I have 90 percent of the wealth. Now imagine we both get richer, but I get richer slightly faster than you. After a year, I have $2,000, but you have $200. In this scenario, we are both better off than before, but I now have about 91 percent of the wealth while you only have 9 percent. Here, saying that wealth has become concentrated obscures the fact that we are both better off. This is not what Marx had in mind. Instead, he thought that there would be fewer and fewer capitalists over time, while in the long run the poor proletariat would see their wages stagnate.

Marx thought that even the remaining capitalists would get a bad deal from capitalism. The rate of profits would fall over time, such that in the end even the few remaining capitalists are doing quite badly. He thought capitalists would gradually saturate and exhaust all possible markets. Over time, the overwhelming majority of people would come to realize that the system was failing them. The workers would revolt, kill the bourgeoisie, seize the means of production, and then instantiate socialism.

Variations of Marxist economics remain quite popular outside of economics departments, though economists reject his theories. Regardless, for our purposes here, Marx is interesting not merely because his work was historically important, as it was used, for instance, to justify revolutions and one-party, anti-democratic states throughout the twentieth century. (Whether Marx himself would have condoned or condemned these revolutions is itself controversial.) Rather, notice that most of the previous authors we have discussed were interested in whether democracy simpliciter is stable or unstable, peaceful or unpeaceful, divisive or cohesive.

Marx cautions against framing our questions this way. Governments are embedded into economic and cultural structures. In his view, democracy with capitalism and democracy with socialism are different things. It might be that one is stable and the other not. (However, pace Marx, our best current empirical work indicates that capitalist democracies tend to be far more stable than socialist democracies.[25]) On Marx's view, in capitalist countries, the market is not subordinate to democratic politics; on the contrary, he thinks democracy becomes the servant of capitalist power.

Group Polarization and Segregation in Contemporary Democracy

A common concern in early democratic theory—including work as late as the *Federalist Papers* or *Democracy in America*—was that democracy would encourage interest-based factions. Their model of democracy was much like—or an extension of—their model of a market economy. This model presumes that people try to promote their self-interest through democratic politics. People with similar goals would form interest-based alliances. For instance, if a tariff, wage law, income tax, or infrastructure project hurts some people but benefits others, they would band together in opposition or support. Political parties would represent people with common interests. Democracy would at least allow the majority to promote their self-interest through politics, but the worry remained that factionalism might lead to incessant internal conflict.

However, later political scientists and economists often argued that properly designed democratic rules could ensure that a wide range of interests—not merely the interests of the majority—get represented. One reason is that majorities generally have disparate interests among themselves. Accordingly, to get things done, with the right rules, any winning coalition would have to make lots of compromises and policy trades with minorities.[26] You vote for this and we'll vote for that. Everyone gets something.

Contemporary political science in many ways vindicates the worry that democracy will suffer from persistent internal factions and conflict. However, perhaps the most surprising finding is that these conflicts often seem *not* to result from disparate interests or ideologies. In contemporary democracies, citizens are highly tribalistic, yet not very ideological, and their voting behavior does not much reflect their self-interest. Plato, Hamilton, and Tocqueville were right to worry about factions, but misdiagnosed their source.

Since the 1950s, political psychologists have studied at great length how people reason about politics and group membership. One major finding is that we suffer from "intergroup bias." That is, we tend to form groups and strongly identify ourselves as members of these groups. We are biased to assume that members of our own group are good, smart, competent, and trustworthy, while members of other groups are bad, stupid, incompetent, and dishonest. We cut our own group slack but damn the slightest transgression on the other side. If this sounds like how contemporary political partisans behave—making excuses for themselves while wagging the finger at others—then you've seen the bias at work.[27]

We often assume the animosity between, say, Republicans and Democrats stems from disputes over justice or policy. But, on the contrary, political scientists persistently find that the overwhelming majority of citizens, including registered party members, are not very ideological, have very few policy opinions, and tend not even to know or support the policies of the party with which they identify. Most citizens have few political opinions, and even fewer stable opinions; what few opinions they have cannot be amalgamated into a coherent position.[28]

In *Neither Liberal nor Conservative*, Donald Kinder and Nathan Kalmoe review the vast empirical literature on voter opinion, including their own. They estimate that fewer than 1 out of 5 voters have a genuine ideology.[29] Many citizens will, if surveyed, describe themselves as "liberal" or "conservative," but most self-described liberals and conservatives lack stable beliefs fitting those ideological self-descriptions. Plenty of other research finds similar results.[30] Further, contrary to popular myth, there are few "single-issue" voters.[31] In general, cognitive elites have ideologies and vote on the basis of ideology, but the majority of voters identify with parties on non-ideological grounds, and simply vote the same way every time.

Given citizens' ideological innocence and lack of strong policy preference, it's strange that they identify so strongly with their political parties. One might think, then, that they at least support their parties because they expect the parties to promote policies that benefit their voters' self-interest, even if those voters don't quite know what the policies are. But yet another surprising finding—supported by numerous empirical studies of voter behavior, using a wide variety of methods—is that voters do *not* vote selfishly. Self-interest is a weak predictor of voting behavior. Voters instead tend to vote for what they believe will promote their nation's common good. They are, in technical terms, sociotropic.[32]

This seems odd because most people are mostly selfish. Overall, people tend to care more about their own interests than society as a whole. But, to preview an issue we'll examine in more depth in later chapters, the reason people might vote sociotropically seems to be because their votes do not matter much. In modern democracies, the chances a vote will make a difference are small. When elections are close enough or small enough that votes have a high chance of making a difference, voters vote selfishly, but when chances are low, they use their votes to express altruistic commitments or their commitment to various groups.[33]

So, if voters are not voting ideologically or in their self-interest, what are they voting for? And why are political partisans so nasty toward each other?

However, political partisanship is more robust than this. Political scientists Christopher Achen and Larry Bartels argue that citizens usually vote from partisan loyalties. These partisan loyalties are grounded in their *identities* but do not track ideology, sincere policy preferences, or their interests. People tend to vote for who they are rather than what they want. Various identities or demographic groups become attached to particular political parties for largely *accidental* historical events or circumstances that have little to do with voters' underlying values or interests.[34] For example, American Jews switched from Republican to Democratic loyalties between 1928 and 1940, not because of policy platform changes, the Wall Street Crash, or ideological changes, but because of reduced antagonism between Jews and Catholics in the 1930s.[35]

Today, in the United States, mutual diffidence between political partisans is high. People tend to see themselves as being on Team Democrat or Team Republican. Since 1960, mutual animosity has gotten worse. For instance, in 1960, most Americans said they would have little problem with their children marrying voters for the rival party. Now, most Americans say they would oppose such marriages.[36] Most partisans will discriminate against job applicants who support a rival party even when party membership is irrelevant to the job.[37]

You may have heard that in the United States and many other democracies, citizens are becoming increasingly politically *segregated*. This is often referred to as "the Big Sort."[38] They are less likely now than in the past to have neighbors who vote differently than they do. Instead, Democrats live near other Democrats and Republicans next to Republicans. As economists Ethan Kaplan,

Jörg Spenkuch, and Rebecca Sullivan find, "At no point since the Civil War have partisans been as clustered *within* the boundaries of individual states as today."[39]

Political segregation is probably an emergent phenomenon. It's not as though Americans or others decided to segregate their country by party, and while there is district gerrymandering and such, it's not as though political segregation is the result of something like political Jim Crow Laws. Instead, the explanation may be simpler. Empirical work generally finds that people dislike members of other parties and dislike having cross-cutting political discussions; they will, if they can, try to live and work in like-minded areas.[40] Indeed, the economist Thomas Schelling (1921–2016) famously demonstrated that segregation can occur even when people want to avoid it. Imagine everyone (A) prefers to be live in a diverse neighborhood but also (B) prefers not to be the *minority* in this diverse neighborhood. The stronger their preference is for B over A (the more they prefer not being the minority to living among diverse neighbors, if they have to choose), the more quickly everyone self-sorts into nondiverse communities. Schelling's depressing results hold even if people *want* diversity and don't want segregation.[41] But, when it comes to politics, most of us prefer not merely to avoid being the minority. Rather, we don't want to interact with the other side at all.

Democratic Backsliding

There's a legend that as Benjamin Franklin left the US Constitutional Convention, someone asked what kind of government they had designed. According to legend, he said, "A republic, if you can keep it."[42]

Theorists have long worried whether we can keep democracy. Indeed, whether *any* form of government is particularly stable remains an open area of inquiry. Even when we see that, for instance, monarchies or dynasties last for centuries, there is often continuous intrigue and bloody fighting over who wears the crown.

Generally, social scientists agree that after World War II, the number of democracies greatly increased. The increase came in waves, first with the end of World War II, then with decolonization in the 1950s and 1960s, and then again with communist states transitioning to democracies at the end of the Cold War. Further, not only did the raw number or percentage of democracies increase, but democratic countries generally became *more* democratic.

In a recent paper, political scientists Valeriya Mechkova, Anna Lührmann, and Staffan Lindberg try to measure just how much democratic backsliding has taken place over the past twenty or so years. They use a database from the "Varieties of Democracy Project," which measures "350 highly specific indicators across 174 currently existing countries as of the end of 2016."[43] They find that the total number of democracies declined by only a small amount (100 to 97), in part because while some countries stopped being democratic, others transitioned to democracy. However, the total degree of democratization has declined. Still, they note that while democracy seems to have peaked in 2011, even today, it is much better than it was in, say, 1974, when only about a quarter of countries qualified as democratic. They caution against alarmist complaints of democratic backsliding, but they also note a trend they find alarming: while the total number of democracies, and the overall measured degree of how democratic these countries are, is fairly stable, these aggregate measures hide that there significant volatility *within* the data. Many countries are volatile, with their scores jumping around year after year, but the *average* happens to wash out to show only a slight decline since 2011. Still, their paper ends with data from 2016, so we might wonder what it would show if it continued today.

The Varieties of Democracy Project itself published a policy in late 2020, during the height of the COVID-19 crisis, on a phenomenon they call "pandemic backsliding."[44] "Pandemic backsliding" refers to when governments, in response to COVID-19, violate or curtail liberal rights, engage in authoritarian practices that limit access to information or control the media, or violate democratic standards in decision-making and accountability. They find that only a small handful of democratic countries had no violations. The majority of democracies, including the United States, France, Spain, and the United Kingdom, had some significant violations of liberal or democratic rights. One might think this is merely a short-term problem but on the contrary, they argue, when states allocate emergencies powers to themselves or curtail civil liberties in the face of an emergency, once the emergency ends, they tend not to relinquish all their new powers. Over time, emergencies allow states to ratchet up their own power and, as a logical consequence, ratchet down the freedom and power of citizens.[45]

As of 2021, there are over 6,000 academic papers published on the problem of democratic backsliding, with about 5,000 of these appearing in the last five years. Some analyze the causes of particular instances of backsliding in particular countries; others try to measure overall changes across the world; others try to assess why backsliding occurs. While there seems to be a consensus that some backsliding has occurred and that it is getting worse, there is no real consensus about *why* it occurs or whether it will continue to do so. So, as of now, it seems that the stability of democracy is a worry, but it is unclear how big of a worry.

What We Should Learn

In the previous chapter, theorists largely argued that democracy would cause peace by reducing and containing factionalism. They claimed that democracy would create stability by ensuring that government serves the people's interests and eliminating their tendency to see government as an alien, occupying power.

In this chapter, we see theorists arguing that this is too simple and unrealistic a take. Instead, they claim, even in democracies, there will always be factions with disparate interests rather than a group with a unified point of view. Democracy might produce new and different kinds. It might be a system in which special interests exploit the many under the disguise of speaking for all.

As we will see in future chapters, this theme will reappear when we consider whether democracy makes us virtuous, equal, or free.

4

For Virtue

Does Democracy Enlighten and Ennoble?

What is the nail for which government is the hammer? In the previous chapters, we discussed how older political theorists tended to think the first virtue of political institutions was to keep order, prevent internal conflict, and provide stability. Nowadays, though, philosophers and theorists tend to take these values for granted, at least when they theorize. Instead, contemporary political philosophy tends to presume that the purpose of government is to produce or preserve equality or freedom, or otherwise provide a range of useful goods and services.

However, an older idea—and an idea that still has defenders today—is that the primary purpose of the state is to help make us *good*. That is, the point of the state is not merely to create law and order, protect rights, preserve equality, or provide public goods like parks. Rather, some philosophers and political theorists have argued that the state should help facilitate and enable us to develop into *virtuous* people. Or, closely related, some philosophers have argued that the state should facilitate "the achievement of human excellence in art, science, and culture," or other (according to them) objectively valuable goods.[1]

Today, philosophers tend to use the word "perfectionism" to refer to such ideas. A political philosophy is *perfectionist* to the extent that it holds that the state should promote moral virtue, intellectual virtue, and/or various forms of human excellence, such as achievements in art, science, culture, engineering, or sport. Perfectionism holds that the state should help make us good people

Democracy. Jason Brennan, Oxford University Press. © Oxford University Press 2023.
DOI: 10.1093/oso/9780197558812.003.0004

and should help us do awesome, impressive things. It should facilitate a culture in which people are honorable, and inquisitive, and in which we climb mountains, fly to the moon, write epic poetry, and split atoms.

As with pretty much everything else in philosophy, there is plenty of debate about what "moral virtue" means.[2] However, following Aristotle, philosophers today tend to say something like the following:

> A morally virtuous person A) does the right thing B) for the right reason, C) knows what they are doing, and D) feels the right way about it.[3]

Notice the different elements. A fully morally virtuous person will perform right actions and avoid performing wrong actions. They *act* properly.

But acting properly is not enough for virtue. A virtuous person also has the right motivations; in particular, they do the right thing because it is right. If I save the drowning child, I act rightly. But suppose I save the child not because I value her life or think saving children is good, but instead *only* because I want personal fame, or hope the child's parents will reward me. In that case, I lack virtue. A sociopath could do the right thing, but virtue requires accompanying good will.

Most philosophers also think virtue requires proper understanding. The general idea is that a virtuous agent has practical wisdom. They don't merely manage to stumble onto the right action, but understand what makes actions right and wrong, and can reliably identify what the right thing to do is in different situations. So, for instance, suppose I am in a complex moral dilemma with six possible actions. I don't know what to do, but I want to do the right thing. Suppose I roll a six-sided die to choose what to do, and by luck, it happens to select what is in fact the right action in that situation. Here, I do the right thing and even in a way have the right motives, but I lack the relevant understanding. So, I am not fully virtuous.

Finally, most philosophers have argued that virtuous people have the right feelings about what they do (or at least lack the wrong feelings). To illustrate, suppose I abstain from plagiarizing or engaging in academic fraud because I know it's wrong. But suppose I am strongly tempted to do so; I want to cut corners, but I resist the urge. Here, philosophers would say I am *merely temperate*. I desire to act wrongly, but I manage to overcome the temptation. A perfectly virtuous person would not have such contrary desires; they would feel good about academic honesty and find cheating revolting.

Thus, virtue seems to have many components. This means that moral perfectionism is a demanding standard for governments. To inculcate moral virtue requires ameliorating citizens' actions, understanding, practical wisdom, feelings, and desires. Similar remarks apply to improving their intellectual virtues. In contrast, insofar as a perfectionist argues that governments should help facilitate or train citizens to produce great human achievements, the demands are more varied. What does it take to produce a culture that creates great works of art or great achievements in science?

In this chapter, we will review why philosophers and political scientists have, over time, argued that democracy of the right sort could contribute to citizens' virtues and excellence. In the next chapter, we will examine why philosophers and political scientists have often argued that democracy instead makes us worse.

Aristotle: For the Sake of Noble Actions

In the *Politics*, Aristotle argues at length that the final end of the state is to produce the good life. The good life is, as he had previously argued in his *Nicomachean Ethics*, a virtuous life. It's worth quoting him at length, because his arguments are somewhat puzzling:

[A] state exists for the sake of a good life, and not for the sake of life only; if life only were the object, slaves and brute animals might form a state, but they cannot, for they have no share in happiness or in a life based on choice. Nor does a state exist for the sake of alliance and security from injustice, not yet for the sake of exchange and mutual intercourse; for then the Tyrrhenians and the Carthaginians, and all who have communal treaties with one another, would be citizens of one state.[4]

He goes on to say that the members of a military or commercial alliance are not members of one state because each state has distinct magistrates and ministers. So, this argument is puzzling because Aristotle seems to be saying, correctly, that cooperation for the sake of mutual commercial advantage or keeping the peace is not *sufficient* to make something a state or to make different people co-citizens. That's right; obviously, the members of NATO are different states. But it's unclear, here, why Aristotle thinks the fact that these bonds do not suffice to make something a state thereby show that the purpose of the state cannot be keeping the peace, security, or facilitating exchange. Maybe both military alliances and states could have the same purpose. It's also unclear what Aristotle's argument about slaves and brute animals forming a state is supposed to do here, but rather than dwell on it, I'll move on to his more careful arguments that follow the passage above.

Aristotle next tries to argue that even if people live and work together with common laws under common rulers, this doesn't suffice to show they have a state. He says:

[I]f men dwelt at a distance from one another . . . and there were laws among them that they should not wrong each other in their exchanges, neither would this be a state. Let us suppose that one man is a carpenter, another a farmer, another a shoemaker, and so on, and that their number is ten thousand: nevertheless if they have nothing in common but exchange, alliance, and the like, that would not constitute a state. Why is this? Suppose . . . they had made an alliance with one another, but only against evil-doers; still an accurate thinker would not deem this to be a state, if their intercourse was of the same character as before their union. It is clear then that a state is not a mere society, having a common place, established for the prevention of mutual crime and for exchange. These are conditions without which a state cannot exist; but all of them together do not constitute a state, which a community of families and aggregations of families in well-being, for the sake of a perfect and self-sufficing life.[5]

Here, Aristotle asks us to imagine men who originally lived and worked apart from each other (though near enough that they could exchange if they wanted to) form a common alliance with common rules to govern them all, all for the purpose of protecting all ten thousand from crime and to facilitate mutually beneficial exchange between them. He thinks we would agree that this doesn't suffice for them to constitute a *state*. However, whether we agree with him here might depend upon further details in the thought experiment that he never supplies. Recall that philosophers tend to define a "government" as the subset of a society that claims a monopoly on the legitimate use of coercion, and which has coercive power sufficient to maintain that monopoly.[6] Aristotle's description does not specify whether these 10,000 men have formed a government so defined for the purposes of keeping peace and promoting commerce, or whether instead they live in cooperative anarchy in which they all follow and privately enforce known common rules. At any rate, if the 10,000 men appointed a king or aristocratic council that had a monopoly on force, but which limited its activities to keeping the peace and facilitating commerce, then I'd call that a state, even if Aristotle would not.

Aristotle continues:

> [T]here arise in cities family connexions, brotherhoods, common sacrifices, amusements which draw men together. But these are created by friendship, for to choose to live together is friendship. The end of the state is the good life, and these are the means towards it. And the state is the union of families and villages in a perfect and self-sufficing life, by which we mean a happy and honourable life.
>
> Our conclusion, then, is that *political society exists for the sake of noble actions, and not of living together.*[7]

In the end, then, what Aristotle seems to be arguing is something like this: if you imagine many people living and working together under common rules (and perhaps rulers?) that keep the peace and promote commerce, this would not suffice to constitute a real *state*. A real state exists when citizens exist in a situation of mutual civic friendship, with a share in each other's happiness and flourishing. Here, Aristotle is counting on readers to already agree and understand that for human beings, flourishing is not a mere condition and happiness is not a mere feeling. Given the kinds of beings humans are—intellectual, political, social, choosing beings—happiness and flourishing instead require virtue. So, he concludes the purpose of a state must therefore be to promote the good life for its members, to enable them to flourish in the ways distinctive to the kinds of human beings who can be citizens in the first place. This means encouraging and facilitating people to become virtuous, excellent agents.

I suspect this argument will be unpersuasive to contemporary readers. Aristotle expects us to agree that a state-like entity that doesn't promote virtue and civic friendship doesn't qualify as a real state. Perhaps you agree or not. But if we agree with him that a true or proper state must also promote virtue, it remains unclear why this proves that the true or central purpose of the state is to promote virtue. In the end, his argument appears to be that a state that does not promote its citizens' virtuous character is obviously a defective state, if we even want to call it a state at all. If the state does *less* than that, it is not a true state, but more like an extended partnership among private people. It is less a coherent whole and more like a military alliance.

Perhaps Aristotle's argument here would be more persuasive if we used a different term from what appears in the translated text above. We could substitute "community" for "state." Let's try recasting his argument this way: imagine a bunch of people living together under common rules, enforced by common rulers, but the rules aim and succeed only in keeping the peace and facilitating commerce. Imagine the people have no intrinsic interest in one another's well-being, happiness, or virtue, nor do they have any interest in working together for common projects that require group input. Here, Aristotle might say—and this seems plausible—that this group is not a proper community. He might then argue that this suggests that proper goals of a community are to enable its members to perform noble acts, develop their virtue, and achieve various kinds of excellence.

In the *Nicomachean Ethics*, Aristotle makes similarly puzzling arguments:

> Now it would seem that this supreme End must be the object of the most authoritative of the sciences—some science which is pre-eminently a master-craft. But such is manifestly the science of Politics; for it is this that ordains which of the sciences are to exist in states, and what branches of knowledge the different classes of the citizens are to learn, and up to what point; and we observe that even the most highly esteemed of the faculties, such as strategy, domestic economy, oratory, are subordinate to the political science. Inasmuch then as the rest of the sciences are employed by this one, and as it moreover lays down laws as to what people shall do and what things they shall refrain from doing, the end of this science must include the ends of all the others. Therefore, the Good of man must be the end of the science of

Politics. For even though it be the case that the Good is the same
for the individual and for the state, nevertheless, the good of the
state is manifestly a greater and more perfect good, both to attain
and to preserve.[8]

Politics is the master science, because it controls what the state and
its citizens will do and how the other sciences will be pursued. All
these other subordinate sciences study particular things, while the
science of politics creates order and includes all these subordinate
ends. Since all these other sciences are aiming at some part of what
is good, politics must aim toward the supreme good of men as well.
But, as Aristotle argues at length (and as most Greek philosophers
seemed to agree), the good of human beings consists, among other
things, in *virtue*.

Aristotle dedicates a great deal of space to establishing the conclusion that virtue is constitutive of human flourishing. In the
Nicomachean Ethics, he asks us to consider possible candidates for
what could constitute the good or "happy" life for human beings.
One might think that happiness is a life of pleasure and enjoyment.
But, Aristotle retorts, pleasure is fit for cattle or lower animals; it's
not a uniquely human form way of living. One might think happiness is a life of honor. But, Aristotle says, honor depends upon
others' recognizing one's excellence or virtue, which makes happiness too dependent on how others think. That seems implausible
as an account of human flourishing. One might think happiness
consists in money-making. But, Aristotle says, money is a means
and not an end in itself.

What's distinctive about human beings is their rationality—
their ability to recognize and act upon reasons. Well-functioning
humans need to have an active life grounded on rational principles.
A happy person enjoys internal harmony, as his life is guided by
reason and his emotions work with rather than against reason. This
requires having a structured life, in which one acts on, balances, and
unifies all of one's reasons, dispositions, and feelings. A person with

such internal harmony is a virtuous person—a person who does the right thing for the right reasons, knows what she is doing, and feels the right way about it. Accordingly, the human good "turns out to be activity of soul exhibiting excellence."[9]

Political theorist David Held refers to Aristotle's (and other related philosophers') conception of democracy as "developmental republicanism."[10] Aristotle and other Greek philosophers who favored active participation (even those who were not in favor of anything we would now call democracy) thought that participation in politics would develop citizens' intellectual and moral capacities. It gave citizens a worthy challenge that required them, in the course of ruling themselves, to think through difficult moral and scientific issues, to persuade one another, to actively work together for the common good, and to learn from experience. Participation in politics supposedly provided a uniquely good opportunity—indeed, a necessary condition—for human flourishing and development.

Spinoza: Achieving Human Perfection through Democratic Society

The Dutch philosopher Baruch Spinoza (1632–1677) is mainly known today for his contributions to metaphysics and epistemology, the branches of philosophy that study the nature of existence and of knowledge. However, he also defended a perfectionist account of politics, and appears—though there is controversy about this—to have been one of the earliest modern philosophers to defend democracy.

At first glance, Spinoza's political theory (as seen in his 1670 *Theologico-Political Treatise*) reads much like Hobbes's *Leviathan* (1651). He describes a state of nature, in which there are no common rules or rulers governing how people interact with each other. As in Hobbes's *Leviathan*, Spinoza argues that in this perilous condition anyone may, by right, do whatever is necessary to preserve and protect themselves, and may regard anyone else as a potential enemy to be used or destroyed.[11] Like Hobbes, Spinoza argues that people would recognize that the state of nature is intolerable and would want to escape it by appointing a common sovereign and common constraints on their actions. In the state of nature, people are free to do anything they please, but the value of this radical freedom is low.

However, Spinoza quickly departs from Hobbes. While Hobbes believes that an absolute monarch is the most stable form of government, Spinoza defends more democratic forms of government on the same grounds. Spinoza argues that monarchy is far more likely to devolve into its degenerate form, tyranny, than is a government consisting of most citizens. After all, he claims, it is easier to corrupt the few than the many and easier to corrupt the one than the few.

Some of Spinoza's arguments advance ideas we will consider at greater length (from other authors, who better develop them) in later chapters. For instance, Spinoza thinks that democracies will tend to make good decisions because the majority will tend to know its own interests. Further, Spinoza thinks that democracy enables people not merely to be subject to the laws but also the authors, which means that in a democracy, people remain free because they live by laws they created.

Spinoza also departs from Hobbes because he defends a different conception of human nature. Hobbes is a subjectivist: your good is the fulfillment of your desires. When Hobbes makes recommendations, such as that all of us would want to escape the state of nature, he is really arguing that the state of nature prevents us from satisfying our subjective desires. Spinoza, in contrast, thinks people have a common nature and a highest good. According to Spinoza, every kind of thing has a nature, and to flourish as a thing is to realize that nature. For human beings, our essential nature is to be rational, which means to act from our own reason rather than to be controlled by external forces. Thus, for Spinoza, human flourishing consists in striving toward increased rationality. (Spinoza doubts that we can achieve perfection in our lifetime—perfection would require immorality. So human perfection is a goal we strive for rather than something we can achieve.)[12]

A traditional objection to this kind of perfectionism goes as follows: even if rationality is a distinctive human trait, it is unclear why maximizing or perfecting this distinctive trait is essential to human well-being. After all, even if, say, bats were the only creatures with echolocation, it wouldn't follow that perfecting echolocation somehow maximizes the well-being of bats. Spinoza would regard this objection as a misunderstanding. He recognizes that different people have different particular goals, ends, and desires. In his view, to perfect rationality is, among other things, to perfect your capacity to order, harmonize, and achieve all of your various goals, and to ensure that your desires and goals work for *you* instead of you being enslaved by your desires. Recall that Hobbes argues that a rational person seeks power after power because power, in the sense Hobbes uses the term, just means the ability to achieve one's goals. For Spinoza, perfected rationality means having control over oneself rather than the mere ability to satisfy whatever desires one happens to have.

Spinoza never claims that democracy is the best or optimal regime. However, he contends that properly constituted democracies have clear advantages over theocracies and monarchies. Theocracies and monarchies tend to be despotic, to stifle human thought (and thus rationality), and to turn people into subjects rather than active agents. Democracy can help promote human perfection (and thus well-being) by turning people into more rational, self-directed agents. An ideal human being is a wise, self-directed, and self-controlled person. Spinoza regards democracy as the institutional arrangement most conducive to creating and most befitting this kind of person.

Tocqueville: Civic Virtue
beyond Narrow Politics

In chapter 2, we discussed how Tocqueville argued that democracy would be more stable than alternative forms of government. But Tocqueville's principal defense of democracy was that it improved citizens' character and behavior, though not in the way Aristotle, Spinoza, or the authors we will consider later in this chapter suspected.

Many philosophers, political theorists, and activists contend that democracy tends to enlighten and ennoble citizens when they participate in politics. (We are considering some such arguments in this very chapter.) Others contend that democracy would tend to produce *smart* decisions, because it allows the people to choose for themselves and because individuals best know how to advance own interests. (We will examine arguments like this in chapters 6 and 7.) Tocqueville disagrees; on the contrary, he regards most political discussion in early American democracy as puerile. Like Plato and others, he thought democratic discussion tended to be emotional, poorly reasoned, and irrational. He thought that democracies rarely produced good legislation and rarely elected competent magistrates. Here, Tocqueville reads like a sharp critic of democracy rather than a fan.

However, Tocqueville thinks the greatest advantage of democratic government comes not from its primary effects, but from its long-term, somewhat hidden side effects:[13]

Democracy does not provide a people with the most skillful of governments, but it does that which the most skillful government cannot do: it spreads throughout the body a restless activity, superabundant force, and energy never found elsewhere, which, however little favored by circumstance, can do wonders. Those are its true advantages.[14]

Later:

> That constantly renewed agitation introduced by democratic gov-
> ernment into political life passes, then, into civil society. Perhaps,
> taking everything into consideration, that is the greatest advan-
> tage of democratic government.[15]

What Tocqueville finds remarkable about democratic Americans is their limitless energy to *do* things; in particular, to do things *themselves*. In most countries, when something bad happens or if there is a social problem, people either do nothing or demand that the government fix it. But, Tocqueville claims, in the United States, Americans constantly form private civic associations in which they themselves solve these problems. Democratic citizens may not govern themselves badly, but they have a robust and lively *civil so-ciety* apart from the government that manages to produce lasting social change and progress. Nonprofit, voluntary "associations" pervade American society. He concludes that the genius of de-mocracy, then, lies not in government, but in that democratic culture energizes citizens to be active agents of progress *outside* government.

Tocqueville goes so far as to claim this explains the different fates of the British and French colonies in North America. The American colonies flourished and expanded because the colonists were energized by the experience of self-government. The French colonies in what are now Louisiana and Canada languished be-cause its members were passive agents unaccustomed to thinking and acting on their own.[16]

Tocqueville is likely correct that that early American democ-racy had an unusually large number of civil associations plus a high rate of participation in those civic associations. Even today, many commentators think the United States enjoys an unusually strong presence of civic associations compared to other advanced democracies. Still, one must wonder whether Tocqueville's diagnosis of *why* Americans are like this is correct. After all, at the time Tocqueville writes, he in effect has a sample size of one democracy versus many non-democracies. It is easy to produce a plausible just-so story about why any features unique to American society might be *caused* by democracy, but hard to verify any such claim, because there are no other democracies to check the theory against. A contemporary political scientist would want to know, to start, are democracy and the size of civil society (in terms of number of organizations, extent of work, and/or percentage of participants) positively correlated? Further, if they are, one then needs to find a way to assess whether democracy causes greater civil society, whether greater civil society in contrast causes democracy, whether they have a common cause, or whether the correlation is coincidental. This remains an active debate in political science today.

Regardless of whether Tocqueville's hypothesis is correct, it is innovative. Political theorists tend to endorse a narrow view of civic virtue, where what it is to be a civically virtuous person is to participate heavily in politics the right way. Tocqueville recognizes that contributions to the polity may come through quasi- and extra-political means. Indeed, we might wonder to what degree normal market activity—if it contributes to the common good and if the participants have public-spirited motives in addition to their self-interested motives—could also constitute civic virtue.[17]

Mill on the Educative Power of Participation

John Stuart Mill (1806–1873) was a prominent English political economist, philosopher, and Liberal Party Member of Parliament. He was an early feminist and co-author of *The Subjection of Women* (1869), which argued that women should be treated as equals to men, and any apparent mental deficiencies women seem to have compared to men result not from their biology, but because of how woman are socialized and miseducated. His essay "The Negro Question" (1850) ridicules the commonly held idea at the time that slavery or oppression *benefited* black people, claims that the existence of slavery means that the United States is a tyranny rather than a democracy, and mocks other racist ideas. His book *On Liberty* (1859) defended fairly radical freedom of speech and lifestyle, and offered a sharp critique of paternalistic legislation, on the grounds that allowing people maximal freedom would ensure social and scientific progress and also best cultivate people's mental and moral virtues. *On Liberty* warns that a close-minded and intolerant society can have more or less the same bad effects as an oppressive government. In *Utilitarianism* (1863), Mill argues that what makes actions right is their tendency to promote happiness, construed broadly to include personal development and virtuous flourishing.

Mill's *Considerations on Representative Government* (1861) offers a sustained defense of representative, popular government. Mill was writing around the time when the label "democracy" started to shift from being a term of derision to an umbrella term for governments characterized by (nearly) universal adult suffrage with equal voting rights. However, Mill is not being coy here with words. *Considerations* advocates representative government but not democracy per se. Instead, Mill defends what he calls a "plurality scheme" or what is today called "plural voting."[18] In plural voting, (nearly all) adult citizens receive one vote, but some citizens—such as those who work in certain professions or who have certain higher degrees—receive two or more votes.

Nowadays, Mill would be labeled an "epistocrat" or a defender of "epistocracy," where "epistocracy" refers to any system of representative government in which the franchise is weighted, by law, according to some criterion of competence or knowledge.[19] We will examine why Mill rejects democracy in favor of epistocracy later in chapter 7.

However, though Mill is not quite a democrat, his arguments for universal adult suffrage and representative government are of interest here because he offers a perfectionist defense of these institutions. Further, one could accept his perfectionist arguments for universal suffrage and then reject his arguments for plural voting; the arguments are independent.

Mill notes that many people believe that an ideal form of government would be something like the absolute rule of a morally perfect king, if only such a king were available. (Remember that both Plato and Aristotle said something similar; or consider how Christians sometimes describe heaven as the absolute kingdom of a perfect God.) Most people of course then add that this is a fantasy; we cannot hope to find a benevolent, wise despot, and even if we did, the next monarch could well be a tyrant. Here, Mill adds that the idea of a wise despot is even more fantastic than people realize. Such a king would have not merely to mean well, but to be "all-seeing." To make wise decisions, he would need to know what is happening in every part of the country and every part of government.[20] In reality, all government requires a genuine division of labor not merely in who *executes* or *administers* decisions, but in who *makes* political decisions. An absolute king has limited knowledge and limited time.

But, Mill says, even if somehow such a wise, all-seeing king could be found, his rule would have bad unintended consequences. Such a monarchy would create a "mentally passive people."[21] He says that sure, under an ideal king, some people might well cultivate the sciences or the arts, while others will pursue intellectual endeavors, while still others will cultivate practical knowledge such as business, engineering, or agriculture. The bureaucracy will carry out the king's will and will be informed about public matters. But the "public at large [will] remain without information and without interest on all great matters of practice."[22]

This is the centerpiece idea in Mill's perfectionist argument for universal suffrage. Mill is a consequentialist; he argues that the best form of government is the one that has the best overall consequences, broadly construed. Mill emphasizes *broadly construed.* Most people who talk about the quality of government consider narrow issues such as whether the decisions are wise, stable, or efficient. But, Mill says, we should also consider how government affects citizens' character. Popular government incentives citizens to be smart, creative, open-minded, tolerant, active, and public-spirited, while other forms of government create close-minded, passive citizens.[23]

Mill says that even if we had an ideal king, the consequences to the citizens' minds and hearts will be dire:

> Nor is it only in their intelligence that they suffer. Their moral capacities are equally stunted. Wherever the sphere of action of human beings is artificially circumscribed, their sentiments are narrowed and dwarfed in the same proportion. The food of feeling is action: even domestic affection lives upon voluntary good offices. Let a person have nothing to do for his country, and he will not care for it. It has been said of old, that in a despotism there is at most but one patriot, the despot himself; and the saying rests on a just appreciation of the effects of absolute subjection, even to a good and wise master.[24]

He adds:

> Leaving things to Government, like leaving them to Providence, is synonymous with caring nothing about them, and accepting their results, when disagreeable, as visitations of Nature.[25]

In effect, in a despotic society—even a benevolent despotic society—people become passive. They don't think much past their own interests. They don't expect to have to solve social problems—and thus barely have any awareness of them. They pay little attention to others' needs. They don't bother learn how the world works, what government can do, or what it takes to solve problems. After all, this is the king's job. The people become sheep under a kind shepherd. Here, Mill might agree that by hypothesis a wise king could make better decisions than a republic, but he says overall that the consequences are worse, because this kingdom renders the citizenry passive, self-centered, ignorant, and stupid.

So, Mill's argument essentially rests on an empirical claim: democracy enlightens, ennobles, and energizes us while other forms of government do the opposite. As an analogy, the idea might be something like this: if you want people to be active agents who can think for themselves, you need to give them responsibility. If you treat people like children, they stay like children. Representative government gives people responsibility while other forms of government do not.

If Mill were writing today, he might try to prove this by finding some way to operationalize and test to what degree citizens in different countries have these good or bad qualities, and then try to see if indeed these qualities are positively correlated with how democratic a country is. He would then try to see whether, say, exogenous changes in how democratic a country is lead to changes in these mental and moral attributes. He would check to see if causation might go the other way—maybe active, smart citizens demand democracy rather than democracy causes citizens to become active and smart. He would check for confounding factors or possible third causes.

However, since Mill is writing before the advent of rigorous political science methods, he instead supports his claim by appealing to what he takes to be well-known historical examples. For instance, he cites Tocqueville and mentions how every visitor to the United States is struck by how smart and active enfranchised Americans seem to be compared to citizens in other countries.[26] He notes differences in behavior between the French (who were once again ruled by an "emperor": Napoleon III) and the British when a problem appears. The British say, "What a shame!" and try to fix it; the French say, "It requires patience" and put up with it.[27] He mentions a wide range of ancient (Greece and Rome) and modern republics (such as late

Renaissance Italian city-states) and asks readers to note how republican citizens tend to be smart and active, while the subjects
of Eastern empires tend to be passive.[28]

Contemporary readers might think Mill is being racist by saying
the citizens of these Western republics tend to be smarter, more enlightened, more open-minded, and more active than subjects in
Eastern despotic kingdoms. But this misunderstands Mill's argument. (And, indeed, Mill was exceptionally progressive on race issues for his time, and perhaps even for our time.) Mill is *not* saying
and indeed *denies* that ancient Greek or Roman people, or white
Americans, are inherently or as a matter of biology better than the
Japanese or Chinese. Indeed, this would contradict his argument.
Rather, he is instead arguing that different institutions create different sets of incentives and different cultural artifacts, which in
turn change how common people behave. If the Chinese had a
long-standing republic and the British a despot, then the Chinese
would be enlightened and ennobled while the British would be
rendered passive.

Indeed, Mill says that despots—even benevolent despots—have
perverse incentives to *encourage* a passive, stupid citizenry. The
problem is not merely that depriving people of the opportunity to
solve problems fails to encourage virtue. Rather, Mill says, if the benevolent despot allows free speech and a free press, this might well
get people interested in and talking about politics. The people will
then either be with him or against him—and it seems likely that
they will often be against him, as different people have different
ideas. What will he do when they oppose his policies? He could
ram the policies down their throats despite their protests, but this
is unstable and a cause of conflict. He could let them share in ruling
or do what the people want, rather than what he (by hypothesis)
knows is best. But then he has become a constitutional monarch in
a partial republic, not a benevolent despot. So, a benevolent despot
would have to stifle political speech. It is easier to rule if people are
passive, ill-informed, and do not think much about politics. The
despot will want to discourage political education.[29]

Just why would political participation enlighten and ennoble us? Here, Mill says:

> Still more salutary is the moral part of the instruction afforded by the participation of the private citizen, if even rarely, in public functions. He is called upon, while so engaged, to weigh interests not his own; to be guided, in case of conflicting claims, by another rule than his private partialities; to apply, at every turn, principles and maxims which have for their reason of existence the common good: and he usually finds associated with him in the same work minds more familiarised than his own with these ideas and operations, whose study it will be to supply reasons to his understanding, and stimulation to his feeling for the general interest. He is made to feel himself one of the public, and whatever is for their benefit to be for his benefit. Where this school of public spirit does not exist, scarcely any sense is entertained that private persons, in no eminent social situation, owe any duties to society, except to obey the laws and submit to the government. There is no unselfish sentiment of identification with the public. Every thought or feeling, either of interest or of duty, is absorbed in the individual and in the family. The man never thinks of any collective interest, of any objects to be pursued jointly with others, but only in competition with them, and in some measure at their expense. A neighbour, not being an ally or an associate, since he is never engaged in any common undertaking for joint benefit, is therefore only a rival. Thus even private morality suffers, while public is actually extinct. Were this the universal and only possible state of things, the utmost aspirations of the lawgiver or the moralist could only stretch to make the bulk of the community a flock of sheep innocently nibbling the grass side by side.[30]

There are a few ways to read this. One less literal way is that perhaps Mill simply means that as a matter of fact, enfranchised people behave one way and unenfranchised people behave another.

But the more literal reading seems to be that political participation *demands* of citizens that they consider others' interests, learn how the world works, acquire information, and so on, because that is what it takes to participate properly and well. Therefore, enfranchised people will heed those demands, become better informed, and develop their moral and intellectual virtues.

But this argument seems unsatisfactory. In short, Mill says that popular government asks citizens to do something, so therefore they will do it and get the resulting benefits. But we can parody this: a state-centered command economy, to work well, requires people to be altruistic, hard-working, and to avoid using the state's power for evil ends, so therefore countries like the USSR will cause their citizens to become altruistic, hard-working, and respectful of rights. Of course, that does not follow; quite the contrary. If a political system *needs* its citizens to behave a certain way to function well, it does not follow that they will in fact behave that way; if it makes demands of them, it does not follow that they will comply.

Deliberative Democracy

In contemporary political theory, "deliberative democracy" refers broadly to various forms of democracy in which people come together to advance ideas, argue about those ideas, weigh pros and cons, listen to one another, and criticize each other's ideas with an open mind. Most deliberative democrats advocate an ideal under which all citizens argue with one another in a dispassionate, scientific way, and then, as a result, reach a consensus about what ought to be done. Many deliberative democrats also present their theory as a theory of political legitimacy and authority; that is, they hold that what makes laws legitimate or authoritative is only when they are passed through what the theorist regards as a properly reasoned process of open deliberation with mass participation and consensus.

"Deliberation" connotes an orderly, reason-guided process. Theorist John Dryzek warns us that most political discussions do not quality as "deliberation" per se.[31] Rather, for something to count as deliberation, participants must follow certain norms of deliberation. For instance, theorist Jürgen Habermas says deliberators should do each of the following:

1. Speakers must be consistent—they must not contradict themselves.
2. Speakers must treat like cases alike.
3. Speakers should use terms and language in a consistent way, to make sure they are all referring to the same things. (No equivocating or switching definitions in ways that would interfere with communication.)
4. Speakers must be sincere—they must assert only what they believe.
5. Speakers must provide reasons for introducing a subject or topic into the discussion.
6. Everyone who is competent to speak should be allowed into the discussion.
7. Speakers are to be allowed to discuss any topic, assert whatever they like, and express any needs—so long as they are sincere.
8. No one may coerce or manipulate another speaker.[32]

Different theorists advance different accounts of what constitutes good or proper deliberation. Some are more stringent and some less. But the important point is that deliberation is not mere political discussion; to qualify as a political deliberation, discussion has to be guided by the right motives, follow the right rules, and perhaps have the right kinds of outcomes.

Deliberative democrats are often seen as some of democracy's biggest fans. But what people often miss, when reading their work, is that deliberative democrats are extremely critical of most actual political discussion, advertising, and processes. Political scientist and deliberative democratic theorist James Fishkin sees the typical citizen as relatively incompetent and apathetic; he regards their discussions as superficial, focused on candidate personalities rather than issues.[33] Habermas and other deliberative democrats do not take citizens' preferences "as a given," as an unassailable basic fact with which democracy must work.[34] Instead, they think citizens ought to interrogate and modify their own preferences in light of high standards of reason. Deliberative democrats and critics of democracy often sound the same at first glance. They often agree that most voters are ignorant of the facts, vote for silly reasons, and reason poorly. The difference is that deliberative democrats think that *more and better* democratic participation can fix these problems.

Deliberative democrats have high standards for what they regard as proper democracy or what constitutes citizens' assent to democratic laws. They hold that most existing democracies fall far below these standards. By analogy, they are like people who think only rock music can be good but at the same time hold that 99 percent of rock music is garbage. Further, when deliberative democracy is offered as a theory of legitimacy, it has the often unnoticed and somewhat perverse implication that almost no actual governments or laws are legitimate. For instance, if I say that a law is legitimate and authoritative only if it is passes after following rules 1–8 above, then—because basically zero laws in the world were passed that way—it follows that no laws are legitimate or authoritative, which means that governments may not enforce any of these laws and we lack have no duty to obey them. But as far as I can tell, no deliberative democrats actually accept this consequence, which means that instead of offering us a theory of legitimacy or authority, they probably mean instead that it would be *better* if laws were passed through deliberative means.

For our purposes here, what matters is that deliberative democrats frequently argue that deliberation will enlighten, ennoble, and educate citizens. Hélène Landemore says, "Deliberation is supposed to . . . Enlarge the pools of ideas and information . . ., Weed out the good arguments from the bad . . ., [and] Lead to a consensus on the 'better' or more 'reasonable' solution."[35] Bernard Manin, Jane Mansbridge, and Elly Stein say that democratic deliberation is a process of training and education.[36] Joshua Cohen claims "the need to advanced reasons that persuade others will help to shape the motivations that people bring to the deliberative procedure."[37] Cohen also claims that *ideal* deliberative procedures can be expected to "shape the identity and interests of citizens in ways that contribute to the common good."[38] Jon Elster claims that in democratic deliberation people will need to advance their proposals by appeal to the common good, and will find it difficult to defend their proposals in such terms unless they really are concerned with common good (rather than just paying lip service).[39] Amy Gutmann and Dennis Thompson claim that even when deliberation fails to produce consensus, it will generally cause citizens to respect one another more.[40]

Different theorists offer different accounts of how deliberation is supposed to go. Bruce Ackerman and James Fishkin suggest that we create a national holiday called "Deliberation Day." Citizens receive a paid day off, but are required to attend moderated, local political discussions.[41] The hope is that citizens will be better informed and more enlightened when the general election comes. Other theorists recommend selecting groups of citizens at random to serve on deliberative councils that will either decide specific laws or offer advice to elected lawmakers. Still others favor even more radical proposals, such as deciding the content of law through Wikipedia-style internet debates.[42]

It often seems straightforward that deliberative democracy would enlighten and ennoble citizens. After all, consider once again Habermas's stringent rules (1–8) of deliberation above. For Habermas, something qualifies as deliberation only if speakers are consistent, treat like cases alike, use language consistently, are sincere, provide reasons for introducing topics, and so on. Cohen says that deliberation requires that every participant have an equal voice, that each participant must offer reasons for their views, that only the reasons expressed during the deliberation should determine the outcome of the deliberation, and that they should aim to reach consensus.[43] Of course, deliberation so described would have to enlighten and ennoble citizens, or cause them to care more about each other and each other's interests. After all, it's perilously close to a tautology that deliberation by definition educates and enlightens people. What it means to deliberate, on their view, is not merely for people to talk, but for them to talk the right way and get the right results. Indeed, when presented with empirical evidence that moderated political discussions failed to produce deliberative democracy's anticipated ameliorative effects, deliberative democrats often respond by saying that this was because the participants did not follow the rules of deliberation and so their discussions do not qualify as deliberation.[44]

It thus sometimes remains unclear whether some deliberative democrats are making a falsifiable empirical claim—that is, this kind of talk will have this kind of positive effect—or making a tautologous claim—that is, to reason together properly by definition produces good results because bad results are proof of improper deliberation or because deliberation, by definition, involves proper reasoning.[45] If that isn't clear, notice the difference between these two kinds of statements:

1. Using difference-in-differences analysis is a good way to discover causation.
2. Using scientific reasoning is a good way to discover the truth.

The first statement makes a substantive claim—a particular method delivers a particular result. The second statement seems like it makes a substantive claim, but the problem is that it might be truism instead. What the speaker means by "scientific reasoning" might simply be "reasoning that tracks the truth."

However, not all deliberative democrats have this problem. Some instead make falsifiable empirical claims and attempt to provide empirical evidence that these claims are true. For instance, Fishkin has run extensive experiments with moderated political discussions, and claims to have shown that deliberation produces, among other things, a greater commitment to the common good and a greater use of reason among participants.[46] However, whether such real-world decision-making on a mass scale, with high stakes, will reliably replicate these positive results remains an open question.

What We Should Learn

Throughout much of history, people took it for granted that good societies make us virtuous and bad societies make us vicious. They presumed that a major goal, if not the only goal, of politics is to inculcate virtue. Nowadays, people tend to assume government should help us develop our potential, protect our rights, and provide for our basic needs, but not to promote good character.

Regardless, both past and present theorists often argued that democracy will make us better people. At base, their argument is simple: properly functioning democracy requires citizens to care about each other and to think carefully. So, they think, participating in democratic institutions is like hitting the gym to build our moral and cognitive muscles. Democracy forces us to be active. This activity overcomes the vices induced by passivity.

5

Against Virtue

Does Democracy Make Us Angry, Mean, and Dumb?

Perfectionist arguments for democracy hold that democracy and widespread political participation are good because they tend to educate, enlighten, and ennoble citizens. As we saw in the last chapter, many of these arguments focus on the supposed direct benefits of democracy itself. They hold that participation itself will make citizens better informed, more rational, and more virtuous. If sound, these arguments imply that some of the supposed deficiencies of democracy are self-correcting. Plato might worry that the mass of citizens are ignorant and biased, but if Mill is right, enfranchising everyone will induce them to be better informed and high-minded. This would be desirable in itself and would help government function better. Many of these arguments—in particular, those by Tocqueville and to a lesser extent by Mill—also held that participation has spillover benefits. According to Tocqueville, while American political discourse is idiotic, enfranchising citizens creates a kind of can-do, go-getter civil and commercial culture that more than compensates for the internal defects of democratic governance.

However, skeptics instead worry that democracy might stultify and corrupt us. In this chapter, we will turn to their arguments.

It's worth pausing, though, to think about the *force* of these kinds of arguments. Suppose I proved, definitively, that aristocracy produces the greatest art and music, while monarchy produces the nicest people. This would indeed show that aristocracy and

Democracy. Jason Brennan, Oxford University Press. © Oxford University Press 2023.
DOI: 10.1093/oso/9780197558812.003.0005

monarchy are *good* in these ways. But you probably would not conclude that this justifies having aristocracy or monarchy overall. You might think that people have a right to a democratic say or a vote, even if legally granting them that right or their exercise of that right turns out to harm the quality of art or the quality of our character.

In parallel, then, you might be suspicious that perfectionist arguments *for* democracy show only that democracy is good in some way, not that people ought to have those rights for those reasons. Suppose someone argued in 1915 that we ought to grant women the right to vote because it would make them better at running charities. You might think that's the wrong kind of justification. Or, if you are skeptical that democracy is just—perhaps because you think it produces bad policies—proof that it makes people better at running charities probably won't override your concern. You might think it's the wrong kind of argument for democratic government.

Plato: The Dangers of Egalitarianism

Recall from chapter 3 that Plato speculates about whether every political system is unstable. Even his ideal political arrangements— the rule of the noble, wise, and selfless guardian class—would degenerate into oligarchy, which would in turn degenerate into democracy, which in turn would fall into despotism. Crucial to Plato's story are the habits of mind and character he thinks each kind of political system engenders.

Plato thinks that democracy propagates a libertine and licentious culture. Democracy promises freedom to everyone—freedom of speech, freedom of lifestyle, and so on. It also encourages egalitarianism. The formal egalitarianism—by law, each person has an equal vote or perhaps an equal chance of being selected by lottery to hold office—encourages people to reject all actual distinctions between people. Democracy says everyone is equal in political standing, but over time citizens falsely conclude that everyone is equal, period. Plato worries than in a democratic polis, this misplaced egalitarianism causes people to lose respect for learning, for wisdom, or for their elders. The young scorn their teachers and in turn teachers, hoping for work, become obsequious to the youth. People stop respecting any kind of authority. They see their own desires and beliefs as inerrant and unchallengeable.

Many egalitarian philosophies acknowledge that we are not in fact equal, but they want us to be treated equally in various ways *despite* our differences. On this kind of view, some people really are wiser, more morally virtuous, more productive, more effective, friendlier, stronger, faster, smarter, or in other respects better than others. Einstein really is smarter than you. Norman Borlaug, the Nobel laureate agronomist, really did make a greater contribution to humanity than you would over 1,000 lifetimes. You are probably an unprincipled coward compared to Hugh Thompson.[1] Nevertheless, many philosophers argue that such differences in aptitude and character do not justify unequal legal status. Jeff Bezos might contribute more to other people's welfare than you do, but he should not enjoy greater protection under the law than you.

However, Plato worries that legal egalitarianism will lead to a more insidious egalitarianism in which people come to insist that they are descriptively equal. The belief that I am legally equal to others leads, over time, to a culture that encourages me to believe I am equal to others, period. No one is or can be better than I am at anything. I come to resent any apparent evidence to the contrary— which leads to resentment and a desire to crush the excellent or exceptional. The belief in human equality—especially moral equality and equality of virtue—becomes a kind of license we grant ourselves to be jerks, to indulge our ignorance, and to treat whatever attitudes, beliefs, or feelings happen to pop into our heads as sacrosanct. If we are all equal, then by assumption we can't be better, which by assumption means whatever we feel or think is *just fine*. That, for Plato, is a recipe for personal corruption.[2]

Plato summarizes his hypothesis here:

> Why, when a democratic city athirst for liberty gets bad cupbearers for its leaders and is intoxicated by drinking too deep of that unmixed wine, and then, if its so-called governors are not extremely mild and gentle with it and do not dispense the liberty unstintedly, it chastises them and accuses them of being accursed oligarchs. . . . But those who obey the rulers, it reviles as willing slaves and men of naught, but it commends and honors in public and private rulers who resemble subjects and subjects who are like rulers. Is it not inevitable that in such a state the spirit of liberty should go to all lengths? . . . And this anarchical temper, my friend, must penetrate into private homes and finally enter into the very animals. . . . the father habitually tries to resemble the child and is afraid of his sons, and the son likens himself to the father and feels no awe or fear of his parents, so that he may be forsooth a free man. . . . and other trifles as these. The teacher in such case fears and fawns upon the pupils, and the pupils pay no heed to the teacher or to their overseers either. And in general, the young ape their elders and vie with them in speech and action, while the old, accommodating themselves to the young, are full of pleasantry and graciousness, imitating the young for fear they may be thought disagreeable and authoritative.[3]

In short: liberty and equality create mindsets that refuse to learn from wisdom or experience and disdain any distinctions. It causes the stupid, ignorant, but self-righteous mob to smother any threat to their self-image and to have contempt for the wisdom of others.

Oddly, as we discussed in chapter 3, Plato thinks radical egalitarianism instills the psychological and cultural mindset that becomes open to tyranny. The thirst to level down, to crush the rich, and eliminate distinctions becomes ever stronger, which in turn induces people to accept any populist flatterer who claims he will act as their representative and voice.

Plato, like Aristotle and many other ancient Greek philosophers, agreed that part of the purpose of the state and of politics was to create conditions that produced virtuous people. Plato and Aristotle both agreed that the state should enable human flourishing and that virtue is a constitutive part of flourishing. They disagreed about what *more* is needed to flourish. Plato sometimes argues that the perfectly virtuous person can flourish through virtue alone, regardless of how badly his life goes, while Aristotle thinks eudaimonia requires virtue *plus* certain external goods.

They both agree that governments should be judged by how conducive they are to virtue, but disagree about how popular, republican governments would work. Aristotle agrees that *the* degenerate form of the rule of the many engenders vice, but thinks that a polity or constitutional government can engender virtue. Plato worries that popular rule engenders vice. Plato does not directly address Aristotle's idea of mixed government, though in his final work, *The Laws* (year of completion unknown), Plato discusses with seeming approval how the Athenian government can help educate citizens toward virtue.

Augustine: Anti-Perfectionism
for Fallen People

Plato worried that democracy corrupts citizens. Below, we will consider other, more recent authors who offer similar views.

But first, it is worth pausing to note one early critic of the idea of perfectionist political theory. Remember that a political philosophy is perfectionist to the extent that it claims that what justifies political or social arrangements is that they engender moral and intellectual virtue or encourage human excellence. The ancient Greek and Roman philosophers didn't quite take it for granted that governments should cultivate virtue and excellence—they did *argue* for those conclusions—but such conclusions were widely endorsed at the time. The typical citizen of an ancient Greek city-state or the Roman republic or empire would have endorsed a perfectionist political philosophy.

However, today perfectionism is far less popular among philosophers and regular citizens alike. We tend to think the job of government is to keep the peace, provide public goods, help facilitate commerce, protect rights, and perhaps promote social or distribute justice. But people in the West do not generally think government should make us *virtuous* or *excellent* per se.

Augustine of Hippo (AD 354–430) was a philosopher and theologian in the Roman province of Numidia, much of which overlapped with what is now Algeria. (The city of Hippo, where Augustine served as a Catholic Bishop, is now Annaba, Algeria.) Augustine is of interest because he is one of the first major Christian philosophers. He lived through the conversion of the Roman empire from paganism to Catholicism but was also writing during Rome's decline. His writing represents a Christian departure from the philosophically pagan past, just as that pagan past was being replaced by a Christian present.

Augustine's most famous work is *The City of God against the Pagans* (AD 426).[4] Much of the book concerns matters of philosophy of religion and theology; it is not predominantly a work of political philosophy. Further, while latter parts of the book contrast a hypothetical history and eschatology of a "City of God" against an "Earthly City," the book is not meant to contrast, say, a worldly Christian theocracy or Christian-centric republic against a pagan republic or empire. (Augustine does discuss putative advantages and disadvantages of a Christian vs. pagan culture, but that is not what the contrast is about.) Augustine is not trying to offer a theory of the ideal human city. However, he does provide a theory of the limitations of what any human polity can achieve on its own.

This account makes Augustine's work a rebuke of Greek and Roman perfectionism. Aristotle, Plato, and other ancient Greek and Roman theorists argued that acquiring virtue is difficult. It requires training and good background conditions. Most people will never achieve full virtue, and many will remain vicious or merely temperate. Nevertheless, they thought that a central goal of the polity should be to nudge, educate, and facilitate the development of virtue and excellence. Augustine in contrast thinks human beings are fallen and depraved. Goodness comes from God's grace, not from human design, and not from a properly created political constitution.

Augustine has a highly constrained view of human nature, which leads to a constrained view of what politics can accomplish. This does not mean he thereby defends a constrained view of the scope of law. He was no liberal or libertarian, though his anti-perfectionism makes him of interest to later liberal theorists.[5]

According to Augustine, human beings are fallen and depraved because of original sin. At our worst, on our own, we are bestial and brutish; at our best, on our own, we are foolish and self-absorbed. Because of the Fall, we are by nature directed toward sin. Our ability to escape sin comes ultimately from God's grace. Nevertheless, by being created in God's image or because we are children of God, we possess a kind of dignity, even if we are inclined toward lust, self-satisfaction, and disobedience.

For Augustine, the Fall does not merely make our hearts depraved. It also corrupts our minds. Before Augustine, many philosophers endorsed Platonic ideas, which held that even if many people are inclined to engage in irrational thought processes, we could nevertheless learn to track the truth and overcome illusion. But Augustine argues that, due to our inherent depravity, we cannot find truth without God any more than we can find morality, justice, or goodness.

Political theorist Paul Miller summarizes Augustine's view of government as follows:

> Humanity's god-like dignity, sociability, sin, wickedness, and brokenness have social and political implications. Because of our

sin, "it is therefore absolutely impossible to establish on earth a society or state made up of saints or true Christians. Thus, if we wish to understand how social, economic, and political life operate, and how, indeed, they *must* operate, we have to start with the assumption that we are dealing, for the most part, with fallen, sinful men." ... As a result, "every human society from the family to the empire is never free from slights, suspicions, quarrels, and war, and 'peace' is not true peace but a doubtful interlude between conflicts."[6]

Miller explains that this leads to a limited style of politics, and indeed could even inspire a kind of "Augustinian liberalism":

Augustinian liberalism does not pretend we are able to definitively solve social and political problems, eradicate evil, eliminate all poverty, or enable flourishing for every person. It does not try to do most of the things that progressivism or nationalism try to do. It does not burden the state with the responsibility of policing identity, of manifesting the unfolding historical idea of American national promise, or of embodying the heritage and culture of the American nation. Augustinian liberalism expects less of politics.[7]

Again, Miller is not saying here that Augustine was in fact a philosophical liberal. Augustine did not think that liberty is the fundamental value that governments ought to protect, and he did not advocate imbuing each person with robust civil and economic freedoms.

Instead, what Miller means here is that Augustine thought that the state could not accomplish all that much. We should put aside grandiose and utopian visions, our hope for fantastic social progress, or the goal of reshaping and remolding of human nature into something better. The Earthly City, composed of fallen people, cannot achieve these. What it can do, perhaps, is keep the peace.

The State cannot be an effective mechanism for achieving social justice or human excellence, but it can be an effective mechanism for preventing barbarism. The State should not try to do much more because it cannot succeed.

Nietzsche: The Problem with Leveling and the Democratic Mindset

Friedrich Nietzsche (1844–1900) is a beautiful and poetic writer. Yet he remains difficult to interpret because he does not write philosophy the way most other philosophers do. Most philosophers write in a direct and heavy-handed way: here is my thesis, my argument, and why my argument matters. Nietzsche, in contrast, is full of surprises. He sometimes outlines arguments, diagnoses problems, and proffers solutions, but he often writes parables, analogies, hyperbolic or polemical language, or poetry. Further, he felt little no need to remain consistent between books or even inside them. Determining what Nietzsche really thinks is no small task. Accordingly, I am far less sure of my presentation of Nietzsche here than I am of the other theorists we discussed so far. While I will discuss Nietzsche's critique of democracy and democratic culture, many scholars think that Nietzsche is nevertheless a kind of progressive.[8]

One of Nietzsche's most famous works is *On the Genealogy of Morality* (1887), a scathing analysis of contemporary moral concepts. According to Nietzsche, the distinction between (A) good and evil and (B) good and bad are not equivalent. Instead, they represent two incompatible ways of seeing the world. According to Nietzsche, the older, pre-Christian, pagan mindset—a mindset that even Plato and Aristotle would have shared—is to conceive of human goodness in terms of various kinds of human excellence and nobility. Goodness is an aristocratic mindset: it involves self-affirmation, assertion, the exercise of power (in the sense of ability, not necessarily power *over* others), and action. Badness, in this aristocratic mindset, is weakness, self-rejection, slavishness, and failure. Nietzsche calls this "master" morality.

The Judeo-Christian culture that supplanted paganism instead propagates a "slave" morality. Slave morality inverts the pagan ideas of goodness. What the noble pagans called "good," the humble Christian calls "evil." What the pagans called "bad," the Christian calls "good." Judeo-Christian slave morality is grounded in the resentment of the strong and efficacious. It celebrates the weak, meek, and meager; it celebrates self-effacement, debasement, altruism, and equality. It scorns accomplishment and excellence. Judeo-Christian morality indeed stems partly from early prosecution of Jews and Christians; the moral code in effect rationalizes self-destructive feelings of resentment, hatred, and envy (which Nietzsche calls *ressentiment*). It turns servility from a vice into a virtue (e.g., by saying that servility before God is necessary for salvation).

Nietzsche scholar Brian Leiter notes that Nietzsche often defends the "value of inequality" because inequality is necessary to create excellent or exceptional people who transcend the mundane people and values around them. Leiter says that for Nietzsche, the "social practice of unequal regard—of looking down on those of lower social rank—conditions people, similarly, to be able to look down upon themselves," which in turn is a close-to-necessary psychological and cultural condition for "an individual to 'overcome' his contemptible current condition, to make of himself something higher and better." He quotes Nietzsche as saying, "Democracy represents the disbelief in great human beings . . .: 'Everyone is equal to everyone else.' 'At bottom we are one and all self-seeking cattle and mob.' "[9]

According to Nietzsche, Christian morality is grounded in *ressentiment*. Nietzsche often claims that democracy or democratic movements are an expression of this Christian ethic. For instance, in *Beyond Good and Evil*, he says:

Now it must sound harsh and cannot be heard easily when we keep insisting: that which here believes it knows, that which here glorifies itself with its praises and reproaches, calling itself good, that is the instinct of the herd animal, man, which has scored a breakthrough and attained prevalence and predominance over other instincts—and this development is continuing in accordance with the growing physiological approximation and assimilation of which it is the symptom. *Morality in Europe today is herd animal morality*—in other words, as we understand it, merely *one* type of human morality beside which, before which, and after which many other types, above all *higher* moralities, are, or ought to be, possible. But this morality resists such a "possibility," such an "ought" with all its power: it says stubbornly and inexorably, "I am morality itself, and nothing besides is morality." Indeed, with the help of a religion which indulged and flattered the most sublime herd-animal desires, we have reached the point where we find even in political and social institutions an ever more visible expression of this morality: the *democratic* movement is the heir of the Christian movement.[10]

Christianity—and the liberal democratic culture it inspired—has the effect of trying to level everyone and everything. It might respect a higher Being in the form of God, but it regards all people as low and indeed celebrates lowness before God. For Christians, in Nietzsche's view, human excellence consists in *kneeling*.

What will this democratic culture achieve? Nietzsche says:

We have a different faith; to us the democratic movement is not only a form of the decay of political organization but a form of the decay, namely the diminution, of man, making him mediocre and lowering his value. Where, then, must we reach with our hopes?[11]

This seemingly hyperbolic conclusion appears at the end of Nietzsche's analysis of modern culture. Modern, egalitarian, democratic culture focuses not on producing excellence, but on alleviating suffering. It focuses not on creating admirable people—or, since not everyone can be excellent or admirable, in teaching the less admirable to admire those admirable—but on sharing pity. Indeed, it makes "shared pity" the highest human emotion. It replaces God-the-savior with a view that the state should be a savior. Rather than making excellent people, it focuses on giving alms.

Oddly, it seems that Nietzsche dislikes liberal or progressive welfare states because he thinks they will *succeed*. Democratic societies want to eradicate suffering. But in doing so, they will create a kind of soft, easy culture. They turn society sort into the equivalent of a cattle feedlot minus the slaughterhouse at the end. This might well produce widespread comfort, but it also turns most citizens into submissive losers who cannot handle adversity, who strive for little, and who resent anyone who exhibits greatness.

Nietzsche also worries that democratic culture will corrupt education:

> All higher education belongs only to the exception: one must be privileged to have a right to so high a privilege. All great, all beautiful things can never be common property.[12]

Nietzsche might say that people are making a mistake in when they advocate widespread, democratic education. The mistake begins because they see that higher education has produced some excellent people—innovators, scientists, philosophers, engineers. They mistakenly infer that opening higher education to everyone produces widespread excellence. They might even be right in the short term—perhaps a few people who would have been peasants become great creators instead. But over the long term, in a democratic, equality-obsessed culture, what happens is instead that institutions of higher education get dumbed down and stripped of purpose. Egalitarians cannot bear seeing some excel and others fail; they regard all differences in outcomes as proof of injustice.

Rather than admit the truth—some people are more excellent than others—they pull the wool over their own eyes by trying to destroy distinction. Democratizing education ensures mediocrity. Nietzsche would say the same fate awaits any other institutions that democratize.

Nietzsche is often seen as defending a kind of aristocratic culture, though whether this is accurate is hotly debated. As Leiter says:

> Although Nietzsche's *illiberal* attitudes (for example, about human equality) are apparent, there are no grounds for ascribing to him a political philosophy, since he has no systematic (or even partly systematic) views about the nature of state and society. As an esoteric moralist, Nietzsche aims at freeing higher human beings from their false consciousness about morality (their false belief that this morality is *good for them*), not at a transformation of society at large.[13]

Rather than asking whether Nietzsche was anti-democratic overall, we should limit ourselves to examining the cultural impediments to human excellence he thinks democracy imposes. Similar remarks apply to Nietzsche's views of other economic or political arrangements. We can see Nietzsche trashing socialism throughout his works, but also trashing liberal market economies. While in the twentieth century, fascists invoked Nietzsche as one of their own, he instead seemed to predict the rise of fascism and mocked fascist ideology.

Whatever Nietzsche's final politics may have been, he worried about democracy's effect on character. A democratic culture thinks every life is valuable and of equal value. It refuses to acknowledge distinctions, but these distinctions *remain*. Thus, democracy must actively work to thwart and undermine excellence to protect the self-esteem of the masses and maintain the illusion of equality.

Nietzsche in turn rejected the Christian/democratic view that every life matters. For Nietzsche, most people are insignificant cattle who lead worthless lives.[14] What matters is the few who achieve genuine excellence. By analogy, the typical starving artist probably deserves nothing better, because their work is terrible. We tolerate a world full of talentless artists as the necessary price to find the few who can produce a *Guernica* or *Starry Night*.

Rational Irrationality Theory

The ancient Greeks and Romans often thought that participation in politics would tend to enlighten and ennoble citizens. As we saw in the last chapter, they offered two basic kinds of arguments. First, they would describe what politics requires from people and then conclude that politics must therefore cultivate those virtues. For instance, just as marathons require fitness, good political activity requires broad-mindedness, thoughtfulness, rationality, and public-spiritedness. Second, they tended to argue that republican participation tended to create a vigorous citizenry.

In addition, many found it plausible that participation ennobles people because they noticed that in their own societies, the people most involved in politics tended to be smarter than the citizenry at large. The problem, though, is that correlation is not causation. Indeed, in ancient Athens, the more educated and advantaged citizens were also the ones with enough free time to participate heavily.

Many of these arguments are highly speculative. However, beginning in the 1950s in the United States, political scientists and economists began studying, with data- and experiment-driven methods, how voters think and what they know. The results are generally regarded as quite depressing. As we'll discuss in chapter 7, the overwhelmingly majority of voters are ignorant; they know nothing or close to nothing about politics. They also appear to reason about politics poorly.

Before getting into the evidence for these claims, let's discuss what the most popular *explanation* is for such results. In 1957 economist Anthony Downs published *An Economic Theory of Democracy* (1957),[15] which uses the tools of microeconomics to analyze political behavior. Downs begins with the presumption that people tend to be *instrumentally rational*, that is, they tend to act in ways that maximize the chances they will satisfy whatever preferences and goals they have.

Downs notes that the rational choice framework applies to all actions, including the choice to acquire or retain information. It makes the following prediction:

> *The economics of information*: People will tend to acquire and retain information if and only if the expected benefits of doing so exceed the expected costs.

For instance, I predict that you, the reader, have not memorized the contents of your local phonebook. Doing so takes tremendous time and effort, but you predict that the payoff to memorizing the phonebook would be tiny. However, if a billionaire credibly offered you $10 million to memorize a single page by next month, you would probably do so.

This theory explains a great deal. It explains why students cram for a test but forget most material afterward. Or consider that people often memorize information simply because they enjoy it; sports fans memorize sports facts, guitar geeks memorize gear facts. Or consider that Europeans from small countries tend to be multilingual, but Americans who speak English as a first language tend only to speak English. If you're from the Netherlands, learning English enables you to communicate with most other Europeans. But if you're from the United States, you could go your entire life without ever needing to speak anything other than English. The few times a second language would be useful don't justify the massive cost of learning that language.

In chapter 7, we will explore how this theory explains widespread ignorance. But in this chapter, we are interested in whether democracy tends to enlighten and ennoble people, or does the opposite. After Downs, many economists and political scientists concluded that the economic theory of information explains not only whether people acquire or retain information, but whether they reason in scientific, truth-tracking ways, or in unscientific, biased, and non-truth-tracking ways. Consider the following theorem:

> *The economics of epistemic rationality*: People will tend to reason about an issue or piece of information in a truth-tracking way if and only if the expected benefits of doing so exceed the expected costs.

This theory has a corollary:

> *Rational irrationality*: In some cases, it can be *instrumentally* rational to be *epistemically* irrational. That is, sometimes people can best serve their goals by reasoning in non-truth-tracking ways.[16]

To illustrate: In the novel *Nineteen Eighty-Four*, thought police agent O'Brien tortures the dissident Wilson. Wilson knows the torture will stop only when he accepts absurdities, such as that 2 + 2 = 5. So, it is instrumentally rational for Wilson to become epistemically irrational.

In mass elections, individual votes do not matter much. It matters how *we* vote, but not how *you* vote. Had you stayed home or voted the opposite way, the election result, and whatever political outcomes result from the election, would have been the same. Your vote makes a difference only if it makes a difference, that is, only if there is a tie and you break the tie. But the probability you will break a tie is very small.

The scary implication here is that democratic voters are liberated to indulge their worst biases or absurd thought processes. Consider: when you reason about which plumber to hire, or whether to do the work yourself, you live the consequences of your decision. So you have a strong incentive to get it right or to learn from your mistakes. But not so for voting: no matter what you do, the same result will occur, so you won't be rewarded for reasoning well or punished for reasoning badly. It might be a disaster if the bad candidate wins, but since your individual vote makes no difference, it's not a disaster for you to vote for that candidate. And because it's not a disaster for you to vote for that bad candidate, it's not a disaster for you to let yourself believe the candidate is good.

Now consider that people seem to get social benefits from being team players. If your friends are Democrats, they might reward you for being a Democrat and punish you for being a Republican (or something else). They will tend to reward you for parroting the party line, but punish you for dissent. Or, if your friends believe the QAnon conspiracy theory, you earn social rewards for agreeing.

All this leads to several predictions: voters will tend to reason poorly about politics. They will tend to believe what their friends and peers believe, to fit in, even if the evidence for this is poor. They will suffer from a wide variety of cognitive biases—that is, systematic deviations from rational thought. They will tend to believe what they *want* to believe rather than what is true. They will evaluate evidence poorly—accepting evidence that helps them believe what they want, but rejecting evidence that refutes what they want to believe.

Contemporary Political Psychology: Motivated Reasoning

Political psychology often confirms the predictions of rational irrationality theory. (Note, however, that these results can hold even if the theory is wrong.)

Political psychologists Milton Lodge and Charles Taber conclude, "The evidence is reliable [and] strong . . . in showing that people find it very difficult to escape the pull of their prior attitudes and beliefs, which guide the processing of new information in predictable and sometimes insidious ways."[17] Political psychologists Leonie Huddy, David Sears, and Jack Levy conclude, "Political decision-making is often beset with biases that privilege habitual thought and consistency over careful consideration of new information."[18]

The problem seems to be that our reasoning skills were not selected for by evolution to make us good philosophers, social scientists, or natural scientists. The real reason we developed the capacity to reason was to form coalitions with one another and persuade others to join our side. As psychologist Jonathan Haidt says:

> [R]easoning was not designed to pursue the truth. Reasoning was designed by evolution to help us win arguments. That's why [psychologists Hugo Mercier and Dan Sperber] call [their theory of why reasoning developed] The Argumentative Theory of Reasoning. So, as they put it . . ., "The evidence reviewed here shows not only that reasoning falls quite short of reliably delivering rational beliefs and rational decisions. It may even be, in a variety of cases, detrimental to rationality. Reasoning can lead to poor outcomes, not because humans are bad at it, but because they systematically strive for arguments that justify their beliefs or their actions."[19]

We can reason well—in a truth-tracking way—when we want to, but people frequently don't want to. People are trying to form coalitions.

"Motivated reasoning" refers to when a person has preferences over what they believe and tries to arrive at and maintain their preferred beliefs. For instance, suppose you have strong evidence your spouse is cheating on you, but you find that truth so painful that you try to evade it. You find convenient excuses to rationalize her absences and convince yourself she is faithful.

Motivated reasoning abounds in politics. For instance, Drew Westen and his colleagues conducted an experiment to determine how people would reason about evidence that various people were hypocritical. The experimental setup involves first showing a famous person making a statement about what they would or would not do, and then shows them acting in ways that contradict their statement. Westen asks subjects whether the behavior is hypocritical or not. Then, Westen shows the famous people making exculpatory statements that explain their behavior. Westen then asks subjects whether it was a good excuse. Westen's subjects included committed Democrats, committed Republicans, and neutral, independent subjects who have no genuinely strong political ties. (Westen is careful here, as many people who call themselves independent are in fact "closet partisans" who always support the same party.) The famous people he asks them to evaluate are obvious Democrats, obvious Republicans, or politically neutral figures. You can probably guess the results: Democratic subjects were quick to judge Republicans as hypocrites, slow to judge their own side, and quick to accept excuses from their side. Republicans did the same for their own team, though they were significantly less partisan. Genuine independents were slow to judge and quick to forgive everyone. Democratic and Republican subjects were also kinder to neutral figures.

Psychologist Geoffrey Cohen has conducted a number of experiments in which he shows that people will rationalize that they agree with a policy when they are falsely told that others in their group support it. As fellow political psychologist Dennis Chong summarizes Cohen's work:

> The experiment presented participants with two contrasting versions—generous or stringent—of a social welfare policy. Judging each policy on its merits, respondents preferred the version that was consistent with their ideological values. But when the policies were attributed to either the Democratic or

Republican Party, liberal respondents favored the Democratic-labeled policy regardless of whether it was generous or stringent, and conservatives favored the Republican-labeled policy regardless of details.[20]

Numerous other studies get similar results. People are not simply following a heuristic. For instance, if I believe theory T, and discover that everyone else who believes T also believes related idea Z, then that provides some evidence that Z is true. Rather, what people are doing is much simpler: they parrot what others say, and are unaware they are parroting. They are not changing their minds in response to evidence others disagree, but—as far as they are concerned—have always agreed with whatever their group says today.[21]

Psychologist Dan Kahan has another ingenious study finding similar patterns of motivated reasoning. First, he gives subjects a hypothetical set of data concerning skin cream and rashes. He makes it clear the data is fake. He asks them, if this data were correct, what conclusion would it support about the efficacy of the skin cream? Here, some people simply cannot do the math or interpret the data. But some subjects can—and they tend to interpret the data correctly. So far, so good. But next he gives subjects the same math problem, only this time the data concerns the efficacy of gun control on crime. Once again, he makes it clear the data is fake, so he is not asking them whether gun control in fact reduces or increases crime. Instead, subjects are only asked what the data would imply if it were correct. Here, though, subjects interpret the known-to-be-fake data as supporting whatever the subjects already believe. If he gives an anti-gun leftist fake data that suggests gun control increases crime, the leftist reads it as saying that gun control reduces crime. If he gives a conservative fake data that suggests gun control works, the conservative reads it as saying it does not work. The better the subjects were at math, the more strongly they rationalize that the data confirms whatever they want to believe. Again, this is *fake* data and the subjects *know* it is fake; they know they are not being asked what the truth is, but what such data would support if it were real. Even then, with nothing at stake, their ability to reason is completely overwhelmed by their desire to believe what they want to believe.[22]

Motivated reasoning explains the presence of two widespread, closely related biases called confirmation and disconfirmation biases. These biases are that we tend to look for and accept evidence only when it supports our preexisting views or what we want to believe. We tend to ignore or reject evidence that disconfirms what we already believe or want to believe.[23] In fact, sometimes giving us evidence that we are wrong convinces us even more strongly that we are right.[24]

Contemporary Political Psychology: Democratic Tribalism and Polarization

The psychologist Henri Tajfel (1919–1982) produced many famous experiments that demonstrate the presence of what psychologists now call "intergroup bias." Intergroup bias is a bias to believe that members of your own group are stronger, smarter, nicer, or otherwise better than members of other groups. What was disturbing about Tajfel's work is that he showed strong versions of this bias would appear almost instantly, among strangers who know almost nothing about each, based on arbitrary and minimal divisions.

His experiments had a common form. First, he would divide subjects—all of whom are strangers who have never interacted and know almost nothing about each other—into groups, usually by falsely telling them that they shared some trivial trait. Second, he would have them play games or perform some activity in which they could display favoritism or bias. He ensured that there was no selfish incentive in the games to be biased toward one's team. (Consider that if I divide a gym class into two basketball teams, each team will try to win because winning is fun. Tajfel ensured nothing like that was going on.) He found that subjects would immediately play favorites. They would, for instance, rate members of their group as smarter or more likeable than members of the other group, or would be willing to discriminate against members of the other group when it came to distributing resources.

If people act this way over *nothing*, then presumably they will act worse when it comes to politics. And that's what the research tends to show. People prefer to live among people who share their political identity. They tend to dislike, mistreat, and discriminate against those with different political identities.[25]

For instance, Shanto Iyengar and Sean Westwood conducted an experiment in which they asked subjects to evaluate fake résumés for a job that had nothing to do with politics. In one phase, the résumés have no political label or affiliation. Here, subjects evaluate the résumés on their merits, which gives Iyengar and Westwood a baseline for the next phase of the experiment. Next, they use similar résumés, but now attach a political label, for instance by including that the applicant was a member of a Young Democrat or Young Republic club. Once that happens, political partisans choose less-qualified members of their political team over clearly better qualified members of the other team. 80.4 percent of Democratic subjects picked the Democratic job candidate, while 69.2 percent of Republican subjects picked the Republican job candidate. When the Republican job candidate was clearly stronger, Democrats still chose the Democratic candidate 70 percent of the time. Once political affiliation was introduced, "candidate qualification had no significant effect on winner section."[26] Politics completely silenced candidate quality.

Relatedly, political scientist Diana Mutz did extensive research on what generates what she calls "cross-cutting political discussion," that is, talking about politics with people with different views. She finds that most cross-cutting political discussion occurs at work, largely because people try to *avoid* talking politics with or listening to the other side, but people tend to have less control over whom they work with than whom they befriend. (In general, people only select friends who share their politics.) She also finds that being white, rich, or educated predicts that people have *less* cross-cutting discussion, while being not-white, poor, or uneducated predicts that people have *more*. Again, the reason is that people tend only to be exposed to different ideas at work. Privileged people tend to have more ability to ensure they work in a bubble, while less-privileged people are more likely to have to accept jobs where they encounter diverse people with diverse perspectives.[27]

One of the most important trends in modern democracies around the world over the past forty years is increasing geographical political segregation.[28] People prefer to live in communities surrounded by co-partisans. Over time, zip codes or the equivalent have thus become more politically homogenous. The result, as the political philosopher Robert Talisse argues, cannot be good for democracy. People of different opinions hardly ever encounter each other in person—at work, at church, at stores, at the park. Their ideas of what others are like, what they want, and how they think are determined not from firsthand experience, but from the caricatures their favorite partisan media channels present (channels that keep viewers viewing by keeping them angry). Social interactions across political divides become increasingly uncommon. As a result, we become "alien and inscrutable to those who are politically unlike ourselves."[29] All this leads to fear and distrust. Rather than being willing to hear, work with, or compromise with the other side, we see them as morally and intellectually bankrupt monsters who must be stopped, squashed, and dominated.

What We Should Learn

In the previous chapter, we saw theorists largely arguing that because properly functioning democracy requires citizens to think and act in virtuous ways, democracy will in fact make them virtuous. This chapter examines the skeptical response that instead, what we get in the real world is dysfunctional democracy that encourages vice.

Theorists argue that democracy contains perverse incentives. Good governance is like safe climate, public roads, military protection, or clean air. Just as you might want to enjoy clean air but pollute to your heart's content, so people might want to enjoy good governance but themselves remain ignorant or indulge their biases. Because democracy spreads out power so much, it makes each individual citizen's share of power insignificant, which incentivizes citizens to treat their political decisions as insignificant.

This seems to be the central dilemma that we face when allocating power. If we concentrate power in the few, they have incentives to be smart but selfish. If we spread it among the many, they have incentives to be foolish and mean.

6

For Wisdom

Two Heads Are Smarter than One

Many political theorists argued what makes political decisions just or legitimate is not merely a matter of *how* they were decided, or *who* decided them, but *what* was decided. A king can be wise or stupid, and so can a democracy. A king's decisions can be right or wrong; so can democracy's decisions.

Not everyone agrees. Some philosophers advocate the view that whatever a democracy decides is good, just, or legitimate *because* the democracy decided it. They might say that because people disagree about what is just or good, the only normative criterion we can use to assess decisions is whether they were made fairly. They claim that properly designed democracies make decisions fairly, and so anything they decide is thereby rendered just. We will examine some arguments like this in more depth in chapters 10 and 11.

Plato would have thought this absurd nonsense. After all, his dialogue *Euthyphro* (c. 399–395 BC) showed that even the Gods cannot make something good or bad by fiat; if almighty Zeus can't do that, then surely the French can't.[1]

Thanks to Plato, one of the central questions in political philosophy concerns whether democracies (and other forms of government) tend to make smart or wise decisions. Do democracies tend to select competent leaders? Do they tend to choose effective means to their ends? Do they tend to choose just ends? How wise are democracies compared to the alternatives? If any alternative form of government can be shown to make consistently smarter or

Democracy. Jason Brennan, Oxford University Press. © Oxford University Press 2023.
DOI: 10.1093/oso/9780197558812.003.0006

wiser choices, how much weight should that be given in deciding between democratic and non-democratic forms of government?

Imagine a jury is deciding a criminal trial. The jury must determine whether the evidence presented removes all reasonable doubt whether a man committed murder. Here, there is an independent truth about whether the man in fact killed someone. Given whatever legal definition the concept "murder" has or what constitutes "reasonable doubt," there is also an independent truth about whether the killing is murder or whether the evidence removes reasonable doubt. Here, we think the jury is supposed to discover truth, not *create* it. The jury is supposed to pronounce someone guilty only if he's in fact guilty.

At least sometimes, then, when we judge how decisions are made, what we care about is whether the decision makers got the right answer, where what constitutes the right answer is an independent truth of the matter the decision maker is supposed to track. The doctor is supposed to give you the medicine that works. The trainer is supposed to give you advice that works.

At the very least, you might agree this applies to the choice of *means* to achieve a goal. If, say, voters authorize Congress to reduce global warming, there is some fact of the matter, given any set of background values and priorities, about whether nuclear or wind energy will be more effective.

You might think that applies not only to means, but also to the *ends* of government. If 90 percent of the United States voted to reinstate Jim Crow (perhaps after amending the Constitution), you probably would not conclude that this would make Jim Crow good or just, but instead that it would show that the majority is unjust.

In this chapter, we will review some of the most important and influential arguments in favor of the view that democracies tend to be wise, in that they tend to make the *right* decision. In the next chapter, we will examine the most important and influential arguments to the contrary.

Aristotle: Two Heads Are Better than One

People possess different levels of intelligence, information, practical and theoretical wisdom, skill in deliberation, and moral virtue. It's probably a pipe dream to think that we all average out to be equal overall. Some people are probably superior on all these dimensions than other people. Further, we can often identify who is superior.

If so, then it seems tempting to conclude that to ensure the best political decisions, what we need to do is identify and empower the person or few people with the greatest overall mix of intelligence, information, wisdom, virtue, and so on. Or, as Plato suggested, we need to *create* such people, rather than merely hope to find them. Further, we need to ensure that these people have a strong institutional incentive to use their power for good rather than for their own self-interest, as even a pretty good person might be corrupted by wearing the crown.

However, Aristotle notes, in some cases two heads are better than one, and three heads better than two. Sometimes a *group* is wiser as a whole than the wisest individual. Sometimes a large group containing fools is wiser than small group comprising only the wisest.

Aristotle makes a few remarks on this point:

The best man, then, must legislate, and laws must be passed, but these laws will have no authority when they miss the mark, though in other cases retaining their authority. But when the law cannot determine a point at all, or not well, should the one best man or all decide? According to our present practice, assemblies meet, sit in judgement, deliberate, and decide, and their judgements all relate to individual cases. Now any member of the assembly, taken separately, is certainly inferior to the wise man. But the state is made up of many individuals. And as a feast to which all guests contribute is better than a banquet furnished by a single man, so a multitude is a better judge of many things than a single individual.[2]

Aristotle follows this paragraph with some explanation intended to serve as evidence for these claims. For instance, he says, it is easier to corrupt single individuals that to corrupt entire masses.

Notice that Aristotle says the multitude is a better judge of "many things" than a single individual. He is not claiming here that the multitude judges all things better than the single individual. Nor does he say that a bigger multitude is always better than a small multitude.

Further, you might wonder whether even the feast analogy holds. You've probably been to single-chef banquets that were superior to potluck dinners, and vice versa. Finally, Aristotle does not say that masses are always less corruptible than the single individual. You can probably think of times where being in a group leads to mob behavior, while single individuals acting alone might resist the temptations that befall mobs. So, we should be careful here not to read Aristotle as saying that no matter what, more heads are *always* better than fewer heads. He probably means *sometimes* more heads are better than fewer.

Aristotle does not elaborate much on this point, but nevertheless, these remarks have spurred a huge amount of work on the issue of collective intelligence. In particular, many theorists today, inspired by Aristotle, now think that sometimes intelligence or wisdom is an *emergent* feature of a group. There might be cases where no group member is wise, but the group on whole is wise. But there might also be cases where groups reinforce and exacerbate foolishness. A good deal of research in collective decision-making concerns trying to find conditions under which groups are intelligent rather than foolish, that is, conditions under which more heads are better than fewer heads.

Further, the research often considers the question of whether adding an additional head is always good or sometimes bad, or whether there needs to be some base level of expertise. For instance, suppose someone has strange symptoms that do not seem to correspond with any obvious disease. Perhaps the three hundred best disease specialists could better diagnose the problem than the single best specialist alone. Perhaps the thousand best doctors would be even better. There might even be cases where "asking the internet" would work better than asking the top thousand doctors, but asking the internet would often return bogus prescriptions of essential oils and gluten avoidance.

Though Aristotle does not offer much reason why the many might outperform the one, we can list some hypotheses here:

1. It is often easier to corrupt one person than many. (This is the main reason Aristotle gives.)
2. Different people know different things, so the group as a whole might know more than any subset of the group. For instance, ten PhD students in a graduate class might collectively know more than the professor teaching the class, though the professor knows much more than any one of them.
3. Different people might have different approaches to solving a problem.
4. A group allows for deliberation and for people to challenge one another; this might induce people to correct their errors and overcome their biases.
5. Groups allow people to learn from one another and to gain information quickly.
6. While any individual might make a random mistake, it is less likely that everyone or most will make the same mistake, and so groups can help correct for error.

And so on. As we will see below, many of the "epistemic" arguments for democracy rely on ideas like this. (An "epistemic" argument for democracy is an argument that holds that democracy is good, just, or legitimate because it has a tendency to make correct decisions.)

Remember that Aristotle did not take these remarks to demonstrate that democracy—in the sense of unchecked majoritarian rule—was the best form of government. Rather, he thought that overall, a kind of mixed regime that combined aristocratic and democratic forms of decision-making in different domains was best. This kind of regime tend to be the most stable. It would rarely make particularly wise decisions, but it also had the lowest chance of degenerating into a worse system that makes particularly bad decisions. Or so Aristotle thought.

Political scientist Josiah Ober recently wrote a comprehensive, data-driven examination of Athens' relative material prosperity, military success, and stability compared to other city-states. He argues that Athens had few distinct advantages in terms of climate, geographic location, or natural resources. What best explains Athens' relative success over the 185-year period in which it was democratic was that it was significantly more *democratic* (in the modern sense of the term, rather than in Aristotle's sense) than its neighbors. Ober's central hypothesis is:

Democratic Athens was able to take advantage of its size and resources, and therefore competed successful over time against hierarchical rivals, because the costs of participatory political practices were overbalanced by superior returns to social cooperation resulting from useful knowledge as it was organized and deployed in the simultaneously innovation-promoting and learning-based contexts of democratic institutions and culture.[3]

Ober does not consider at length whether *other* institutional arrangements explain the difference (for instance, Athens was also generally more liberal and capitalistic than other city-states, two traits that can be expected to produce prosperity and stability). Further, in his analysis, democratic city-states taken as a group outperformed tyrannies and monarchies, but do not appear to outperform oligarchies and aristocracies. Athens itself made some notoriously disastrous decisions, such as an invasion of Sicily that caused it to lose the Peloponnesian War and its empire.[4]

Recall, though, that even in Athens, participation was restricted to the few, not the many. Indeed, Ober argues that one of the reasons Athenians could overcome the knowledge deficits possessed by most individual eligible is that these citizens participated and deliberated early and often. The people allowed to self-govern became good at self-governing because they practiced.[5] If Ober is right, then, a good question for us is to what degree a modern democratic government governing a larger polity, and which does much more, could scale these practices up or emulate what makes Athens work.

Condorcet: A Formal Proof of the Wisdom of Crowds

In 1785, the mathematician Nicholas de Condorcet (1743–1794) published a mathematical proof that vindicates the idea that under some conditions, a group making a collective decision is more likely to arrive at the correct answer than a single individual. Further, the proof shows that the larger the group becomes, the more likely the group is to decide the issue correctly. The associated conclusion of this proof is usually referred to as "Condorcet's Jury Theorem." The proof is formal and requires the reader to understand some issues in probability theory, but we can discuss it here in terms mathphobic readers can appreciate.

First, Condorcet has us imagine a jury tasked with assessing an issue with an objective truth—for instance, is a person guilty of a crime? Condorcet's original proof is limited to considering cases in which the question has a yes or no answer; he does not consider questions where there might more than two possible answers. (For instance, the jury in the proof might consider a question such as, "Is

Jason Brennan the present king of France?" but not the question, "Which of these fifty people, if any, is the present king of France?" or "Which of these following twenty economic theories is the best to use to govern our country?")

So, this is gives us an idea of what kinds of questions Condorcet's proof applies to, at least in its original form. (Below, we will discuss how recent authors argue that the theorem can be relaxed and apply to other cases.) Now we need to consider how Condorcet models the voter behavior.

When I toss a "fair coin," the probability of heads is exactly 0.5. If I toss a fair coin, say, 15 times, I might get 11 heads and 4 tails. Burt the more tosses, the more I will approach 50 percent heads and 50 percent tails. (Of course, each toss of the coin is *independent* of the last.)

What's interesting, from Condorcet's perspective, is if the individual jurors or voters are like *weighted* coins. A weighted or "unfair" coin is a coin that has a higher chance of landing on heads than tails, or vice versa. For instance, suppose I have a coin that is very slightly weighted toward heads. Each time I toss it, I have a 50.1 percent chance of landing on heads rather than tails. Each toss, I still have a good chance (49.9 percent) of getting tails. But consider what happens when I toss the coin 10,000, 100,000,000, or 1,000,000 times in a row. The more tosses, the more likely it becomes that heads will outnumber tails. In fact, as the number of tosses (of a coin weighted toward heads) approaches infinity, the probability that heads outnumbers tails approaches 1 (100 percent). Even if the coin is barely weighted toward heads, the point holds. If a coin has a 50.0000001 percent chance of landing on heads, then as the number of tosses approaches infinity, the probability that the majority will be heads approaches 1 (100 percent).

So, Condorcet asks, what if each juror is like a weighted coin, tossed independently of the last? Suppose the jury is asked to decide whether a man is guilty or not. Suppose that each juror is a little more likely than not to get the right answer: not guilty. That is, suppose each juror, on their own, has a 53 percent chance of saying not guilty and 47 percent chance of saying guilty. Or suppose the vote is between a Nazi and a Liberal presidential candidate. Suppose the Liberal is the right choice over the Nazi. But suppose voters are only slightly reliable: Each voter has a 53 percent chance of picking the Liberal and a 47 percent chance of picking the Nazi. If, as Condorcet suggests, each juror or voter is like a coin slightly weighted toward the correct answer, then an amazing thing happens here. As one adds more and more jurors to the pool or voters to the electorate, the probability that the jury or electorate picks the right answer approaches 1 (100 percent). If a coin has a 50.0000001 percent chance of landing on heads, then as the number of tosses approaches infinity, the probability that the majority will be heads approaches 1 (100 percent). If a juror is like that coin, with a 50.0000001 percent chance of selecting the correct answer, then as the number of jurors approaches infinity, the probability that the majority will vote for the correct answer approaches 1 (100 percent).

So, Condorcet's Jury Theorem offers a formal mathematical proof that under certain conditions, a crowd can be wise, indeed wiser than any member of that crowd. Note, however, that Condorcet himself cautions against interpreting this as vindicating crowds under all conditions. On the contrary, he states that the theorem can just as easily prove the stupidity of the crowd. Above, we asked what would happen if the jurors are even slightly more likely to pick the right answer over the wrong answer. As the number of jurors increases, the probability that the majority would select the right answer approaches 1. However, Condorcet says, by the very same logic, if instead the individual jurors are even slightly more likely to select the wrong answer over the right answer, then as the number of jurors increases, the probability that the majority will select the wrong answer approaches 1 (100 percent). This is often referred to as the "Dark Side of Condorcet's Jury Theorem."

So, to summarize, the theorem says the following:

1. If individual voters are more likely than not to select the right answer, then as the number of voters increases, the probability that the majority picks the right answer increases.
2. If individual voters are equally likely to select the right answer as the wrong, then as the number of voters increases, the probability that the majority picks the right answer over the wrong approaches zero. Instead, the chance of a 50–50 split increases.
3. If individual voters are more likely than not to select the wrong answer, then as the number of voters increases, the probability that the majority picks the wrong answer increases.

In short, a large group of slightly wise voters is expected to be smarter than a smaller group, while a larger group of slightly dumb voters is expected to be dumber than a smaller group.

Condorcet's Jury Theorem does not say that larger groups are always smarter than smaller groups or single individuals. It does not even say that two smart heads are better than one. Instead, if the assumptions of the theorem hold, then whether a larger group, smaller group, or individual is smartest or most reliable *depends* on the size of the group and reliability of an individual person. For instance, suppose you have a 90 percent chance of being right. At some point, a group of people who each have reliability of a 50.0000001 percent will outperform you, but the group will need to be large.

Or, suppose you have a 90 percent chance of being right. If so, you by yourself are more reliable than jury of you plus two people who have only a 51 percent chance of being right. The other two bring the average reliability down.

Or, imagine a case where each person voter has a reliability of 45 percent. That is, each person is more likely to be wrong than right. Here, asking a single person to decide is better than asking a group to decide. Condorcet's Jury Theorem says that if everyone is unreliable, a larger group is expected to perform worse than a smaller group, which will perform worse than a single unreliable individual.

Even on the "Light Side" of the theorem—that is, when voters are more reliable than not—the theorem does not necessarily suggest that *everyone* should vote on everything. The reason is that while each additional reliable voter increases the chance that the majority will select the right answer, it turns out that each voter also has diminishing marginal returns. To illustrate, imagine that voters have an average reliability of 0.51, that is, they have a 51 percent chance of selecting the right answer. Here, going from 101 to 103 voters increases the probability that the majority will select the right answer by about 0.00039 (0.039 percentage points). Going from 5,001 to 5,003 to increases the probability that the group will select the right answer by only about 0.000021 (0.0021 percentage points). In short, as the number of voters increases, the *added value* of each additional voter approaches *zero*. What this means is that we can in principle calculate the *optimal* group size for a voting electorate by knowing (A) how important getting the right answer is; (B) how competent the average voter is; and (C) what the *opportunity cost* is for each voter. I once calculated some dummy examples out and found surprising results. If, say, the value of the right answer in an election were an astounding $10 trillion, and if the average voter has a 0.51 probability of selecting the right answer, then the 100,003rd voter adds only 26 cents worth of competence to the group! So, on Condorcet's theorem, while adding more heads in this example (where each voter has the same reliability) improves the group's reliability, there's no value in having tens of millions of voters, even when the stakes are high.[6]

No one criticizes Condorcet's proof per se. The debate is over whether and how the theorem applies to real-life voting.

More recent scholars have derived variations of the theorem that relax some of his assumptions. For instance, Condorcet discussed cases where every voter is equal in probability to every other, but it turns out that what matters is the average probability of the voters.

(If on average voters are more likely than not to get the right/wrong answer, then as a group becomes larger, the probability that the majority selects the right/wrong answer approaches 1.) It also turns out that the theorem can be generalized for non-binary questions.

Perhaps most important issue is that Condorcet models individual voters as if they were independent coin tosses. In the real world, though, voters are not independent. When I toss a coin a second time, how the first toss landed has no effect on how the second toss lands. But voters tend to follow each other and follow thought leaders. If I am a Democratic Party primary voter, and I learn you, my friend, voted for Biden over Sanders, that increases the chance I vote for Biden. Numerous scholars have examined how to model these effects. In short, the result is probably what you would expect: smart thought leaders and voters make other dependent voters smarter; dumb or unreliable thought leaders and voters make other dependent voters dumber and less reliable.

Thus, a great deal of current debate about the applicability of Condorcet's Jury Theorem concerns whether we are on the Light Side or Dark Side of the theorem in any given election. If you think voters are on average smart and listen to smart thought leaders, you expect large democracies to get the right answer. If you think voters are on average unreliable and listen to unreliable thought leaders, you expect democracies to get the wrong answer. What Condorcet's Jury Theorem says about the wisdom or stupidity of the crowd depends on crowd dynamics.

It's worth noting one further implicit controversy about Condorcet's Jury Theorem. One of the big questions in political science concerns how best to model voting to calculate the probability that a vote will be decisive. Condorcet's Jury Theorem models voters as coin tosses; it asks what the chances are that some number of weighted coin tosses will come out one way rather than another. It is an instance of a class of models (of the probability of decisiveness of individual votes) known as "binomial models." However, thanks to recent work by political scientists Aaron Edlin,

Andrew Gelman, and Noah Kaplan, binomial models of the probability of a tie are now largely seen as incorrect, because *if* the binomial model were true, then there would almost never be an upset in an election, and indeed it would be amazing that so many real-life elections are so close as they are.[7] Oddly, though, I have noticed that in person, if not in print, many people reject binomial models (of the probability of a vote being decisive) because such models usually imply that individual votes don't ever matter, but then those same people will trot out Condorcet's Jury Theorem as an argument for group wisdom. But one cannot have it both ways; if Edlin, Gelman, and Kaplan are right about what's inadequate about binomial models, then Condorcet's Jury Theorem does not apply to actual elections.

Madison: Constitutions and the Pace of Decision-Making

US president and *Federalist* coauthor James Madison's most famous written work is Federalist No. 10 (1787), which attempts to diagnose how to contain factions. Previously, in chapter 2, we discussed how the *Federalist* authors believed the proposed US Constitution could maintain stability and reduce strife. Here, we will examine why Madison thinks divided government can improve the wisdom or reliability of collective decisions.

Madison begins with a preamble of sorts:

> The friend of popular governments never finds himself so much alarmed for their character and fate, as when he contemplates their propensity to this dangerous vice. He will not fail, therefore, to set a due value on any plan which, without violating the principles to which he is attached, provides a proper cure for it. The instability, injustice, and confusion introduced into the public councils, have, in truth, been the mortal diseases under

which popular governments have everywhere perished; as they continue to be the favorite and fruitful topics from which the adversaries to liberty derive their most specious declamations. The valuable improvements made by the American constitutions on the popular models, both ancient and modern, cannot certainly be too much admired; but it would be an unwarrantable partiality, to contend that they have as effectually obviated the danger on this side, as was wished and expected. Complaints are everywhere heard from our most considerate and virtuous citizens, equally the friends of public and private faith, and of public and personal liberty, that our governments are too unstable, that the public good is disregarded in the conflicts of rival parties, and that measures are too often decided, not according to the rules of justice and the rights of the minor party, but by the superior force of an interested and overbearing majority.[8]

Notice that Madison is not merely talking here about instability and conflict, but also about questions of what he would consider objective right and wrong. (Madison was no moral relativist or subjectivist; he probably advocated some version of a natural law theory in which people have rights and obligations in virtue of being human. Of course, his slave ownership violated this theory.) Madison is worried that factionalism can lead popular governments to make wrong choices.

Madison worries about "passion" overtaking groups. He mentions "passion" ten times in Federalist No. 10 alone. Madison claims that impassioned factionalism is a necessary byproduct of liberty. If we allow people freedom of thought and opinion, they will of course disagree with each other, and fall into various factions. Liberty is to factionalism what air is to fire. However, he says, we should no further wish to eliminate liberty than air, despite the costs.

Madison offers a quick theory of political psychology. He says that people are fallible, and he notes that "opinions and passions will have a reciprocal effect on each other."[9] He then notes that people do not merely disagree about what is best, but also tend to view each other with "mutual animosity." Almost as if he was predicting what Henri Tajfel's (see chapter 5) minimal group experiments would show, he says that even "where no substantial occasion presents itself, the most frivolous and fanciful distinctions have been sufficient to kindle [people's] unfriendly passions and excite their most violent conflicts."[10]

Madison concludes that trying to eliminate the causes of faction, to eliminate passions and biases, or trying to achieve a consistently enlightened citizenry are pipe dreams. To put his argument anachronistically, you might see him as having a pre-scientific understanding of the political psychology discussed toward the end of chapter 5. People are biased, emotional, and motivated reasoners prone to tribalism; they are not rational deliberators. Madison thus concludes that instead of trying to stop these problems from occurring, the friend of popular government should try to contain their effects.

Here, Madison thinks representative government offers two basic sets of solutions to the problem of "passions." First, he outlines at length how representative government prevents the great mass of people, whether a sizable minority or even the majority, from simply imposing its will at once. Instead, a voting population overcome or afflicted with some passion must still choose representatives. Different people from different places will choose different representatives, so the representatives will not all be afflicted with the same passions. Further, Madison expects that people will tend to choose, if not perfect leaders, at least more knowledgeable, less impassioned, and more even-headed representatives. In turn, even these representatives cannot simply do as they please at will. The Constitution requires both the House and Senate to pass a law and offers the president an opportunity to veto it. (Today we would add that the Supreme Court can also, in effect, veto or modify laws.) So, in short, the familiar story about checks and balances applies here.

Internally divided government tends to be smarter government in part because it makes it difficult to pass stupid laws.

The second reason the Constitution offers a solution, per Madison, is less obvious. In a recent book called *Madison's Metronome*, the Madison scholar Greg Weiner catalogs Madison's various arguments and positions on questions of majority rule and constitutionalism, in the *Federalist* and elsewhere.[11] Weiner finds that Madison wanted a system of checks and balances in large part to *slow down* the process of political decision-making. Democratic bodies are prone to fits of passion, which impede their ability to make sound, rational decisions. But passion fades over time. The cure for such passions is not good arguments—impassioned people don't listen to reason!—but *time*. Thus, Madison's goal, in designing such a convoluted political process, was to prevent impulsive and impassioned decision-making. If passing a law takes months, then cool heads will prevail; only laws appealing to cool heads are ratified. Wiener notes that the modern United States has imposed rules—such as massive congressional delegation of its powers to the president or to bureaucracy—that speed up decision-making and remove these time constraints. Madison might say these changes eliminate the safeguards.

In contemporary political science, these issues are still debated. Unicameral legislatures in parliamentary systems tend indeed to be faster, but have fewer checks and balances. Bicameral legislatures and presidential systems tend to be slower in making changes, but have more checks and balances. It's probably fair to say that among empirically minded political scientists who work on this issue, the consensus seems to be that parliamentary systems outperform more convoluted systems, all things considered. Still, part of the issue here concerns what we mean by "outperform," even if we agree on the same values. After all, Madison probably does not mean to say that convoluted democracies will be more likely than less convoluted democracies to select the *right* answer. He probably means that they are less likely to select a *disastrous* answer.

James Mill and Jeremy Bentham: Democracy as the Extension of Market Liberalism

Liberal political philosophies hold that each person should be permitted a wide sphere of liberty to make personal, religious, and economic choices free from the threat or presence of interference from others. A liberal polity is a society that realizes and acts upon this philosophy.

Democracy and liberalism are closely associated historically. As a matter of intellectual history, the philosophers who developed liberal theory tended also to be more democratic than others. As a matter of political history, as countries liberalized their economies by strengthening property rights and removing government constraints on trade, they also tended to become more democratic, by extending and strengthening the franchise. As a matter of logic, a country could be extremely liberal and entirely undemocratic, or extremely illiberal but very democratic. But as a matter of fact (see chapter 8), democracy and liberalism tend to be found together. For that reason, people often conflate the two.

The English utilitarian philosophers Jeremy Bentham (1748–1832) and James Mill (1773–1836) were early radical liberals who advocated extensive political and economic reforms. (James Mill was the father of John Stuart Mill, whom we discussed in chapter 4.) Both also wrote extensively on political economy and helped develop classical economics. Classical economists generally regarded economies as spontaneous orders—much like ecosystems—bound and regulated by internal rules and norms. As the Scottish sociologist Adam Ferguson (1723–1816) argued, human institutions and social order tend to be products of "human action, but not the execution of any human design."[12]

If, say, hip-hop displaces rock as the most popular form of music, this results not because a music czar ordered it so, but because of individual people making strategic individual choices. Similarly, economists today would say that the actual market price of a freely traded commodity results from the forces of supply and demand, which ultimately are simply the emergent products of individual people making strategic individual choices.

Liberal philosophers and economists tend to emphasize how many trends result from individual action without anyone intending to produce the results. As an analogy, ecosystems maximize biomass, though individual living things do not aim to maximize biomass. They aim to survive and reproduce. But the emergent effect of numerous organisms acting to reproduce, under the selection pressures of evolution, is that ecosystems maximize possible biomass given the environmental constraints. Similarly, liberal economists argue that market economies tend to maximize productivity and promote the general welfare, though no participant aims at these general goals.

Because economics is not our concern here, we won't go into much depth about Bentham, Mill, or other related liberal philosophers' defense of the market economy. What's of interest here is that they believed their arguments for personal and economic liberty also worked, with modification, as arguments for representative and democratic government.

They made two major moves. First, they were skeptical of *administrative or bureaucratic power*. Second, they were optimistic about individuals' capacity to make good choices for themselves. So, their arguments for democracy consisted of a negative part—a critique of unelected officials' incentives—and a positive part—a defense of personal choice in light of individuals' incentives.

The story Bentham and Mill tell is probably familiar. This does not mean they were unoriginal; rather, their arguments were so influential that the average person living in a democracy can probably recite them without knowing who Bentham and Mill were. Both argued that the main purpose of government is to secure the peace, maintain a degree of order, and provide various public goods that markets or civil society might underprovide. However, once we create positions of power, the people who hold this power will have a strong incentive to use it to promote their personal interests rather than serve the public. To avoid rebellion, these government agents might do *some* good and avoid the worst abuses, but nevertheless, they will serve themselves and exploit the public when they can.

The best though imperfect solution to this problem is to align the interests of the governors with the governed. Consider as an analogy what happens in a market: if people have the right to walk away from a deal, then the only way to get rich is to provide products or services at a price that makes your customers better off. This holds even if the customers only have bad options—you can make a deal only by providing them a *better* option than they already have. So, markets align the self-interest of buyers and sellers; they require people to serve each other to serve themselves.

Similarly, Bentham and Mill thought that requiring leaders to stand for periodic elections with a secret ballot would tend to ensure that these leaders served the interests of the governed. To win election, leaders must promise good policies—policies that voters could recognize would help them—and provide evidence they could deliver. To win re-election, they must deliver.

This argument presupposes that voters are good judges of which policies would best help promote their interests. Here, Bentham and Mill again use the analogy of the market. Consider what happens when you buy music, clothing, food, or whatnot for yourself. Sure, you can make mistakes. Still, you have the best knowledge of what is good for you, including what kinds of trade-offs are best for you. Further, when you make mistakes on the market, you'll suffer the consequences. So, over time you'll tend to learn from your mistakes. You'll become a smarter and better consumer.

Sure, we can identify times when someone else can identify your mistakes—for instance, perhaps a dietitian could see that you eat too much sugar, and perhaps you'd be healthier if she could veto your food choices. But, overall, most adults are best served by relying on their own judgment than by being subject to the continual control of others. In general, no one cares more about you than you do, so no one takes your interests quite as seriously as you do.

Bentham and Mill think similar remarks apply to voters. Sure, voters can make mistakes. But overall, they have a stronger incentive to determine which candidates and policies are best for them than others do. (In the next chapter, we will consider challenges to this market analogy.)

While Bentham and Mill made similar sorts of arguments here, they disagreed about just how democratic society should be. Mill was less democratic than Bentham, though by the standards of his time, he was a radical democrat. In public, Mill advocated extending the suffrage to all male householders over the age of forty, though in private he probably wanted to extend the suffrage even more than that.[13] In contrast, in public, Bentham advocated extending the suffrage to all adult men first, and then to women after universal male suffrage had been achieved, though in private he advocated universal adult suffrage. (Since they were often writing for an audience they regarded as backward and prejudiced, they were willing to hedge their public remarks.)

David Held says that Mill's view occupies the happy medium between more radical democrats and more radical elitists, like Burke. Some democrats believed that representative democracy always reduces liberty, because in an election, one selects a representative to decide for you and in your place. On this view (which we will examine in greater length in chapter 8), anything other than direct democracy forfeits freedom. Others, like Burke, thought that having good representation in government required only that the leaders promote your interests, not necessarily that you personally voted for them or had a say in electing them. (Indeed, Burke worried that typical voters would not know how to select good candidates who would in fact promote their interests.) Mill thought representative government ensured that government agents would tend to promote the interests of the governed. But, in contrast to direct democracy, it takes less *time* and so is more efficient. Direct democracy takes adults away from their other valuable pursuits. So, for Mill, direct democracy doesn't survive cost-benefit analysis; the benefits of increased participation are dwarfed by their opportunity cost.[14]

Contemporary Epistemic Theories

Over the past two hundred and especially one hundred years, the number of countries that have experimented with various forms of democracy has greatly increased. Further, we have many instances where countries transition to or away from democracy or become more or less democratic. We have far more data about how democracy performs, when it works and when it doesn't.

However, part of the problem is measuring what counts as democracy, what counts as a good or bad result, and determining whether those results come from the fact that a country is democratic or from some other confounding factor. Part of the problem is that we rarely get good natural experiments in the social sciences.

Nevertheless, contemporary epistemic defenses of democracy often begin by noting that in general, democratic countries seem to outperform non-democratic countries on most measures a reasonable person might care about. In general, the best places to live right now are liberal democracies, not dictatorships, one-party governments, oligarchies, or absolute monarchies. Democratic forms of government have generally been the best performing systems we've had so far in human history. Indeed, in chapter 8, we'll review some of the empirical evidence on behalf of the claim that democracies tend to do a better job protecting and promoting citizens' freedom and promoting their welfare than other countries. It seems obvious that in the long run democracies outperform most other forms of government we've tried, and if so, then there must be something about democracy that explains why it tends to make what are comparatively good decisions.

In 1776's *Wealth of Nations*, Adam Smith argued the main reason some countries are prosperous and others poor is not because of different natural resources, fortuitous geography, or the spoils of empire, but instead because some countries have institutions that foster prosperity and others have institutions that prevent it. Fast forward to today, and this thesis—the institutional thesis—is probably the dominant theory in standard economics. A good example of this can be found in *Why Nations Fail* by leading economists Daron Acemoglu and James Robinson.

Acemoglu and Robinson argue the main difference between good and bad institutions concerns whether they are what they call *inclusive* or *extractive*.[15] Inclusive institutions empower people across society, and thus tend to benefit all. Extractive institutions empower only some, and thus tend to benefit only those small groups of people at others' expense. On the political side, inclusive institutions generally require a state that strikes a tricky balance between a reasonable level of centralized power and pluralism. Pluralist governments represent many different groups and interests in society, through free and competitive elections, and governed by the rule of law.

Inclusive political institutions uniquely avoid destructive outcomes that fall on the opposite extremes on a spectrum of political violence. On the one extreme, there is anarchy and civil war. These are the result of insufficient political centralization. On the other extreme, there is tyranny, oppression, and rent seeking. These are the result of too much concentration of power into the hands of some. Societies that find themselves too close to either extreme contain extractive political institutions.

In contrast, Acemoglu and Robinson claim, extractive political institutions create extractive economic institutions. The effects, Acemoglu and Robinson summarize, are ugly:

> Nations fail today because their extractive economic institutions do not create the incentives needed for people to save, invest, and

innovate. Extractive political institutions support these economic institutions by cementing the power of those who benefit from the extraction. . . . In many cases, as . . . in Argentina, Colombia, and Egypt, this failure takes the form of lack of sufficient economic activity, because the politicians are just too happy to extract resources or quash any type of independent economic activity that threatens themselves and the economic elites. In some extreme cases, as in Zimbabwe and Sierra Leone . . . extractive institutions pave the way for complete state failure, destroying not only law and order but also even the most basic economic incentives. The result is economic stagnation and—as the recent history of Angola, Cameroon, Chad, the Democratic Republic of Congo, Haiti, Liberia, Nepal, Sierra Leone, Sudan, and Zimbabwe illustrates—civil wars, mass displacements, famines, and epidemics, making many of these countries poorer today than they were in the 1960s.[16]

One way of framing the difference between extractive and inclusive institutions is that the first are either zero- or negative-sum, where a few quite literally live high by preying upon the many. The inclusive institutions are positive-sum, in which most people engage in wealth-producing and wealth-sustaining activities, activities that do not just benefit themselves, but benefit others.

In philosophy and political science, epistemic democrats often focus on trying to provide models that are meant to explain why democracies might make smart choices. Above, we discussed how contemporary defenders of Condorcet's Jury Theorem have shown that the certain assumptions in the theorem can be relaxed. There are also two other formal theorems that are meant to demonstrate that under certain circumstances, a crowd as a whole can be wise even if most members of the crowd are not.

From at least Plato onward, critics of democracy have worried that voters might be ignorant. But whether ignorance hurts depends on how ignorant voters vote. Some think that ignorant voters might turn out to be harmless—so long as there's lots of them!

That might sound paradoxical, but consider the following analogy. Imagine that you toss a fair coin 10 times in a row. Though the coin has a 50–50 chance of landing on heads or tails, after only 10 tosses, there's a decent chance you'll get a majority of heads or majority tails rather than 5–5 split. However, the more you toss the coin, the more the split will approximate 50–50. If you toss the coin 100 million times, while you probably won't get a literally 50 million to 50 million split, but the split should be close.

A theorem called the Miracle of Aggregation models ignorant voters as being like fair coins. On this analogy, a truly ignorant, being ignorant, voter would have no reason to prefer one candidate to another. Thus, the argument goes, they should vote randomly. So, if the ignorant voting public is very large, then their votes should be evenly distributed among all the candidates.

Suppose there are two candidates, Good and Bad. Suppose 98 percent of voters are completely ignorant and thus vote randomly. Suppose 2 percent of the electorate is well-informed, and thus prefers Good to Bad. Suppose the electorate is very large. Under these assumptions, Good should receive about 51 percent of the vote, while Bad will get 49 percent. Good and Bad split the ignorant votes but Good gets all the informed votes.

Thus, according to the Miracle of Aggregation, an electorate composed almost entirely of ignorant voters will select the same candidate or vote for the same policies as an electorate made up entirely of informed voters, so long as the electorate is *large*. We can solve the problem of ignorant voters by adding lots more ignorant voters!

In general, if the errors of a crowd are randomly distributed and centered on the correct answer, then making the crowd larger improves the wisdom of the crowd. Some examples include having people guess someone's weight or the number of jelly beans in a jar.

In 2004, Lu Hong and Scott Page developed a mathematic theorem that, according to them and to sympathetic readers, provides a different reason to believe that large crowds can be wise. They say there are two ways to increase the overall reliability of a group. One is to increase the reliability of individual people within the group. A second way is to increase the degree of cognitive diversity within the group. If people have diverse perspectives, diverse mental models, and diverse problem-solving techniques or heuristics, and if they are working together on a common problem and willing to listen to one another's good ideas, then adding diversity to a group should improve group performance.[17]

Hong and Page have offered what they regard as a mathematic formalization and proof of the idea (along with computer simulations meant to demonstrate it). These are subject to considerable controversy. Many critics claim that the "proof" of the theorem is question-begging and that the concept of diversity within the formal proof has little to do with cognitive diversity in the real world.[18] Some contemporary political theorists, such as Hélène Landemore, use the Hong-Page theorem as the foundation for arguments that full democracies should outperform any less democratic decision-making process, and that the rule of the many always beats the rule of the few.[19]

What We Should Learn

Democracy spreads power out without concern for the competence or wisdom of the people. But the quality of governance matters. A morally vicious citizenry might choose unjust leaders and policies. A misinformed citizenry could "mean well," but choose leaders and policies that undermine their goals.

This chapter reviewed a variety of arguments that hold that even if the typical citizen is badly informed, democracies nevertheless make it up in bulk. Maybe errors cancel each other out. Maybe two heads are better than one, so having a big committee of average people beats a small committee of experts. Maybe the advantages of diversity of thought outweigh the advantages of concentrated expertise. Or, maybe the issue is simply that democracy forces politicians to serve the people, because bad leaders lose re-election. Maybe that's enough to make democracy function better than dictatorship, monarchy, aristocracies, or single-party states.

7

Against Wisdom

Garbage In, Garbage Out

Skepticism about democracy's wisdom was pervasive throughout most of Western intellectual history. The argument seems simple: the masses are ignorant, passionate, unwise, and easily bamboozled by flatterers and demagogues into voting against their own interests. Politics is difficult. Most voters lack the information they need to vote well. Most voters reason poorly. Democracy gives citizens the opportunity to serve themselves, but they instead shoot themselves in the foot.

You probably already believe something like this is true. I've noticed my academic colleagues—many of whom have a quasi-religious reverence for democracy—bristle at the claim that many voters are too ignorant or irrational to vote well. But these same academics generally agree that, for instance, Republican or Trump voters in the United States voted against their own interests. They generally do not say that Trump voters help themselves at the expense of others or of justice, but instead think Trump voters hurt themselves *too*. They do not say that most Republicans are well-informed and self-interested voters, but instead cast them as misguided fools. The difference between my academic colleagues and Plato, then, is that Plato would say most Democratic voters are *also* misguided fools.

This chapter reviews some of the most important arguments against the collective wisdom of democratic decision-making. While most chapters have focused heavily on historical figures and

Democracy. Jason Brennan, Oxford University Press. © Oxford University Press 2023.
DOI: 10.1093/oso/9780197558812.003.0007

then ended with recent work, this chapter will focus mostly on re-cent empirical work in political science and economics. The reason is that starting in the 1950s, there has been tremendous amounts of research into what voters know, how they think, and why they vote. Most of the intellectual history of political ignorance and irration-ality is *recent* history. Part of the reason for this is that many of the other issues we have discussed or will discuss in this book—such as whether democracy promotes liberty or virtue—are to a great ex-tent *philosophical*. But what citizens know or don't know is largely a social scientific issue. Rigorous methods in researching this did not appear until after World War II.

Plato: Who Should Steer the Ship of State?

Sometimes people compare choosing candidates to choosing ice cream flavors. Choosing how to vote is subjective. There can be no right or wrong answers. The best candidate for you is the candi-date you choose because you chose them. Since there are no right and wrong answers, there can be no question of skill or aptitude, or better or worse voters.

It's unclear whether this argument works even for ice cream flavors. It's an objective fact about me which flavors cause pleasant or unpleasant sensations in my mouth. I cannot simply decide to find peanut butter ice cream tasty. I cannot simply decide to make ice cream healthy or unhealthy. If I spent $100 a year on ice cream, it's at least partly objective—given my other preferences and other values—whether this spending promotes or demotes my interests, or whether the opportunity cost of that spending exceeds the benefits. People can and do make mistakes in consumption, saving, spending, and investing. They can and do make mistakes in choosing ice cream flavors.

Indeed, an entire subfield of economics called behavioral ec-onomics challenges the assumption that economic actors are al-ways rational or informed. Many behavioral economists then argue that consumer irrationality justifies government paternalism. If people make bad choices on the market—choices that undermine individuals' interests as the individuals themselves see it—the government should force them to make better choices.[1] However, it seems that the flaws in consumers are much worse in voters.[2] (We will discuss *why* below.)

Plato would have regarded such subjectivist arguments as non-starters. Of course, people can be mistaken about what is in their self-interest, for instance, by choosing poor means to their ends. Plato gives numerous examples, but we can focus on contemporary equivalents. A smoker might ignore the long-term health threats. An anti-vaxxer might discount the threat of a disease or overestimate the vaccine's risks. An unhappy person might think they can fill the void in their heart with jewelry, travel, or food. An art history master's student faces a negative return on investment. And so on.

Further, Plato thinks that politics is not merely about self-interest. Of course, government should promote citizens' objective interests, all things equal. But throughout the *Republic* and other works, Plato notes that individuals might have conflicts of interests. Here, Plato thinks that there are matters of *justice*. Among other things, justice is about finding the morally right way to mediate or resolve conflicts of interest.

Sometimes there is an objective truth of the matter about justice; it's not simply a matter of taking a vote or finding a fair procedure. You probably already agree with this point. For instance, suppose 90 percent of people are whites who hate blacks. They enjoy seeing the black minority suffer. Suppose 10 percent of people are blacks. Suppose everyone can vote. If we have a fair and equal vote on what policies to implement, you'd expect the policy to implement racist policies that thwart black interests. Would you call that just? Or suppose instead we randomly select a person to serve as queen, who may then do whatever she wants. This procedure is fair in that everyone an equal chance to become queen. Again, there is a 90 percent chance the polity will end up with racist policies which thwart black interests. Would you call that just?

You probably conclude that the resulting racist policies would be evil and unjust in either case. This mean that you already think that the *substance* of the law matters. A fair or equal decision can still be a wrong decision.

Plato argues that knowledge and skill are not evenly dispersed. For any issue, some people know more than others. A trainer might know better than you which exercise regimes promote your health. A medical doctor might know better than you which medicines cure your diseases or treat their symptoms. A captain might know better how to steer the ship, even if you are allowed to decide the destination. A travel agent might know better than you which destinations are good, given your budget and preferences.

Plato thinks similar remarks apply to politics. At the very least, when it comes to selecting *means*, some people know better than others what to do. And, since Plato is not a moral nihilist or sub-jectivist (just as you probably aren't), some people might also know better which *ends* of government ought to be selected. Some people have more moral wisdom and insight than others. (If you disagree, then notice you are thereby committed to saying that Hitler, Stalin, Martin Luther King Jr., Gandhi, Jesus, and you have equal moral insight.)

In Plato's view, morality and justice matter. It matters that we do the right thing, which means it matters that we implement forms of government that tend to do the right thing. That means, among other things, we should implement forms of government that will select for people with both the skill and moral motivation to do what's right, and which reduce the power of those with neither the skill nor good faith to act rightly.

Plato worries that democracy allows a mob to steer the ship of state:

Picture a shipmaster in height and strength surpassing all others on the ship, but who is slightly deaf and of similarly impaired vision, and whose knowledge of navigation is on a par with his sight and hearing. Conceive the sailors to be wrangling with one another for control of the helm, each claiming that it is his right to steer though he has never learned the art and cannot point out his teacher or any time when he studied it. And what is more, they affirm that it cannot be taught at all, but they are ready to make mincemeat of anyone who says that it can be taught, and meanwhile they are always clustered about the shipmaster importuning him and sticking at nothing to induce him to turn over the helm to them. And sometimes, if they fail and others get his ear, they put the others to death or cast them out from the ship, and then, after binding and stupefying the worthy shipmaster with mandragora or intoxication or otherwise, they take command of the ship, consume its stores and, drinking and feasting, make such a voyage of it as is to be expected from such, and as if that were not enough, they praise and celebrate as a navigator, a pilot, a master of shipcraft, the man who is most cunning to lend a hand in persuading or constraining the shipmaster to let them rule, while the man who lacks this craft they censure as useless. They have no suspicions that the true pilot must give his attention to the time of the year, the seasons, the sky, the winds, the stars, and all that pertains to his art if he is to be a true ruler of a ship, and that he does not believe that there is any art or science of seizing the helm with or without the consent of others, or any possibility of mastering this alleged art and the practice of it at the same time with the science of navigation. With such goings-on aboard ship do you not think that the real pilot would in very deed be called a star-gazer, an idle babbler, a useless fellow, by the sailors in ships managed after this fashion?[3]

A government is like a ship. It must go somewhere and do something. The question is who decides. According to Plato, the great mass of people in a democracy—even a highly constrained and elite democracy like ancient Athens—are like the impertinent, uninformed, and narcissistic sailors in the story above. They lack the knowledge of statecraft needed to steer the ship of state properly. They deny there is any such knowledge to be had. They would not choose an expert pilot if given the chance.

When people enter politics, they deny a truth they understand outside politics: some people know better than others. In chapter 5, we discussed why Plato thinks we think this way: democracy's institutional egalitarianism leads people to falsely believe everyone is equal in character, skill, and judgment. Its liberalism induces citizens to focus on satisfying their desires rather than doing what's right. Believing everyone is equal means believing no one can be better, which means believing *I* cannot be better, which turns into a license for allowing myself to remain incompetent.

Contemporary scholars would offer a different explanation. Recall the discussion of "rational irrationality" in chapter 5. Citizens reason poorly because the expected costs of processing political information exceed the expected benefits. As we will see below, many also argue that something similar explains why citizens are ignorant.

Who should decide? Plato thinks the answer depends on who, when given power, will tend to make the right choice and avoid wrong choices.

This is a more complicated question than it seems. Consider three doctors:

1. Doctor One has a 75 percent chance of curing your fatal disease, a 20 percent chance of killing you immediately, and a 5 percent chance of sexually assaulting you instead of treating you.
2. Doctor Two has a 50 percent chance not of curing you, but of extending your life by five years, and a 50 percent chance of extending it by ten years.
3. Doctor Three has a 100 percent chance of extending your life by 7.5 years.

Which doctor counts as "tending" to make the right choice? Doctor One has the biggest upside but also the biggest downsides. Doctors Two and Three have less variance in the quality of their outcomes.

Aristotle uses reasoning like this as part of his defense of constitutional polities. He claims that constitutional government is best not because it tends to make the best decisions, but because it tends to avoid terrible decisions. Its decisions are moderate—neither very good nor very bad. In contrast, he thinks monarchies and aristocracies tend to make much better but also much worse decisions. Monarchy might be like Doctor One, while a polity is like Doctor Two or Three.

In general, Plato thinks that the people who know best about what justice requires, and who are most apt to do it (keeping in mind the complications we just discussed), should rule. But to be clear, Plato is not making any of the following controversial claims: we always can determine what's right. The experts are always right. When the experts and people disagree, the experts are always right. We can always identify who the experts are. Political and moral experts are uncorruptible. The rule of experts will always prevail.

Attributing such bold but implausible claims to Plato makes it easier to dismiss him, but it's uncharitable and not supported by the textual evidence. For one, he does not assert them. Two, we have already seen in previous chapters how Plato worries that even his idealized state, ruled by a guardian class, would degrade over time. In the *Republic*, he explicitly states that creating and maintaining a guardian class would be difficult. Third, it clashes with much of his other work on epistemology and metaphysics. Plato was a philosophical skeptic. His dialogues are supposed to show both that there are objective truths but also that we face serious cognitive difficulties in discovering them.

Consider, for instance, Plato's famous Allegory of the Cave. Plato asks us to imagine prisoners chained to a wall who cannot move their heads. They spend their entire lives facing a different wall. Behind the prisoners, other people—whom the prisoners cannot see—hold up puppets, which casts shadows on the wall the prisoners can see. The prisoners develop a language, metaphysics, and epistemology that reflects their experience. They think the shadow puppets are all that exists. After some time, we imagine that one prisoner is freed and allowed to come to the surface. He sees how the other prisoners are held. After he adjusts to the surface light, he learns that the shadows he had seen on the wall correspond to real objects on the surface. Now suppose the man returns to the cave and is allowed to tell the prisoners what he saw. The other prisoners would regard his claims as fantastic and absurd. They wouldn't believe him. The prisoners might even conclude that leaving the cave is dangerous and would try to kill anyone who wanted to "free" them.

Philosophers debate what the allegory is supposed to mean. For instance, are the masses in a democracy supposed to be like the prisoners? But, generally, scholars think the meaning is not inherently political. Rather, we are all somewhat like those prisoners, seeing only a shadow of a deeper truth, with most unable and defiantly unwilling to see more.

Plato thinks that those with more wisdom about justice, statecraft, and politics should rule. In response, the contemporary philosopher David Estlund claims that Plato's argument—and others like it—rests upon three tenets:

1. *The truth tenet*: There are correct answers to some political questions.
2. *The knowledge tenet*: Some people know better than others what the correct answers are; some people are more reliable than others at determining the truth.
3. *The authority tenet*: Knowing better entitles you to more power than those who know less.

Estlund himself accepts the truth and knowledge tenet but rejects the authority tenet. He says that it commits the "expert-boss fallacy."[4] The expert-boss fallacy occurs when someone concludes that because one person knows better than another, that person should be in charge. For instance, a dietitian might know better than you what you should eat, but it doesn't follow that she should have the right to choose your meals.

Still, you might think Estlund's example works for personal choices but not *political* choices. A dietitian should not be able to force you to eat the way she knows is best because it's *your* body. Maybe we have the right to choose poorly for ourselves. It's less obvious whether this also applies to *collective* choices.

Mill: Democracy as Classism

Many philosophers claimed that different forms of government would be, in effect, rule by different economic classes. An aristocracy is supposed to be the rule of the best, but it ends up being the rule of the rich. Plato claimed a democracy is supposed to be the rule of the many but ends up being the rule of the poor (because the poor are the majority).

Plato's comment may have been correct 2,500 years ago, but it's perhaps not so today. In the contemporary mature democracies, the middle class is often the majority. Different economists and political scientists define "middle class" differently, so whether that statement is true depends in part on what we mean by the words. Further, what we mean by "poor" today isn't what we meant by "poor" 100 or 2,500 years ago. An American at the US poverty line today is, *after* adjusting for the cost of living and inflation, in the top 1 percent of income earners ever; a "working-class" British citizen has a standard of living at least twenty times higher than his counterpart from a thousand years ago.[5]

In chapter 4, we saw how John Stuart Mill believed that (nearly) universal enfranchisement would enlighten and ennoble citizens.[6] This argument—that we should extend the franchise as a means of

educating citizens' intellectual and moral virtues—remains popular among democratic theorists today. Nevertheless, while Mill
thought political participation would improve citizens' character,
he did not think it would perfect them.

In *Considerations on Representative Government*, Mill worries
that democracies will suffer from class bias:

> [In democracy] absolute power, if they chose to exercise it, would
> rest with the numerical majority; and these would be composed
> exclusively of a single class, alike in biases, prepossessions, and
> general modes of thinking, and a class, to say no more, not the
> most highly cultivated. The constitution would therefore still be li-
> able to the characteristic evils of class government: in a far less de-
> gree, assuredly, than that exclusive government by a class, which
> now usurps the name of democracy; but still, under no effective
> restraint, except what might be found in the good sense, moder-
> ation, and forbearance of the class itself. If checks of this descrip-
> tion are sufficient, the philosophy of constitutional government
> is but solemn trifling. All trust in constitutions is grounded on
> the assurance they may afford, not that the depositaries of power
> will not, but that they cannot, misemploy it. Democracy is not
> the ideally best form of government unless this weak side of it
> can be strengthened; unless it can be so organized that no class,
> not even the most numerous, shall be able to reduce all but itself
> to political insignificance, and direct the course of legislation and
> administration by its exclusive class interest. The problem is, to
> find the means of preventing this abuse, without sacrificing the
> characteristic advantages of popular government.[7]

In short, Mill thinks there are both advantages and disadvantages
to universal suffrage. The advantages include that suffrage
enlightens and ennobles citizens. Following Tocqueville, Mill
claims that (as of the time he writes) the American lower classes
have superior intellectual development compared to lower classes

elsewhere. Further, Mill agrees that widespread suffrage increases the diversity of ideas on the table. It helps citizens believe that their government serves them and reduces strife.

But, he thinks, democratic government faces certain problems. Like Plato, he worries that democracy would become the rule of the poor, who are intellectually uncultivated.[8] The poor are likely to exercise power for their own interests at the expense of others. They might not govern in good faith.

However, Mill thinks, even if the poor tried to rule well, they would tend to share various "biasses [sic], prepossessions, and general modes of thinking."[9] Even if they wanted to govern for the benefit of all, they would nevertheless get mired in particular mental models or modes of thought that impair their ability to solve problems.

If that isn't clear, consider an analogy. Imagine a country in which only white people may vote. Suppose that whites *want* to govern fairly and want to serve the interests of non-whites. Or imagine that only men may vote, but all men nevertheless want to govern fairly and serve the interests of other genders. Or suppose only the young could vote, but they wanted to help the old. You probably suspect that in all three cases, the governing demographic would nevertheless fail to acknowledge or understand certain issues or problems, and thus would systematically fall short of passing laws optimal for the excluded demographics. Mill thinks the same thing would apply if any particular economic class has (close to) exclusive power. Indeed, Mill is even more pessimistic here, because I am asking you to imagine that, for instance, whites may vote but blacks may not. Yet Mill is arguing that since the majority gets its way even when the minority is enfranchised, universal suffrage will not protect us from biased outcomes.

Thus, Mill concludes that democracy will be class-based government, just as much as aristocracy or monarchy are. Perhaps he'd agree that today, thanks to changes in the distribution and degree of income, democracy has become government for the middle class rather than for the poor. He would probably even agree with Aristotle that government by the middle class is superior to government by the poor. But he still argues that *any* class-based government is deficient.

Further, Mill claims that governments function well only when the citizens trust the government. But trust in government requires trust that the government makes *wise* decisions. While he argues that universal suffrage could improve citizens' intellectual and knowledge, he does not conclude that it will thereby render every citizen an expert. Instead, Mill thinks that most citizens will remain significantly uninformed, underinformed, misinformed, or prejudiced.

Ideally, we want the ship of state to be piloted by a competent body. The citizens themselves want this. If the majority gets its way, but its way turns out to be mistaken and harmful to the majority itself, the majority will lose faith in their own government. So, Mill agrees with Plato that the fact that some people know much more than others is a reason to imbue them with power, if not by itself a decisive reason.

In Mill's view, (nearly) universal suffrage has advantages, but rule by an educated elite also has advantages. Both have disadvantages. He argues that the solution is to *mix* a kind of aristocracy of the informed with the universal suffrage of democracy. He thus advocates what is called a "plural voting scheme" or plural voting. In a plural voting scheme, all (or nearly all) adults have at least one vote, but some adults have more than one. (Exactly *how many* extra votes is up for debate. Mill doesn't try to resolve this question.)

Mill suggests three possible ways for acquiring multiple votes: by exam, by education, or by profession. He does not consider these competing policies. Instead, a country might adopt all three.

His first proposal is to acquire additional votes though an impartial system of national tests and qualifications. Consider, by analogy, that most countries require foreigners applying for citizenship to pass an exam on the new country's history, culture, and form of government. In Mill's view, we might use the same method to earn extra votes. At age eighteen, everyone gets one vote, but if you want additional votes, you must pass an exam demonstrating your knowledge of history, social science, culture, and basic political facts.

Another alternative would be to assign votes to those with sufficient education. More highly educated people tend to know more than the less educated. So, perhaps everyone with a bachelor's degree should get additional votes.

A third alternative is to allocate extra votes by profession, because certain professions have more knowledge than others. Mills says:

> [T]he nature of a person's occupation is some test. An employer of labour is on the average more intelligent than a labourer; for he must labour with his head, and not solely with his hands. A foreman is generally more intelligent than an ordinary labourer, and a labourer in the skilled trades than in the unskilled. A banker, merchant, or manufacturer is likely to be more intelligent than a tradesman, because he has larger and more complicated interests to manage.[10]

Mill suggests that votes might be apportioned to individuals by their work.

However, right before the quoted passage above, Mill notes that citizens could become jealous or contemptuous of power if they perceive it to be distributed by income or wealth. The typical banker is richer than the typical laborer. The typical college graduate is richer than the typical high school–only graduate. The plurality voting scheme does not directly distribute power by income or wealth. Instead, it distributes power based on real qualifications that happen to be positively correlated with wealth. In the same way, medical licenses tend to go to higher-income people, but that doesn't mean medical licenses are distributed according to wealth.

Still, the (mistaken) perception that they are distributed by wealth could be a problem.

Mill anticipates objections: isn't this scheme unfair to those who receive fewer votes? Doesn't it treat them as inferior? Might they perceive it as mistreating them? He responds:

> There is not, in [the plural voting scheme], anything necessarily invidious to those to whom it assigns the lower degrees of influence. Entire exclusion from a voice in the common concerns is one thing: the concession to others of a more potential voice, on the ground of greater capacity for the management of the joint interests, is another. The two things are not merely different, they are incommensurable. Every one has a right to feel insulted by being made a nobody, and stamped as of no account at all. No one but a fool, and only a fool of a peculiar description, feels offended by the acknowledgment that there are others whose opinion, and even whose wish, is entitled to a greater amount of consideration than his. To have no voice in what are partly his own concerns is a thing which nobody willingly submits to; but when what is partly his concern is also partly another's, and he feels the other to understand the subject better than himself, that the other's opinion should be counted for more than his own accords with his expectations, and with the course of things which in all other affairs of life he is accustomed to acquiese [sic] in. It is only necessary that this superior influence should be assigned on grounds which he can comprehend, and of which he is able to perceive the justice.[11]

To summarize, Mill agrees that everyone should have a say in politics. To be denied a vote is to be rendered a political spectator, a mere subject. But only a fool would deny that some people know more than others and some have better judgment than others. Further, a civic-minded person would recognize that power is not merely about serving personal interests, but about promote justice and outcomes good for all. So, a civic-minded person should *want* a system to defer to whoever has the best judgment, and should want to adhere to a system that has the best chance of producing good judgments. In short, if you find plural voting intrinsically offensive, you're probably a self-serving jerk who doesn't care about justice.

A critic might respond that in practice a plural voting scheme is ripe for abuse. Perhaps governments will take advantage of the system to distribute votes on sham qualifications. They will try to ensure that their constituents or loyalists get more power, thus allowing the ruling party to solidify its control. As a parallel, consider that current debates about whether the District of Columbia should become a state seem motivated by partisan politics rather than principle. DC is overwhelmingly Democratic. Democrats support statehood and Republicans don't. If DC's party numbers were reversed, the parties' positions would switch.

Hayek: You're Asking the Wrong Question

So far, most of the arguments for and against democracy have rested upon a common assumption, an assumption you might not have noticed. The assumption is that the debate is about whether to have democracy or *some other form of government*, such as monarchy, timocracy, epistocracy, aristocracy, or whatnot. The theorists we've discussed have been asking whether democracy promotes or demotes stability, virtue, or wisdom, and how well it compares to other political alternatives.

Another possibility is that perhaps government shouldn't make certain decisions at all. Sometimes, the correct answer to "who should rule?" is *no one*.

Suppose we want to improve the quality of decision-making. We could do so by modifying any of the following aspects of government:

1. *Scale*: The number of people or geographic range over which a particular decision, law, or policy applies. It might turn out that governments over a certain geographic size or over a particular number of people are optimal.
2. *Timing*: How quickly or slowly decisions are made, or when the decisions are made. For instance, we saw in chapter 6 how Madison believed that slowing down decision-making improves it.
3. *Form*: Who rules and how power is distributed among the people who rule. For instance, should we have democracy, plural voting representative government, Plato's guardians, or something else?
4. *Scope*: Which issues and topics are regularly or in principle subjected to political or decision-making. For instance, it might turn out that governments of any form are bad at making certain decisions, in which case the decisions might be left to private individuals.

Most of the debates we've seen so far have concerned the form of government, but these other questions matter too.

Unless you are a totalitarian, you already believe governments ought to have limited scope. You probably think that government ought not to assign you a religion or a marriage partner. You probably think that you have the right to decide for yourself and that governments are not competent to choose for you.

In the early 1900s (and even now), many intellectuals and others advocated subjecting almost everything to democratic (or some other governmental) rule. In their view, the scope of government should be, well, everything. In particular, many advocated extensive or complete government control of the means of production, with democratically elected representatives overseeing expert technocratic administration of the economy. In short, they advocated having a command socialist economy. ("Socialism" here refers not to an extensive welfare state or government regulation, but to a system in which the government owns the means of production and makes all important economic decisions.)

The Nobel laureate economist F. A. Hayek (1899–1992) threw some cold water on this mode of thinking. Early on, when socialism was new and the evidence was not yet in, socialists often claimed that socialist economies would outperform capitalist economies. Hayek argued instead that socialist planners are by necessity too uninformed to plan an economy.

Hayek's argument is technical, but we can simplify it in an accessible way. Think of an economy as an extended system of cooperation. An economy consists of people working together to produce various goods and services. To get them to work together, we need to coordinate what different people will do at different times. Thus, every economy needs three basic things:

1. *Information*: Something must signal to individuals what would be useful to do.
2. *Incentives*: Something must induce people to act upon that information.
3. *Learning*: Something must correct people's mistakes and teach people to become better at responding to information and incentives.

Other critics of socialism often focus on its incentive problems. They claim that systems of equal reward do not incentivize workers or managers to be productive. "To each according to their needs and from each according to their abilities" means, in effect, punish productive people by making them work more and reward unproductive people by giving them more. Or, critics claim that the concentrated and total economic power inside socialist governments ends up being captured by murderous tyrants such as Mao, Lenin, Stalin, Pol Pot, Ho Chi Minh, and Castro.

But, while Hayek agrees that real-life socialism has these problems, he thinks the problems are even deeper than that. Even if people were angels who were inclined to work hard for equal reward and never inclined to abuse concentrations of power, they could not become *informed* enough to plan an economy.

Consider what looks like a simple economic decision: should we make nylon or vinyl belts? In fact, that's a complicated choice: how many belts ought you make? In what size, color, or style? Where should you make them? With what kinds of tools? What mix of labor and capital should you use? Of what sort? What *else* could you use those raw materials, capital, or labor for? Finally, after you decide, how do you know whether your choices were right or not, that is, whether you added value to the world or not? After all, everything you do has a cost—including an opportunity cost (i.e., the best option you didn't choose).

For a small firm in a market economy, these are incredibly difficult questions. But a socialist planner—or committee of planners—has to decide all these questions, all at once, for every good and service, all while conditions constantly change. Hayek points out that to make proper decisions, planners in any economy need to know not merely generally statistical facts—such as that there are exactly 132 million waists in the country—but also local opportunities, trade-offs, preferences, and costs. Worse, these facts are not static. Even if, somehow, all that information could be transmitted to the planners, as soon as the information is transmitted, it's obsolete.

Markets coordinate economic activity and solve the calculation problem because market prices are an information transmission mechanism. You probably have heard that market prices are a function of supply and demand. Let's think about what that means.

All things equal, as things become costlier, we tend to stop pursuing them and instead look for substitutes. For instance, if your favorite restaurant triples its prices, you might find a new favorite. When you learn no one wants to buy your poetry but they are willing to pay you to do accounting, you'll probably switch to accounting.

A store manager can put whatever sticker price she wants on an item, but cannot decide the actual market price. Instead, here's what she can expect. If the price is too high, the item won't sell. She'll have to discount it. If she sets it too low, the product will fly off the shelf—and she might see people buying it only to resell it for a higher price. So, she'll have an incentive to adjust her prices to match market demand. Similar remarks apply to buyers. If I pay too much for something, I lose more than I gain, and the opportunity cost of my purchase is too high. But if I refuse to pay enough, I get nothing.

Market prices emerge as a function of supply and demand, which are in turn emergent forces created by everyone acting in response to everyone else on the disparate information each individual has. The forces of supply and demand are determined by all the choices and trade-offs that every individual in the economy makes, given the information they have. The forces of supply and demand are in turn determined by all of us, as individuals, acting on our disparate knowledge and disparate desires as we react to the world around us.

Market prices thus convey information about the relative scarcity of goods considering the effective demand for those goods. What this means, then, is that market prices convey *information* about the relative scarcity of goods considering people's desire for those goods. Market prices thus tell producers and consumers how to adjust their behavior to other people's wants and needs. And, importantly, they do so without actors in the market needing to understand what prices are. Few people, aside from economists, understand that market prices encapsulate the knowledge and desires of everyone in the market. But people act on the information signal markets provide, even though they don't *know* that prices are a signal.

For instance, imagine that a disaster destroys much of the electrical grid, which then needs to be replaced. Governments and utilities buy as much copper as they can, which causes the price to rise, because demand is now up. As a result, acoustic guitar string manufacturers now must compete to buy copper for bronze strings. They must pay more, which means they can make a profit only if their customers are willing to pay more. As a result, guitar string manufacturers might decide to charge a lower price for "80/20 bronze" strings, which contain 80 percent copper, than "phosphor bronze" strings, which are 92 percent copper. Guitar players, seeing the price difference, will shift toward lower-priced strings. Though it was no part of their intention, guitar players will thereby start conserving copper, allowing it to be used for a higher-value, more important goal. Price changes induce people to act on changes in facts about scarcity or value *even though* consumers and suppliers do not know those facts.

Relatedly, you might notice that soda cans now have a curved top and bottom, unlike the straight cylinders of fifty years ago. This change in shape allows them to be stacked high despite containing significantly less metal than the old cans. Coca-Cola and other companies made the switch not because they were concerned about sustainability, but because finding a way to get the same results using fewer resource nets them a higher rate of profit. Market prices induce people to conserve even when they don't care about conservation.

Most of the objects you buy result from amazingly complex processes involving millions of people, who work together without even knowing it. Consider a number 2 pencil. The person who mines the iron that goes into the ball bearings in machines that make the paint that coats the pencil helped make the pencil. The person who taught engineering to the engineer who designed the crank on one of the machines that helped get the oil that went into the grease on the ball bearings helped make the pencil. Market prices induce millions of people to work together.

Further, because market prices are a function of supply and demand, they tell individual agents whether their work creates or destroys value for others. For instance, suppose I want to create new art. I buy $100,000 worth of MacBooks, smash them, and then make a self-portrait bust from the pieces. Suppose I have fun making the bust, so we don't have to treat my labor as a cost. Suppose I put the sculpture for sale. If I find a buyer willing to pay more than $100,000, that shows I took materials others valued at $100,000 and transformed them into something the world values more. I created value for others, and I get a profit as a reward. If, instead, I can only sell the statue for $100, I lose $99,900. I destroyed value—I turned what others valued at $100,000 into something they value only at $100—but the market makes me eat a loss as a punishment. Market prices again thus induce people to work for others' benefit and to create rather than destroy value. Over time, then, market prices help people learn to behave in more cooperative and value-creating ways.

As we said above, every economy needs information, incentives, and learning processes. In market economies, these are the mechanisms:

1. *Information*: Market prices.
2. *Incentives*: The ability to acquire private property and wealth for one's own disposal, as one sees fit.
3. *Learning*: Profits and losses.

But, Hayek notes, centralized command economies—whether democratic or not—dispense with market prices. For most economic tasks, planners lack anything that is even a moderately good substitute. As a result, they must either guess, or—if they are surrounded by market economy countries—they can approximate or copy what these market economies. Neither method is very good, and this explains both (A) why genuinely socialist countries tend to remain or become poor, with low-quality goods and poor levels of productivity and (B) why so-called socialist countries rarely try to have genuine socialism, but instead quickly move to having mixed economies.

This is a book on the theory of democracy, not on economics. But this argument from Hayek is important because it reveals that democratic theorists often ask the wrong questions. Instead of asking, "Should we have democracy vs. some other form of political rule?," the right question is instead often, "Should we have democracy or leave this question outside of politics?"

Rational Ignorance: The Tragic Commons of Ideas

Recall this point, from Anthony Downs, which we discussed in chapter 5:

> *The economics of information*: People will tend to acquire and retain information if and only if the expected benefits of doing so exceed the expected costs.

Downs identified that this principle has a corollary:

> *Rational ignorance*: If the expected costs of information exceed the expected benefits, people will tend not to acquire or retain that information.

For instance, I suspect that you, the reader, are not and do not plan to become fluent in Sarcee. You expect that learning the language—which you probably didn't know existed until the last sentence—would cost more than whatever benefit you'd derive.

Consider a hypothetical case: imagine that Calculus I has 1,000 students. Imagine on day one the professor tells students that she is an egalitarian. She plans to administer one final exam worth 100 percent of students' final grade. She will average all 1,000 students' final exam grades together and they will each receive the same score. Imagine she somehow can get away with this grading scheme. You would expect that the average grade in the class will be lower than normal—perhaps even an F—because students face perverse incentives. If a student studies hard and as an individual scores 100 percent, this will barely affect her grade. She bears all the costs but gets hardly any benefit. If she slacks off, watches Netflix, and never learns calculus, this will hardly affect her grade. Since this holds for every student, we would expect most students to fail to learn much calculus.

You've probably heard people talk about the "marketplace of ideas." Just as we try to find the tastiest item on the menu or the best-looking shirts at the store, we select politicians who offer the best policy ideas given our values. Indeed, as you saw in the intro-ductory paragraphs of this book, this is probably the most common and important argument *for* democracy: democracy serves the interests of most citizens because citizens know which policies are good for them, and representatives win power only by promising to implement such policies.

What Downs claimed, in effect, is that this metaphor is mistaken. When you buy a sandwich, you *get* the sandwich *you* ordered, and *you* eat it. When you vote . . . you get what the majority or largest plurality wants, period. That's true for everyone, including every member of the majority. So voting is not like a market, and the spread of political ideas is not quite a market either. It's some-thing else.

Economist Bryan Caplan explains:

The analogy between voting and shopping is false: *Democracy is a commons, not a market.* Individual voters do not "buy" policies with votes. Rather they toss their vote into a big common pool. The social outcome depends on the pool's average content.

In common-pool situations, economists usually fear the worst. Heedless of the aggregate effect, people will foul the waters. The main reason that they are complacent about democracy, I suspect, is that the pollution is hard to visualize. It is not run-of-the-mill *physical* pollution. Democracy suffers from a more abstract externality: ... *mental* pollution.[12]

As a better analogy, think of the climate. The climate is something we all hold in common. No one owns it, but everyone has access to it. Your individual behavior has only negligible effect on it, but our collective behavior has massive effect. The result: too much carbon emission and climate change. Democratic voting faces the same structural problem.

In short, Downs claims, the incentive structure of democracy predicts widespread political ignorance. Is that what we find?

The Empirics of Ignorance

In the late 1950s, researchers in the United States began collecting data about what citizens know and don't know. The studies focused on "basic political information," such as which party controls Congress, what major laws have passed, who voters' elected officials are, and so on. The studies did not test more advanced political knowledge, such as what comparative advantage tells us about free trade or what effect carbon has in the atmosphere.

In general, these studies find that some voters know a lot, but most Americans know very little, many know nothing, and many are systematically misinformed. (They know less than nothing.) Studies of other countries generate similar results. Even when smartphones and the internet became widespread, citizens remained as ignorant as before. The price of information went down, but the value did not go up.

There are thousands of studies and hundreds of books documenting what citizens don't know. Good overviews include Michael X. Delli-Carpini and Scott Keeter's 1996 *What Americans Know about Politics and Why It Matters* and Ilya Somin's 2013

Democracy and Political Ignorance. Here, I will summarize a few persistent findings.

In a typical election year, most Americans cannot identify their congresspeople or which party controls Congress. During election years, most citizens cannot identify any congressional candidates in their district.[13] Most cannot guess the unemployment rate within a few percentage points. Most have little memory of recent events.[14]

In the 2000 US presidential election, most Americans knew that Al Gore was more "liberal" than Bush, but most did not know what that label means. Fewer than half understood that Gore was more supportive of abortion rights, more supportive of welfare-state programs, favored a higher degree of support for issues of concern to black Americans, or was more supportive of environmental regulation.[15]

A month before the Brexit vote, the polling form Ipsos Mori discovered that the British public was systematically misinformed about facts relevant to the decision. For instance, Leave voters believed that EU immigrants comprised 20 percent of the UK's population. Remain voters estimated 10 percent. They were both wrong, though the Leave voters were further from the truth. On average, both Leave and Remain voters overestimated by a factor of 40 to 100 how much the UK pays in child benefits to people in other countries. Both vastly underestimated the amount of foreign investment from the EU and vastly overestimated the amount from China.[16]

And so on. In general, studies tend to find that voters know who the chief executive is, but not much else. They generally do not know relevant geography, the shape or content of the budget, recent changes in law, changes in social indicators, the overall measures of relevant social indicators, or the shape of their own government or who has the power to do what in government.

Even when such studies sometimes indicate voters know general trends, they often do not know the extent of those trends.

In 2000, most Americans knew that the federal deficit decreased under Clinton. But they could not identify by how much.[17] Many Americans in 1992 knew that unemployment had risen under George H. W. Bush, but most could not estimate the unemployment rate within 5 percentage points of the actual rate. When asked to guess what the unemployment rate was, most voters guessed it was twice as high as the actual rate.[18]

Democratic Realism

In chapter 1, we discussed the sixth-grade model of democracy—the model that we learn in primary school. This model says that citizens first have values, then form political beliefs and policy preferences, who then find and vote for parties and candidates who share those political beliefs and promise to enact those policies. As a result, the winning candidates tend to do what the majority want. Thus, the story goes, democracy makes leaders serve the public.

If voters are ignorant or irrational, this casts doubt on the model. Voters are not like reasonable patients seeking evidence-based medicine. They are more like silly hippies who think crystals will cure cancer.

However, a theory of voter behavior called democratic realism is even more erroneous than this. We can summarize democratic realism with these two sentences by philosopher Kwame Anthony Appiah: "People don't vote for what they want. They vote for who they are."[19] Let's unpack what that means.

Many studies of voter ideology tend to find that, well, most voters don't have ideologies. In a comprehensive review of the research on voter belief, political scientists Donald Kinder and Nathan Kalmoe estimate that fewer than 1 out of 5 voters have something like a political ideology.[20] There are few "single-issue" voters.[21] In general, cognitive elites have ideologies and vote from ideology, but most voters support the same party year after year on non-ideological grounds. This creates a puzzle. What are citizens voting for? If they do not agree with their party or share its ideas, why do they support it?

Consider an analogy: why do you support one sports team rather than another? Probably you picked the teams closest to you because your peers and friends support them. But then why root for a team at all? You might like the sport, but it goes deeper than that. When a Bostonian wears a Red Sox shirt, this signals to others that you are in a way loyal to the community—you're really one of us! And that brings all sorts of social benefits.

Political scientists Christopher Achen and Larry Bartels suggest that roughly the same mechanism explains political affiliation. Most citizens possess some regulating self-identity (which may be complex), such as "college professor" or "Boston Irish" or "Southern evangelical Christian." Politically active citizens learn how others with the same regulating identity vote, and then usually vote the same way.[22] Just as a person from Boston looks around and decides to be a Red Sox fan to fit in, so Southern Evangelicals become Republican to fit in.

They claim that various groups become attached to different parties for largely accidental historical events or circumstances that have little to do with voters' underlying values or interests.[23] For example, to repeat a point from chapter 3, American Jews switched from Republican to Democratic loyalties between 1928 and 1940, not because of policy platform changes, the Wall Street Crash, or ideological changes, but because of reduced antagonism between Jews and Catholics in the 1930s.[24]

Some voters *appear* to be ideological, but, realists claim, the appearance is somewhat illusory. It's not that they pick the party that matches their ideology; rather, they get attached to a party for arbitrary reasons, and then match their apparent ideology to whatever their party says today. Rather than "I vote Democrat because

I support gun control," it's "I support gun control because I vote Democrat." These partisan voters learn what their party stands for and claim/convince themselves that they also stand for it. If their party changes platforms, they will change too, usually unaware that they changed.[25]

The evidence for the realist hypothesis is multifold. First, there is independent evidence that most voters lack many political beliefs and that what few beliefs they have are unstable.[26] Second, most voters who express beliefs "change their minds" whenever their party changes platforms. If you were voting Republican because you advocated free trade, then when the Republicans turn protectionist, you would support them less. On the contrary, realists claim that most voters not only switch to defending protectionism, but also claim that they have *always* been protectionist. Third, we see that people cluster their political beliefs around whatever the party happens to endorse. As psychologist Dan Kahan says:

> Whether humans are heating the earth and concealed-carry laws increase crime, moreover, turn on wholly distinct bodies of evidence. There is no logical reason for positions on these two empirical issues—not to mention myriad others, including the safety of underground nuclear-waste disposal, the deterrent impact of the death penalty, the efficacy of invasive forms of surveillance to combat terrorism to cluster at all, much less form packages of beliefs that so strongly unite citizens of one set of outlooks and divide those of opposing ones. However, there is a psychological explanation. . . . That explanation is politically motivated reasoning.[27]

These issues are logically independent of each other, yet if you take a stance on one issue, we can predict with near certainty what stance you have on all the others. Thus, it seems that people adopt whatever their party's stance is. They advocate policies because their party advocates them; they do not choose a party because they share its policy ideas.

Realism, if correct, is bad news for wisdom-based defenses of democracy, including Bentham and Mill's interest-based defense from the previous chapter. Elections are not mechanisms by which politicians are incentivized to do what the people want. Elections are more like mechanisms by which people publicly signal loyalty to their social group. Politicians gain power as a by-product. People support parties and candidates for largely arbitrary reasons, so democracy does not deliver what the people really want.

What We Should Learn

The empirics are clear: most voters are badly informed and reason about politics in motivated and irrational ways. The best explanation appears to be that democracy creates perverse incentives and citizens take the bait.

Most democratic theorists model citizens as trying to use their votes for the purpose of generating government that will serve their interests and goals. But recent empirical work challenges even this. Democratic realism suggests instead that voters use politics for building and signaling social alliances. Since their individual votes have little effect on government or policies, they don't even try use them for the purpose of producing policy.

These past two chapters cover some of the most crucial issues in democratic theory today. We have to ask hard empirical and normative questions. What are voters really doing when the vote? Why do they form ideologies, if they even do? Are voters smart on the whole even if most are not "smart" as individuals? Is there a way to fix these persistent problems of ignorance and irrationality? And, if not, what does this say about the justice of democracy itself?

8

For Liberty

The Consent of the Governed?

Are Democracies Free or Is Democracy Itself a Kind of Freedom?

Democracy rests on the consent of the governed, or so the story goes. Democracy is unique among forms of government because—regardless of how smart the laws might be—the people *choose* the laws for themselves. In monarchy, the king *imposes* laws upon subjects. In democracy, the people *authorize* the laws themselves, if indirectly. Thus, the story goes, democracies have a special connection to freedom.

We often describe democracies as free countries and people living in other forms of government as unfree. Why? There are two different (though compatible) answers we might give.

One is that democracies also happen to be liberal. As a matter of empirical fact, countries with democratic regimes tend to be *liberal* in the philosophical sense. In philosophy, the word "liberal" doesn't mean "anything left of center." Rather, a liberal philosophy is any political theory that holds that each individual ought to be imbued with an extensive set of strongly protected personal freedoms. A political regime qualifies as liberal to the extent it recognizes and protects such freedoms. In principle, democracies could be illiberal, but as a matter of empirical fact, most turn out to be liberal. This view holds that there is an empirical regularity or connection between liberal freedom and democracy.

Democracy. Jason Brennan, Oxford University Press. © Oxford University Press 2023.
DOI: 10.1093/oso/9780197558812.003.0008

A second view holds that democracies are *inherently* free and all non-democracies are inherently unfree, because (part of) what it *means* to be free is to have a vote and a right to say (or a right to an equal say) over what affects you. On this view, democracies do not simply turn out to be liberal, but rather, the rights to vote and run for office are themselves constitutive of freedom. This is the "consent of the governed" kind of view.

Conceptions of Liberty

"Liberty" and "freedom" are contested concepts in political theory. Philosophers and theorists dispute what the terms mean and what counts as liberty and freedom. They do not merely disagree about which freedoms people ought to have—for instance, should people have the freedom to snort coke or to refuse government-mandated vaccines—but what the proper definitions of the words are.

Part of the fault for this lies with the British political philosopher Isaiah Berlin (1909–1997). In his "Two Concepts of Liberty" (1958), Berlin claims that historians have documented over a hundred different ways natural English speakers tend to use the terms "liberty" and "freedom."[1] So far, so good. Berlin says that in natural language, the terms refer to lots of distinct things. The terms do not have a singular meaning. This suggests, I think, that rather than fighting over whether this or that really counts as a form of freedom, we should simply identify the thing we are interested in and ask whether people ought to have it.

Berlin instead identifies two principal ways that philosophers and others have tended to use the terms, which he dubs "negative" and "positive" liberty. Note that a "negative" conception of liberty is not somehow worse than a "positive" conception. Rather, the distinction goes as follows:

Negative conceptions of liberty: Hold that to be free requires the *absence* of something.

Positive conceptions of liberty: Hold that to be free requires the *presence* of something.

Negative liberty connotes the *absence* of impediments, constrains, interference, or domination from others. When you say you are free to choose your own religion, what we mean is that no one else may force you to accept their religion. Freedom of religion is the absence of interference from others.

In contrast, positive liberty connotes the *presence* of something, usually some power, ability, or capacity. Berlin himself originally meant "positive liberty" to refer to self-mastery, that is, the capacity to choose one's goals and actions in a rational, autonomous way.[2] As we will see below, certain democratic theorists who think democracy is necessary for freedom share a version of this conception. Other philosophers use the term "positive liberty" to refer to the capacity to achieve one's ends or goals. When we say a bird is free to fly, we mean the bird has the *power* to fly.

By pointing out that in natural language, the words "freedom" and "liberty" refer to related but distinct things, Berlin might have helped us avoid turning definitional questions into ideological battles. Unfortunately for philosophy, Berlin argued that different conceptions of liberty tend to lead to different political ideals. For instance, for much of the twentieth century, liberal philosophers argued that true freedom is negative, consisting in rights *against* various kinds of interference. Socialists often argued that true freedom consists in a positive right to acquire various goods and services.

Somehow, this led philosophers to assume that because socialist *philosophies* held that people should have positive freedom, that in fact socialist *societies* would deliver that freedom to people. But that's a mistaken inference. Suppose for the sake of argument that one important form of freedom is the power to achieve one's goals, and suppose that for most people, adequate wealth and income are necessary to achieve many of their goals. Suppose we agree for this reason that it's important that most people have adequate wealth and income. We cannot then settle from the armchair which economic system delivers freedom so defined. Rather, it's an empirical, social scientific question which kind of economic system (capitalist, socialist, some mix of the two, or something else entirely) actual delivers that freedom.

This is a book on democracy, not liberty, so I won't belabor these debates. Instead, I offer this as a kind of cautionary tale. When thinking about freedom or liberty, we need to be careful. The point of defining terms is not to cut off debate but to help make debates more productive. Once somebody identifies what is plausibly a form of freedom, we can then ask follow-up questions: do people have a right to that kind of freedom? How strong are those rights? As a matter of social scientific fact, what kinds of institutions in fact tend to promote or demote those freedoms, and why?

The Liberty of the Ancients?

In many of these chapters, we started with the ancient Greeks and moved forward toward the present. However, as far as we know given the surviving manuscripts we have, ancient philosophers spent far less time discussing and debating liberty than modern and contemporary philosophers do. (Explicit debates about liberty really take off during the Enlightenment.)[3]

Nevertheless, scholars interested in liberty find nascent elements of modern debates in the old texts. To some degree, though, they tend to project their own ideas and concerns backwards.

The Swiss philosopher and politician Benjamin Constant (1767–1830) wrote a famous essay called "The Liberty of the Moderns

Compared to the Ancients" (1819). Here, Constant argues that modern Europeans have a view of liberty distinct from that of citizens of ancient Greece or Rome. Constant's goal in making this distinction is not merely theoretical, though. Instead, he thinks certain conceptions of liberty can be dangerous, as they can seduce people, activists, and politicians alike. For instance, he warns that "France [during the Revolution] was exhausted by useless experiments, the authors of which, irritated by their poor success, sought to force her to enjoy the good she did not want, and denied her the good which she did want."[4]

Constant notes that as representative government was in fact rare among the ancients. Most ancient Greek city-states had either no or very limited political participation among adult male citizens and excluded everyone else. Even Rome, during the Republican period, limited the power of its citizens. Most power was held by the senate's aristocratic families behind it. Still, he contends, even though the "moderns" in fact experience and live under representative government far more than the ancients, the moderns tend to regard freedom in terms of liberal rights over oneself and liberal protections against governmental intrusion. In contrast, he claims that the ancients thought of freedom as the right to participate in politics and were not much concerned with liberal freedom.

Constant claims that citizens of modern England, France, or America conceive of liberty as

the right to be subjected only to the laws, and to be neither arrested, detained, put to death or maltreated in any way by the arbitrary will of one or more individuals. It is the right of everyone to express their opinion, choose a profession and practice it, to dispose of property, and even to abuse it; to come and go without permission, and without having to account for their motives or undertakings. It is everyone's right to associate with other individuals, either to discuss their interests, or to profess the religion which they and their associates prefer, or even simply

to occupy their days or hours in a way which is most compatible
with their inclinations or whims.[5]

In short, for the moderns, liberty consists both of procedural rights
that protect the individual from their government and also general rules and rights that allow individuals to choose for themselves
where and how they will work, how they will spend their time,
what they think will think, believe, or say, and with whom they
will associate. For the moderns, liberty is about creating a sphere of
autonomy around individuals protecting them from others. The institutional framework that best enables such spheres of autonomy
is a liberal, democratic government characterized by the rule of law.

Constant continues:

> Now compare this liberty with that of the ancients. The latter
> consisted in exercising collectively, but directly, several parts of
> the complete sovereignty; in deliberating, in the public square,
> over war and peace; . . . But if this was what the ancients called
> liberty, they admitted as compatible with this collective freedom
> the complete subjection of the individual to the authority of the
> community.[6]

Constant claims that the ancients did not regard personal liberty and personal self-control as important overall. Instead, they
regarded rights of participation, deliberation, and voting as essential to freedom. For them, freedom was not about what the government could or couldn't do to individuals, or whether individuals
could make choices for their own individual lives, but instead
about whether those individuals were able to participate in collective decisions. Constant claims that the for the ancients, individual
subjugation was fine so long as we choose collectively to subjugate
everyone.

He illustrates:

You find among them almost none of the enjoyments which we have just seen form part of the liberty of the moderns. All private actions were submitted to a severe surveillance. No importance was given to individual independence, neither in relation to opinions, nor to labor, nor, above all, to religion. The right to choose one's own religious affiliation, a right which we regard as one of the most precious, would have seemed to the ancients a crime and a sacrilege. In the domains which seem to us the most useful, the authority of the social body interposed itself and obstructed the will of individuals. Among the Spartans, Therpandrus could not add a string to his lyre without causing offense to the ephors. In the most domestic of relations the public authority again intervened. The young Lacedaemonian could not visit his new bride freely. In Rome, the censors cast a searching eye over family life. The laws regulated customs, and as customs touch on everything, there was hardly anything that the laws did not regulate.[7]

Constant concludes that individuals were sovereign in public affairs but effectively slaves to the public in their private affairs.

Constant claims that whatever merits or demerits the ancient conception of freedom had, it is nevertheless not available to us in modern politics. The ancients lived in largely homogeneous city-states with small populations living in small territories. They had a different economic system, with far less division of labor. In a way, their political problems were less complex, so it was more reasonable to expect every "citizen" to have the time and knowledge needed to participate actively in politics. (Remember that only a minority could participate.) Contemporary countries are larger, more diverse, and more geographically dispersed. It is less reasonable to think people have the time or knowledge to govern themselves collectively; it makes more sense to have every individual chose for themselves.

Not everyone agrees with Constant's assessment of ancient politics. The classics scholar Kurt Raaflaub, in his *The Discovery of Freedom in Ancient Greece*, thinks Constant is mistaken. He claims on the contrary that for Athenian democrats, "sharing in power was essentially a means to an end: their goal was life in freedom and happiness."[8] Raaflaub says the "core of the value of freedom guaranteed by democracy" to an average citizen was that it let him

> develop a political identity and over time made it so attractive that it became his primary identity. . . . Democracy guaranteed him the integrity of his house and person, put him on a par with all other citizens in essential areas of life (especially before the law and politics), and made him independent of the power of the mighty. For all these reasons, democracy met an extraordinarily important sociopsychological need: it was the only political system that enabled the freeman to develop and realize his potential to the fullest.[9]

Raaflaub argues that the ancient Greeks, and especially the Athenians, came to develop a largely liberal conception of freedom.

During the Athenian empire, Athens was free because it was autonomous, not under any other city's control. The Athenians applied this view of international relations to relations between citizens. Citizens were free not merely because they were not slaves, but because they were autonomous, lacking any sort of masters, able to see each other as equals, able to live as they choose, and able to participate in governance. During the fourth century BC, Athenian democracy strengthened, and freedom became identified *in part* with participation in democratic government. However, Raaflaub contends, our textual evidence from speeches, legal documents, and elsewhere shows that at no point, though, did Athenians regard democratic participation as *sufficient* for freedom. Freedom meant a host of civil and economic liberties, not just the right to vote or hold office.[10] According to Raaflaub, Athenians were both democrats and liberals; they care about the so-called liberty of the moderns and not just the so-called liberty of the ancients.

Republicanism: The Political Mechanisms of Non-Domination

Recent contemporary political philosophy has witnessed the revival of "republicanism," an old set of ideas about freedom and representative government. (Note that "republicanism" as a philosophical concept has little to do with the contemporary Republican Party in the United States, just as "liberal" has little to do with the Democrats.) Let's start by examining the motivation behind the revival, and then we'll jump back to consider the ancient origins of these ideas.

Recall that Isaiah Berlin claimed that there were two basic conceptions of liberty that tend to dominate political philosophy. Berlin claimed that liberal political philosophies tend to conceive of liberty in negative terms. Liberals, he claimed, say that a person is free insofar as there is an absence of interference from other people.[11] At first glance, this kind of definition seems sensible. After all, totalitarian governments continuously interfere with their citizens.

The political theorist Philip Pettit thinks this definition of freedom—freedom as the absence of interference from others—is inadequate. To illustrate, he asks us to imagine a slave with a kindly, absent master. The master has the right to interfere with the slave at will and with impunity. But the master in fact never exercises that right and lets the slave do whatever the slave wants. Pettit might agree that this slave is freer than most slaves, but the slave is nevertheless unfree compared to non-slaves. If freedom were merely non-interference, then this hypothetical slave would be free, but the slave clearly isn't, so freedom is not merely non-interference.

Pettit concludes that we need a better theory of freedom: freedom is not the absence of interference; rather, freedom is the absence of *domination*. Domination occurs when:

1. The dominator has the capacity to interfere with the victim's choices.
2. The dominator can exercise this capacity at will, with impunity.[12]

This applies to groups as well. A group can dominate an individual, a group can dominate another group, or an individual can dominate a group.

Pettit regards this conception of freedom as in a way rather old. We can find variations on this among the ancient Romans who defended the Roman republic, as well as among Renaissance Italian thinkers who defended Italian city-states. Notable republican thinkers include Cicero (106–43 BC), Livy (59 BC–AD 17), Marsilius of Padua (1275–1342), and Machiavelli, among many others.

What these thinkers share is the view that political power must be spread out and checked, through various kinds of institutional processes, to ensure that leaders do not abuse that power. For instance, Marsilius argues—and you've seen this kind of argument before—that if a law is embraced by the many, it will have to serve the interests of the many, because people would not knowingly choose a law that harms them. In contrast, when a king may decide a law by personal fiat, the king can shape the law for his personal benefit and externalize any harms onto others.[13]

Republicans tend to hold that representative government of the right sort is essential to realizing freedom as non-domination. Like liberals, they advocate due process of law, checks and balances, separation of powers, and constitutionally protected rights of free speech and assembly.[14] Ancient, medieval, and Renaissance republicans were not usually *democrats* per se—they did not advocate universal suffrage—but they did tend to be highly democratic compared to others of their time. Many advocated having citizen councils, or councils that represent different ethnic groups and tribes, which had some sort of check or at least advisory role for more central governments. They also tended to advocate some devolution of powers within larger countries.

Further, ancient and medieval republicans tended to think that proper republics required certain background economic conditions. They often argued that having an extensive system of small artisans, craftspeople, merchants, and traders was important. The idea is that a middle class of independent small-business owners would help ensure that a sufficiently large percentage of the voting population is *economically independent* and thus better positioned to be *politically independent*. (Until the 1800s, many otherwise quite democratic thinkers often held that wage earners should not have the vote because they were too dependent and dominated by their employers; giving them votes would be in effect giving their employers extra votes.)

Contemporary republican theorists tend to think that due process and ordinary liberal checks and balances are not enough. For instance, Frank Lovett says:

> The standard republican remedy [to the problem of arbitrary power] is enhanced democracy. . . . Roughly speaking, the idea is that properly-designed democratic institutions should give citizens the effective opportunity to contest the decisions of their representatives. This possibility of contestation will make government agents wielding discretionary authority answerable to a public understanding of the goals or ends they are meant to serve and the means they are permitted to employ. In this way, discretionary power can be rendered non-arbitrary in the sense required for the secure enjoyment of republican liberty.[15]

To "enhance" democracy in this way, contemporary republicans generally advocate two major sets of changes. First, they support creating opportunities for more extensive and more inclusive public deliberation. For instance, they advocate having political decision makers, such as legislative bodies, courts, or bureaucracies, present their decisions in public forums, where the public may challenge and debate the leaders. Some contemporary republicans even argue that some such forums should serve as "courts of appeals," in which citizens can modify or even vote decisions.[16] Second, republicans claim there should be greater inclusion and real political equality. All citizens must have an equal right to participate in such public contestation. Republicans hold that legal political equality is insufficient to create genuine political equality, because citizens from richer or more prestigious backgrounds tend to have more influence than others. They thus advocate limits on campaign financing, advertising, and lobbying. In summary, republicans think that regular, contested, competitive elections are not enough. Some argue that ensuring equal power requires equal incomes and wealth.

Contemporary republicans thus tend to be far more radical than ancient and early modern republicans. Early republicans tend to advocate familiar liberal rules of due process and checks and balances but want politics to remain an occasional side vocation for most people. Contemporary neo-republicans often advocate radical societal change to ensure politics remains pure. They want frequent and widespread political participation.

Contemporary neo-republicans are not hyper-charged liberals; instead, they often reject liberalism in favor of what Constant calls the liberty of the ancients. Recall Pettit's concern: the slave with the absent master is unfree because the master *could* interfere with impunity, though the master chooses not to. You might think that republicans thus one-up liberals by saying freedom is about non-interferences *plus* institutional rules that ensure no such interference takes place. However, surprisingly, many contemporary republicans, including Pettit, are fine with the state having rather extensive power to interfere with and control individual citizens' choices and lives, so long as this power is not *arbitrary*.[17] For Pettit, if the state imposes significant paternalistic or other kinds of interference upon you, you are still free, provided the institutional mechanisms behind these decisions properly include you as an equal participant, are subject to checks and balances, and properly track your interests. Liberals find this bizarre. Pettit somehow moves from the view that non-interference is not sufficient to render a person free to non-interference is not necessary for a person to be free.

Rousseau: Autonomy in Law

The Swiss philosopher Jean-Jacques Rousseau (1712–1778) was one of the most important political philosophers in Western history. A great deal of contemporary political philosophy is a reaction to him.

As we saw in chapter 2, Hobbes wanted to answer the question, if government didn't exist, would we want to invent it? He argued that in a hypothetical state of nature, mutual diffidence would lead to conflict, which a common authority could reduce. Rousseau has a far different view of the so-called state of nature. (Whether Rousseau intends this to be a thought experiment or an actual history is up for debate.) In his *Discourse on the Origins of Inequality* (1755), Rousseau wants to explain how inequality emerged. In Rousseau's view, inequality is an unnatural social creation.

In the state of nature, Rousseau imagines people living as lone, self-sufficient "savages." They have little language and are barely capable of thought. They attend to their own immediate needs, driven by instinctual self-love, aversion to suffering, and natural compassion. Men and women might come together briefly to mate, but Rousseau imagines that they do not even form family units, so the women raise any resulting offspring alone. While Hobbes claims that the state of nature would face incessant conflict, Rousseau claims that Hobbes is projecting attitudes that arise from living in a society (such as selfishness, a desire to dominate, or mistrust) backward.

Over time, though, Rousseau claims that as these lone individuals multiply, they will spread out to different environments. As the population increases, they might start working together. Over time, they develop families, language, ideas of conventions, and the idea of property. Rousseau pulls no punches on his feelings about the invention of property:

> The first man who, having enclosed a piece of ground, bethought himself of saying *This is mine*, and found people simple enough to believe him, was the real founder of civil society. From how many crimes, wars and murders, from how many horrors and misfortunes might not any one have saved mankind, by pulling up the stakes, or filling up the ditch, and crying to his fellows, "Beware of listening to this impostor; you are undone if you once forget that the fruits of the earth belong to us all, and the earth itself to nobody."[18]

Rousseau was no friend of free-market capitalism, but he does not mean this passage to imply that we should therefore dispense with private property. Further, he qualifies the sentences above and claims instead that the concept of property must have developed gradually.

Rousseau thinks it was perhaps unavoidable that human society, with conventions of property and law, would develop. Such society has many benefits, but also many costs. For as society develops—along with conventions of property and law, and then institutions to enforce those laws—so comes inequality, servitude, venality, vice, poverty, and a whole host of other evils. Rousseau recognized that his savages lived at a subsistence level, with just barely enough to get by and with no real property of their own. But he claims that nevertheless they did not experience real poverty because—lacking reason, comparisons, or foresight for the future—they *needed* less.

Rousseau recognizes that people in his time could do much more than these hypothetical savages can, but he sees his contemporaries as *unfree* in part because they are mutually dependent upon each other, and in part because they are subject to laws created by and enforced by masters. As he opens *The Social Contract* (1762): "Man is born free, and everywhere he is in chains."[19]

Rousseau thus thinks modern society sets up two major and closely related normative problems: Is it possible for people to live together, under common laws, as free and equal? In chapter 10, we'll spend more time discussing how Rousseau thinks a properly designed democracy can promote equality of the right sort. Here, we're interested in Rousseau's view of the connection between democracy and liberty.

Governments generally claim—and most people believe at least some governments have—two moral powers:

Legitimacy: Governments have permission (within certain limits) to create and enforce new rules.

Authority: Within certain limits, when governments issue new rules or commands, citizens have a duty to obey those rules or commands because they were issued by the government.

That is, most people think governments may create rules, and when they do, we are supposed to be obey them because they are laws.

Rousseau's *The Social Contract* is meant to investigate what, if anything, could justify governments having these two special moral powers. After all, imagine that I, Jason Brennan, command local restaurants to include calorie counts on their menus. I threaten to fine them $500 if they don't obey. You would conclude that I have no right to act like this and the companies have no obligation to comply. But if your county or state government does the exact same thing, you probably think their behavior is permissible and that companies ought to obey. This illustrates one of the basic puzzles of political philosophy: why would governments have any right to act this way and why would anyone have any duty to obey?

Rousseau says that everywhere, people are in chains, pushed around by masters who claim authority and legitimacy. He thinks the existing justifications for this situation fail. No person, he argues, has greater natural authority than others; we are not born as slaves and masters, subjects and kings. These are conventions rather than natural relations. Further, might does not make right; the fact that someone is powerful enough to subjugate others and enforce his will does not imply he is permitted to do so or that others are morally obligated to obey. So, Rousseau concludes, the only possible source for authority must come from agreements: a social contract.

However, Rousseau thinks other philosophers' conceptions of the social contract are nonsense. For one, many—such as Hobbes—argue that people would rationally agree to be subject to an absolute leader. But Rousseau thinks no sane person could consent to a complete alienation of their freedom:

> To renounce your liberty is to renounce your status as a man, your rights as a human being, and even your duties as a human being. There can't be any way of compensating someone who gives up everything. Such a renunciation is incompatible with man's nature; to remove all freedom from his will is to remove all morality from his actions. Finally, an "agreement" to have absolute authority on one side and unlimited obedience on the other—what an empty and contradictory agreement that would have to be![20]

(Remember, though, that in Hobbes's social contract, the citizens contract with each other to obey the sovereign; they do not have a contract with the sovereign per se.)

While Hobbes's social contract is hypothetical, some other philosophers thought there was a literal social contract. They argued that previous generations literally agreed to live together under common authority. But Rousseau argues, even if that were valid for those people, it would not bind *us*. Your parents can bind themselves, but not you. A social contract would have to be continuously renewed or would otherwise be invalid.

Rousseau concludes that people cannot rationally renounce their own liberty or consent to be subject to the authority of others. This, he thinks, creates a dilemma he intends to solve:

> [E]ach man's force and liberty are what he chiefly needs for his own survival; so how can he put them into this collective effort without harming his own interests and neglecting the care he owes to himself? This difficulty, in the version of it that arises for my present subject, can be put like this:
>
>> Find a form of association that will bring the whole common force to bear on defending and protecting each associate's person and goods, doing this in such a way that each of them, while uniting himself with all, still obeys only himself and remains as free as before.
>
> There's the basic problem that is solved by the social contract.[21]

In other words, Rousseau thinks that we need to find a form of government in which there are genuinely binding laws and rules, but nevertheless in which all people remain *free and equal*.

Here, Rousseau doesn't mean that people should be free in the liberal sense, that is, that they have an extensive set of personal, civil, and economic rights protected by the state. We could imagine a benevolent dictator who enforced liberal rights better than any existing state.

Rather, the "liberty" Rousseau has in mind here is autonomy, in the sense of setting rules for oneself. Rousseau worries that if other people make rules for you, then you are to that extent unfree, because you are bound by their will rather than your own. So, he wants to devise a political system in which every person is bound by the same rules, yet every person can rightly say that she set the rules for herself rather than the rules being imposed upon her by others.

Rousseau's statement of the problem is beautiful. His proposed solution is perplexing. He thinks that a properly designed democracy—with deliberation and involvement by all individuals—could something produce a situation in which we each are subject to only our own wills.

Let's be clear about what Rousseau does not mean. He does not mean that in a democracy, because we vote, we thereby consent to being governed or to the rules. After all, at first glance, if the majority votes one way and you vote another, the issue Rousseau identifies would still remain: you would not be free because the resulting rules are imposed upon you by others. Further, Rousseau thinks you cannot rationally consent to lose your freedom to a boss, regardless of whether the appointed boss is a monarch or a democratic majority.

Instead, Rousseau's idea is that a properly constituted, egalitarian democracy could lead to the emergence of something called the "general will," a will that is supposedly shared by all people, and which in some way represents each person's own true will. What precisely this is general will is supposed to be is unclear. As philosopher Christopher Bertram says, in an encyclopedia article (aimed at other specialists):

> Rousseau's account of the general will is marked by unclarities and ambiguities that have attracted the interest of commentators since its first publication. The principal tension is between a democratic conception, where the general will is simply what the citizens of the state have decided together in their sovereign assembly, and an alternative interpretation where the general will is the transcendent incarnation of the citizens' common interest that exists in abstraction from what any of them actually wants. Both views find some support in Rousseau's texts, and both have been influential.[22]

On the one hand, sometimes Rousseau seems simply to be saying that in a general assembly, citizens might agree or converge upon a set of laws. But, given Rousseau's own statement of the problem—for someone to be free, she must remain under her own will and not under the will of others—it seems that people can only qualify as free if literally every member agrees to those laws. A majority vote would mean at the very least that the minority lacks autonomous control of itself.

On the other hand, Rousseau sometimes instead seems to say that when people deliberate, if they take the proper mindset, they will conceive of themselves not as selfish, self-centered individuals, but as proper members of a mutually respectful collective of individuals. This new conception somehow represents their proper selves. These people who now identify themselves as members of a public of free and equal individuals will recognize that they have shared interests and converge on shared rules and laws. The "general will" that emerges from equal, democratic deliberation from individuals who conceive of themselves this way is supposed to represent or be each person's *real* will. (Rousseau thinks we could still think of narrow self-interest or conceive of ourselves as identifying with a subset of society, but these are somehow less proper or fitting of our true selves.)

Exactly how this is supposed to make sense remains hotly debated among Rousseau scholars. Some see him as doing something brilliant: at our core, our true selves have shared goals and interests and allow us to converge upon a common set of rules that each of us supports; thus, it is possible for us to live under laws that bind us and yet remain free because each of us chooses those laws for ourselves.

Others see the story as bogus nonsense—and dangerous nonsense too. Rousseau describes the problem correctly: how can we have common rules if individual people in fact didn't agree to those rules and don't have any real power to change them? Isn't every government—democracy included—a system in which some people tell others what to do, and thus every government is that extent unfree? But then, to avoid this problem, Rousseau tries to argue that our *real* selves correspond to some *idealized* version of ourselves, with different attitudes and values, and further that these idealized versions of ourselves would agree to common laws under a system of free and open deliberation. To many, that sounds like saying, "You are free even when bound by laws you in fact oppose, because a better version of you with different ideas and values would want those laws." People almost never find philosophical moves like this satisfactory outside of social contract theories. For instance, suppose the state forced you to get married by proving that an idealized version of you would agree to the marriage. You'd regard this as subjugation, not as freedom.

It's hard to overstate how influential Rousseau's style of theorizing remains, even if most philosophers find his arguments puzzling, and there isn't much agreement about how exactly his argument is supposed to go. For instance, Immanuel Kant's general moral theory was based on a generalization of Rousseau's worry. Kant thinks that what makes a moral agent special—and what makes us a moral agent, period—is that we are free. We are not simply pushed around by desires. But, he thinks, for a moral agent to be free, he must act on his own wills, which means that freely acting moral agents must act on moral rules they set for themselves. So, Kant tries to show that for each of us, our own rationality presupposes and contains a universal set of moral rules that we will for ourselves.

A version of Rousseau's problem persists in contemporary academic philosophy. Many political philosophers today subscribe to "public reason liberalism." Public reason liberals hold that every citizen should be treated as free and equal. They think that in order to justify a coercive law, there must be a "public" justification that in some way is grounded in each distinct person's values and beliefs. The law should not be forced down people's throats. It should be something each can see is justified given one's own beliefs and values.

Exactly what this means varies from public reason theorist to theorist. Still, public reason theorists face a problem like Rousseau's. In fact, people disagree about lots of things. For any actual law, it's easy to find lots of people subject to that law who not only in fact reject it, but for whom the law is incompatible with their deeper beliefs and values. Public reason liberals respond as Rousseau did by *idealizing* citizens to some degree, that is, by saying a better, more informed, and more reasonable version of each citizen would accept various coercive laws. But this often seems to violate the very spirit of the project. Instead of publicly justifying principles and policies to the *actual* public subject to those policies, theorists instead try to justify their preferred policies to their preferred *hypothetical* public with different beliefs from those held by the actual public. To that degree, the public reason project seems to fail on its own terms. (Public reason theorists of course disagree.)

Regardless of whether Rousseau's proposed solution works, the puzzle is fascinating. Rousseau's interest is not primarily whether democracies promote liberal rights like free speech or religion. Rather, it is whether in a democracy or any other form of government we remain in control of ourselves or are instead subject to other people as bosses. Rousseau wants to argue that a properly constituted democracy creates a situation in which each of us is the author of the laws that bind us. We remain free because we set the laws for ourselves.

Rousseau's ideal democracy requires heavy participation from citizens. Rousseau is extremely skeptical about political representation or delegation. If we choose leaders who choose laws, we thereby have bosses and are not fully free. The fact that you chose your boss doesn't change the fact that you have a boss.

Accordingly, Rousseau thinks that the right kind of freedom-preserving democratic republic could work on a small scale—such as his contemporary Geneva—but he was worried that larger countries would create a need for delegation and representation, which would in turn make freedom impossible. The increasing scope of cooperation renders the division of labor unavoidable, which renders hierarchy unavoidable, which ultimately reduces our freedom. In modern democracies as we find them, some people issue orders and some people obey.

Liberal Democracy and Liberal Freedom

Liberalism and democracy are separate things. In principle, a dictatorship could be highly liberal.[23] You could imagine that if, say, a radical libertarian became a dictator, that he might instantiate and enforce radical freedom of speech, lifestyle, choice, economic decision-making, and so on, and no one could stop him. You can also imagine a completely illiberal democracy—and indeed, many democratic theorists want democracy but not liberalism. An illiberal democracy might guarantee freedom of political speech but not other speech. It might have strong safeguards to ensure everyone can participate and vote as equals. But it might otherwise tell everyone what to do, what to wear, where to work, and how to live. Contemporary philosophy journals often publish papers in which a theorists argue that individual freedom must be constrained to protect the democratic process.

Nevertheless, as a matter of fact, liberal countries tend to be democratic and democratic countries tend to be liberal. Illiberal countries tend to be undemocratic and undemocratic countries tend to be illiberal. Liberal freedom and democracy are not the same thing, but tend to be found together. The hard question—a question social scientists today heavily debate—is why.

We cannot measure degrees of freedom or democracy as easily as we measure GDP, life expectancy, or height. Asking whether the United States is more democratic than France, or whether the United States is less democratic today than last year, involves hard value judgments.

That said, various institutes, think tanks, and foundations try to measure and assess how democratic or liberal different countries are. For example, Canada's Fraser Institute produces the widely cited annual "Economic Freedom of the World" index. The *Wall Street Journal*, in conjunction with the Heritage Institute, also produces an annual Index of Economic Freedom. Freedom House and the *Economist* magazine's research institute each produces similar ratings of protection for civil liberties, as well as indices that score countries on how well they implement basic democratic electoral procedures.

Freedom House's "political rights" score and the *Economist*'s "electoral process and pluralism" score are both meant to measure the degree to which countries have universal adult suffrage and free, open, competitive, and uncorrupt elections. Countries that fail to have these things—whether they are active monarchies, dictatorships, communist single-party states, or whatnot—receive bad scores. Both indices try to avoid conflating political rights with *other* civil or economic liberties. Thus, if there turns out to be any correlation between, say, Freedom House's "political rights" score and various measures of economic or civil liberty, this is an interesting rather than trivial result.

Many countries that Freedom House or the *Economist* describes as authoritarian are democracies *on paper*. They have constitutions that formally "guarantee" competitive elections, universal suffrage, and fair voting rights. But Freedom House and the *Economist* do not rate a country as democratic unless it actually implements democratic procedures. Similarly, the Fraser Institute and the *Wall Street Journal* do not rate countries as economically free merely because their constitutions "guarantee" the rule of law or substantive due process in protecting property rights. They score countries by what they do, not by what their constitutions say they will do.

As Figure 8.1 shows, there is a clear and strong positive correlation between democracy and economic freedom. Note that

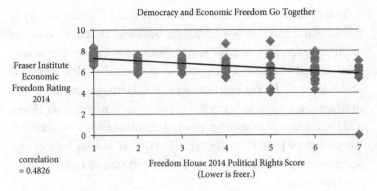

Figure 8.1 Democracy and Economic Freedom

in the figure, a *lower* political rights score counts as *more* democratic. Freedom House scores the freest countries a 1 and the least free countries a 7. Thus, the negative slope of the regression line shows a positive correlation between political rights and economic freedom.

Using different measures gets similar results. If we substitute the *Wall Street Journal*'s rankings for the Fraser Institute's, the correlation increases slightly to 0.4994. If we substitute the *Economist*'s electoral process and pluralism ratings for Freedom House's political rights scores, the correlation drops slightly to 0.4669. Regardless, the correlations are similar and robust.

As Figure 8.2 shows, there is an even stronger positive relationship between democracy and civil liberties. Here, I graph the *Economist*'s measure of civil liberties against Freedom House's Political Rights score. Once again, for Freedom House, a lower political rights score indicates a country is *more* democratic. Thus, the negative slope represents a positive correlation.

Once again, substituting different rating systems yields similar results. (The correlation holds steady at around 0.9.)

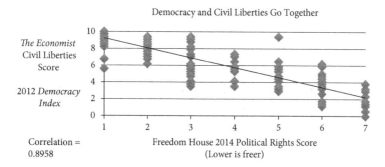

Figure 8.2 Democracy and Civil Liberties

Figure 8.2 might be misleading because it provides a snapshot of conditions at any given year. Sometimes democratic countries elect bad leaders who seize power for themselves. When democracies collapse into authoritarianism, leaders tend to suppress democratic procedures and civil liberties at the same time.[24] Since the protection of political rights and civil liberties tend to fall in tandem, the correlation seen above might overstate just how much protection democracy offers on behalf of liberal rights. Countries that currently have high political rights scores also have high civil liberties scores, but some such countries are vulnerable to collapse.

These two graphs are mere snapshots of different measurements at different years. If we created the same kinds of graphs over different years, the patterns would persist. But, as you've probably heard, correlation does not guarantee causation. It is an open question whether the relationship seen here is a coincidence. Perhaps democracies tend to choose liberal policies, or perhaps liberal cultures tend to choose democracy. Perhaps historical accident leads cultures to develop democracy and liberalism simultaneously. Nevertheless, while democracy and liberalism are not the same thing, they tend to come and go together.

What We Should Learn

We tend to say democracies are free societies. Why?

Sometimes what people mean to say is that democracy and freedom are different things, but as a matter of fact, democracies tend to preserve, promote, enhance, and protect freedom. As an empirical fact, it turns out that democracy and civil and economic liberty tend to come and go together. Just why this is so is a matter of open debate.

Sometimes people mean that democracy is itself a form of freedom. Rousseau in particular had an intriguing idea: in every other form of government, some people rule and some people obey. You are forced to obey orders from others, which means you are not really free. He thought that in a properly functioning democracy, the laws you are forced to obey are nevertheless laws you issued yourself.

9

Against Liberty

Democracy as the Many-Headed Master

Back in October 2020, the fast casual restaurant chain Nando's Peri Peri did a public relations stunt encouraging people to vote.[1] During the stunt, customers could choose their own meal or instead select an "UnDemocratic Meal." Anyone who tried the UnDemocratic Meal was then served whatever disgusting, random food combination the public relations people chose for them, such as cheesecake with spicy mayonnaise or brownies on rice.

The stunt offers a good critique of dictatorship. A dictator might not care or know about your interests and thus might deliver bad policies. But notice that Nando's didn't offer a Democratic Meal. Instead, the other option was that you buy what you want. That's not a Democratic Meal. That's a Market Meal.

How might Democratic Meal work?: You go to the counter and state your preferences. Then, instead of getting what you asked for, you receive whatever menu items have received the most votes so far. If you want an XX Hot sauce quarter chicken with rice, but the lemon and herb chicken sandwich with fries is the most popular, then you get the lemon and herb chicken sandwich with fries.

A system in which we each get what we each order isn't democracy, but a market. As we've seen in previous chapters, some theorists have argued that democracy would tend to serve the interests of the governed, or would itself constitute a kind of freedom, because they equate democracy with a system in which people choose for

Democracy. Jason Brennan, Oxford University Press. © Oxford University Press 2023.
DOI: 10.1093/oso/9780197558812.003.0009

themselves. But we must be careful: *each of us individually chooses for ourselves* is not the same thing as *we collectively choose for us as a collective*. Markets are the former. Democracy is the latter.

The last chapter explored historically important arguments that held that democracy either tended to encourage liberty, or that democracy was itself an important form of liberty. This chapter examines historically important skeptical responses to such views.

David Hume: Consent Theory and Social Contract Theories Are Bogus

People who accept the sixth-grade model of democracy (see chapter 1) sometimes say that democracy rests on the consent of the governed. Elected leaders serve us and we consent to their lead. To vote is to consent to government.

The social contract tradition in philosophy—exemplified by Hobbes, John Locke, Rousseau, among others—often portrays government as the product of a tacit, explicit, or hypothetical agreement among equals. Even the absolute monarchist Hobbes (see chapter 3) argued that in the state of nature, people could and would consent and contract with one another to create an absolute king or some other absolute sovereign. Hobbes probably meant his argument to be hypothetical—government is justified because in its absence people would unanimously want to create it—but other theorists argued that society rests on an actual social contract.

The Scottish philosopher and historian David Hume (1711–1776) thought social contract theories were mostly nonsense. Hume was one of the first thinkers to develop a plausible account of how stable social institutions could arise without being the product of anyone's intention or design. In his work on the philosophy of religion, he produced a plausible proto-evolutionary theory that could help explain how order could arise without a designer. Hume recognized that most people are biased to assume that any big social change or natural event must have been intentional, but he sought to explain order without having to posit an *order-maker*.

His 1752 essay "Of the Original Contract" finds the historical social contract theory—and the idea of historical consent—rather silly. He notes that philosophers want to believe that government arose from rational agreement:

> [P]hilosophers . . . assert, not only that government in its earliest infancy arose from consent, or rather the voluntary acquiescence of the people; but also, that, even at present, when it has attained its full maturity, it rests on no other foundation.[2]

But reality shows otherwise. As a matter of historical record, almost every government everywhere began with conquest.

> The chieftain, who had probably acquired his influence during the continuance of war, ruled more by persuasion than command; and till he could employ force to reduce the refractory and disobedient, the society could scarcely be said to have attained a state of civil government. No compact or agreement, it is evident, was expressly formed for general submission.[3]

Subsequent governments almost always arise from conquest as well—a new king defeats and replaces the old:

> Almost all the governments, which exist at present, or of which there remains any record in story, have been founded originally, either on usurpation or conquest, or both, without any pretense of a fair consent, or voluntary subjection of the people. When an artful and bold man is placed at the head of an army or faction, it is often easy for him, by employing, sometimes violence, sometimes false pretenses, to establish his dominion over a people a hundred times more numerous than his partizans. He allows no such open communication, that his enemies can know, with

certainty, their number or force. He gives them no leisure to as-
semble together in a body to oppose him. Even all those, who are
the instruments of his usurpation, may wish his fall; but their ignorance of each other's intention keeps them in awe, and is the
sole cause of his security. By such arts as these, many governments
have been established; and this is all the *original contract*, which
they have to boast of.

The face of the earth is continually changing, by the increase
of small kingdoms into great empires, by the dissolution of great
empires into smaller kingdoms, by the planting of colonies, by
the migration of tribes. Is there anything discoverable in all these
events, but force and violence? Where is the mutual agreement or
voluntary association so much talked of?[4]

Philosophers ignore these historical facts, and instead tend to argue
that even present governments rest on the consent of the people.
But, on the contrary, when we look around, we do not find government by consent.

But would these reasoners look abroad into the world, they
would meet with nothing that, in the least, corresponds to their
ideas, or can warrant so refined and philosophical a system.
On the contrary, we find, every where, princes, who claim their
subjects as their property, and assert their independent right of
sovereignty, from conquest or succession. We find also, every
where, subjects, who acknowledge this right in their prince,
and suppose themselves born under obligations of obedience to
a certain sovereign, as much as under the ties of reverence and
duty to certain parents. These connections are always conceived
to be equally independent of our consent, in Persia and China;
in France and Spain; and even in Holland and England, wher-
ever the doctrines above mentioned have not been carefully
inculcated. Obedience or subjection becomes so familiar, that
most men never make any inquiry about its origin or cause,

more than about the principle of gravity, resistance, or the most universal laws of nature.[5]

Hume thinks it's bogus to claim that Athens was a government of the people, for the people:

> The republic of Athens was, I believe, the most extensive democracy that we read of in history: yet if we make the requisite allowances for the women, the slaves, and the strangers, we shall find, that that establishment was not, at first, made, nor any law ever voted, by a tenth part of those who were bound to pay obedience to it: not to mention the islands and foreign dominions, which the Athenians claimed as theirs by rights of conquest. And as it is well known, that popular assemblies in that city were always full of licence and disorder, notwithstanding the institutions and laws by which they were checked: how much more disorderly must they prove, where they form not the established constitution, but meet tumultuously on the dissolution of the ancient government, in order to give rise to a new one? how chimercial must it be to talk of a choice in such circumstances?[6]

So, Hume thinks, the idea that society is grounded on an original, voluntary social contract is plainly false. In fact, governments everywhere arose through conquest. Governments today are the offspring of these original conquests, subsequent conquests, and territorial amalgamations and divisions. For instance, democratic France today is descended from various French kingdoms that are descended from tribal conquests. It wasn't as though a bunch of people unanimously chose to create what we now call France. On the contrary, "French" identity is largely something invented by government and foisted onto more local linguistic groups despite their resistance.

Still, Hume acknowledges, some might object that even if most governments were founded on war, perhaps we nevertheless consent to them now. Perhaps the fact that we choose to live in a country proves that we consent to its laws and the authority of its government.

An early instance of the social contract idea appears in Plato's *Crito*. Crito and his friends offer to help the condemned Socrates escape to Thessaly. Socrates knows that his conviction was wrongful. Nevertheless, Socrates argues that he has made an implicit contract with the laws of Athens themselves. (He does not claim to have a contract with the *Athenians* or the democratically selected *leaders* of Athens; rather, the contract is directly with the laws.) Socrates claims that the laws educated him, nurtured him, and gave him a home. In exchange for these goods, he implicitly promised obedience. Further, the laws allowed him both voice and exit. If he believed the laws unjust, he could have tried to change them earlier, or he could have freely left Athens earlier for another city-state. Yet on the contrary, Socrates hardly ever left the city despite having this freedom. Accordingly, Socrates concludes, if he chose to escape, he would break his compact with the laws, and his critics would ironically turn out to be correct: he would indeed corrupt the youth by showing disregard for law and order. Thus, Socrates concludes that even he was not guilty of those crimes, he has a duty to accept the sentence.

Hume find this reasoning unpersuasive when applied to most people:

> Should it be said, that, by living under the dominion of a prince, which one might leave, every individual has given a tacit consent to his authority, and promised him obedience; it may be answered, that such an implied consent can only have place, where a man imagines, that the matter depends on his choice. But where he thinks (as all mankind do who are born under established governments) that by his birth he owes allegiance to a certain prince or certain form of government; it would be absurd

to infer a consent or choice, which he expressly, in this case, renounces and disclaims.

Can we seriously say, that a poor peasant or artizan has a free choice to leave his country, when he knows no foreign language or manners, and lives, from day to day, by the small wages which he acquires? We may as well assert, that man by remaining in a vessel, freely consents to the dominion of the master; though he was carried on board while asleep, and must leap into the ocean, and perish, the moment he leaves her.

So, Hume offers a few responses to the idea that we tacitly consent to government by remaining in a territory. First, many people believe they owe allegiance to their government by birth or by natural authority; for them, the idea that they consent to government is absurd because they do not even seriously consider the idea that they could dissent. Second, he says that most people cannot be said to consent to government because they have no reasonable way of opting out.

Let's examine the ship captain analogy more closely. Here, Hume asks us to imagine a person has fallen asleep, is kidnapped, and then brought onto a ship. When the person awakens, the captain says, in effect, you can either accept my authority or *leave*. But here, leaving means death.

Maybe that's not quite fair. It's true that some countries will not allow their citizens to leave, but most have a right of exit. Still, consider that for most of us, moving away is tremendously difficult and costly. As Hume says above, the typical person in his day cannot financially afford to emigrate and lacks the knowledge or language skills to do so.

But—and Hume would not have anticipated this—even if today more people can afford to move, they still aren't allowed to do so. Their own governments might let them leave, but foreign governments won't let them enter. For instance, it is tremendously difficult for a Canadian to get the right to move to and work in the United States for any significant length of time, and vice versa.

So, today Hume might say that for the typical Canadian, it is as if you've been kidnapped and placed on a ship. The captain—the Canadian government—tells you that you may leave. It doesn't build a wall to keep you in, but it turns out every other government has built a legal wall to keep you out—they'll let you visit but usually won't let you stay long or work. And Canadians have it relatively easy. The reality, Hume would say, is that most people are stuck with whatever government they're born with. We consent to our governments about as much as we consent to gravity and the sun.

Lysander Spooner: The Anarchist Challenge

Lysander Spooner (1808–1887) was a prominent American abolitionist, anarchist, individualist, and workers' rights activist of the nineteenth century. As a natural law theorist, he held that every person—including blacks, women, and other minorities—are endowed with the same rights and should be treated as equals. Spooner's most famous works include *The Unconstitutionality of Slavery* (1845) and *No Treason: The Constitution of No Authority* (1867). The former argued that the US Constitution did not, despite appearances, permit slavery. The latter argued that the US Constitution lacked authority and legitimacy and does not constitute any kind of binding agreement. Spooner believed the US federal government—indeed, any actual existing government in the world—lacked the right to rule. Spooner's argument in *No Treason* is of interest to us here because it further critiques the idea that democracy is consensual, that it is founded on a social contract, or that democracy is itself a kind of freedom.

Two central questions in political philosophy are whether it is permissible to enforce an unjust law and whether we could ever be obligated to obey an unjust law. The question here is not whether one merely *thinks* the law is unjust. Rather, the question is whether a law that is *in fact* unjust may nevertheless be enforced or be authoritative.

Spooner thought the answer was no. He would say that even if most people vote to do something unjust, that would not somehow grant them permission to perform the unjust action, or somehow imbue others with an obligation to follow the unjust law. In Spooner's view, the reason is that people really do have rights; rights are not mere social conventions granted by the people in power. Morality and justice really matter; they are not mere conventions or ways of talking to be changed at will. Spooner would say that if you believe, as most people today seem to, that an unjust law can be rendered legitimate and authoritative so long as it comes about the right way, then you in effect believe that justice and morality have a special escape clause. Spooner might mock this reasoning as follows: hey, do you want to kill some people in an unjust war? Or, do you want to violate people's rights? Normally, you can't do that, But, no worries, it turns out that there's a loophole!: If people with equal voting rights first deliberate about this stuff and then the majority vote to do it, then this magically makes it permissible! Spooner thinks such views are absurd. You cannot render evil permissible by following a convoluted decision-making process, democratic and egalitarian or not.

Americans might say that the Constitution represents their social contract. But, Spooner says this does not survive scrutiny:

> The Constitution . . . does not so much as even purport to be a contract between persons now existing. It purports, at most, to be only a contract between persons living eighty years ago. And it can be supposed to have been a contract then only between persons who had already come to years of discretion, so as to be competent to make reasonable and obligatory contracts. Furthermore, we know, historically, that only a small portion even of the people then existing were consulted on the subject,

or asked, or permitted to express either their consent or dissent in any formal manner. Those persons, if any, who did give their consent formally, are all dead now. Most of them have been dead forty, fifty, sixty, or seventy years. *And the Constitution, so far as it was their contract, died with them.* They had no natural power or right to make it obligatory upon their children. It is not only plainly impossible, in the nature of things, that they *could* bind their posterity, but they did not even attempt to bind them.[7]

Here, Spooner's point is similar to Rousseau's critique of original social contracts. In real contracts, people are bound only when they freely agree themselves. A parent cannot bind their future children to a contract. A person living in Boston cannot bind all future Bostonians to a contract. So, Spooner says, those who adopted the Constitution cannot somehow bind all of us to it because *they* agreed to it.

Further, Spooner argues, the idea that the Constitution is binding is especially bogus because hardly anyone had a say in it, or even had a *right* to say:

> In the very nature of things, the act of voting could bind nobody but the actual voters. But owing to the property qualifications required, it is probable that, during the first twenty or thirty years under the Constitution, not more than one tenth, fifteenth, or perhaps twentieth of the whole population (black and white, men, women, and minors) were permitted to vote. Consequently, so far as voting was concerned, not more than one tenth, fifteenth, or twentieth of those then existing, could have incurred any obligation to support the Constitution.[8]

Hardly anyone was allowed to vote, and of those who were permitted, a sizable minority did not actually vote:

Of the one-sixth that are *permitted* to vote, probably not more than two-thirds (about one-ninth of the whole population) have *usually* voted. Many never vote at all. Many vote only once in two, three, five, or ten years, in periods of great excitement.[9]

Further, it is unclear that voting could even bind voters themselves into perpetuity.

No one, by voting, can be said to pledge himself for any longer period than that for which he votes. If, for example, I vote for an officer who is to hold his office for only a year, I cannot be said to have thereby pledged myself to support the government beyond that term. Therefore, on the ground of actual voting, it probably cannot be said that more than one-ninth, or one-eighth, of the whole population are *usually* under any pledge to support the Constitution.[10]

So, Spooner concludes, the idea that the Constitution binds us is absurd. At the time of its ratification, only a minority of people who were subject to it had a right to say it in it. At most, a minority of past people voted for it. No other contract founded this way would be binding on us today.

Spooner recognizes that others might claim that what makes the Constitution binding today is instead that we, today, perform acts that signify our consent to its authority and show we have entered into a kind of social contract. In particular, some say that by voting, a person consents to the authority of their democratic government. (Spooner might note that if that voting signifies consent, then those who abstain do not consent to the social contract.)

At any rate, Spooner thinks that the view that voting signifies consent is bogus. As a matter of fact, most people are stuck under whichever government claims authority over them, and there is little most people can do to escape that. Instead, Spooner argues, the right way to see voting is that people are stuck with a government that will exercise power over them, which can deprive them of life, liberty, and property, and which can greatly affect their welfare. Given this state, then of course it is reasonable for them to try to influence that government in ways that benefit rather than hurt them. But this does not signify consent or a contract:

> On the contrary, it is to be considered that, without his consent having even been asked a man finds himself environed by a government that he cannot resist; a government that forces him to pay money, render service, and forego the exercise of many of his natural rights, under peril of weighty punishments. He sees, too, that other men practise this tyranny over him by the use of the ballot. He sees further, that, if he will but use the ballot himself, he has some chance of relieving himself from this tyranny of others, by subjecting them to his own. In short, he finds himself, without his consent, so situated that, if he use the ballot, he may become a master; if he does not use it, he must become a slave. And he has no other alternative than these two. In self-defence, he attempts the former. His case is analogous to that of a man who has been forced into battle, where he must either kill others, or be killed himself. Because, to save his own life in battle, a man attempts to take the lives of his opponents, it is not to be inferred that the battle is one of his own choosing.[11]

A citizen in a democracy is forced to live under a government she did not choose. The government will exercise power over her, period. So, if she tries to influence the government, this no more signifies consent to government than I would signify consent to battle by fighting back against a mugger. Or, Spooner might say, suppose you lived under an absolute monarch, but you had the opportunity to write letters or petition the monarch to decide this rather than that. This would not signify consent to the monarch's rule. Spooner say that by voting, you petition your many-headed master rather than a one-headed king. There's no real difference. Spooner illustrates with another such example:

> As taxation is made compulsory on all, whether they vote or not, a large proportion of those who vote, no doubt do so to prevent their own money being used against themselves; when, in fact, they would have gladly abstained from voting, if they could thereby have saved themselves from taxation alone, to say nothing of being saved from all the other usurpations and tyrannies of the government. To take a man's property without his consent, and then to infer his consent because he attempts, by voting, to prevent that property from being used to his injury, is a very insufficient proof of his consent to support the Constitution.[12]

So, at this point, Spooner thinks he has established that the original ratification of the Constitution does not somehow bind posterity to it; at most, it binds only the people who wrote it and voted for it, if even them. But, secondly, the fact that some of us participate in government now by voting, paying taxes, or using public goods does not signify consent to that government, because we have no real choice and are simply doing the best we can, given circumstances we did not choose.

Spooner goes on to say that even in a democracy, we are unfree and subject to the authority of others:

> Neither is it any answer to this view of the case to say that the men holding this absolute, irresponsible power, must be men chosen by the people (or portions of them) to hold it. A man is none the less a slave because he is allowed to choose a new master once in a term of years. Neither are a people any the less slaves because permitted periodically to choose new masters. What makes them slaves is the fact that they now are, and are always hereafter to be,

in the hands of men whose power over them is, and always is to be, absolute and irresponsible.

The fact that you get to vote for a new master every few years does not change the fact that you are subject to a master. Rousseau would agree with this point—he thought that representative democracy always involved a loss of liberty because it involves giving others the power to decide for oneself (see chapter 8).

But Rousseau argued that in an equal, direct democracy, it's possible that no one is a master because we can adopt the General Will. Spooner instead claims that even in a direct democracy, each of us is unfree. Each of us, as individuals, is subject to whatever the majority decides. Even the members of the majority are unfree because, for each of them, had they voted or chosen differently, the same outcome would have occurred and they would be forced to do what the majority wants. While a monarchy subjugates individuals to the king, democracy subjugates each individuals to the collective.

Further, Spooner thinks it's absurd to claim that our elected officials are our servants:

But these men who claim and exercise this absolute and irresponsible dominion over us, dare not be consistent, and claim either to be our masters, or to own us as property. They say they are only our servants, agents, attorneys, and representatives. But this declaration involves an absurdity, a contradiction. No man can be my servant, agent, attorney, or representative, and be, at the same time, uncontrollable by me, and irresponsible to me for his acts. It is of no importance that I appointed him, and put all power in his hands. If I made him uncontrollable by me, and irresponsible to me, he is no longer my servant, agent, attorney, or representative. If I gave him absolute, irresponsible power over my property, I gave him the property. If I gave him absolute, irresponsible power over myself, I made him my master, and gave myself to him as a slave. And it is of no importance whether I *called him* master

or servant, agent or owner. The only question is, what power did
I put into his hands? Was it an absolute and irresponsible one? or
a limited and responsible one?[13]

Spooner says that as a matter of fact, elected officials have tremendous power in modern democracies. As individuals and even as a
collective, we have very limited capacity to check their power. It is
absurd to think of them as servants. Consider what that analogy
would mean. Suppose I hire a captain to steer my yacht. The captain goes where I tell him to go; that makes him my servant and
me the master. I can tell the captain to change course and he will.
When we "hire" politicians by electing them, they might promise to
bring the ship of state to one destination rather than another. Still,
once in power, they are free to do as they please, and move the ship
where they think is best, even against our expressed wishes or our
commands otherwise. At most, we can "fire" them a few years later.

The consent theory of government is not the only viable theory
of legitimacy or authority. Spooner may have succeeded in showing
that the typical citizen of a modern democracy cannot be said
to consent to their government, but perhaps some *other* theory
explains why governments nevertheless sometimes have legitimacy or authority. Still, for our purposes here, Spooner has shown
that equating democracy with freedom and consent is problematic
at best.

Carl Schmitt: Who Is the Sovereign?

The German political and legal theorist Carl Schmitt (1888–1985)
eventually became a prominent member of the Nazi Party. He
was not alone among philosophers or theorists in extolling totalitarian politics. Martin Heidegger (1889–1976), perhaps the most
prominent German philosopher of the twentieth century, was
also a prominent Nazi. In *When Reason Goes on Holiday* (2016),

Neven Sesardic chronicles how Bertrand Russell (1872–1970), Otto Neurath (1882–1945), Rudolf Carnap (1891–1970), Ludwig Wittgenstein (1889–1951), Gerald Cohen (1941–2009), and a wide range of other prominent twentieth-century philosophers spent large portions of their lives as sympathizers and apologists for totalitarian regimes, oppression, and mass murder. So much for the view that philosophy makes us wise or moral.

While Schmitt was a fascist, his political thought is still of interest to us here even if fascism is not. He might have insightful ideas about parliamentary democracy even if his preferred alternative is worse.

In *The Crisis of Parliamentary Democracy* (1923), Schmitt argues that much of the justificatory apparatus of democracy—the story we tell ourselves about why democratic decisions are justified—is false. We say that democracy is special because the people rule themselves. Democracy eliminates the distinction between those who rule and those who obey because they people rule themselves. But, Schmitt says, this is a gloss over what really happens. In fact, people have disparate goals and interests, and they vote in different ways.

Instead, when we claim that democracy expresses the will of the people, what we are in effect doing is identifying the will of the people with whatever the majority decides—or, rather, with whoever ends up ruling in the name of the majority. After all, even if the majority votes for one candidate over the other, it's not as though the majority speaks as one voice or agrees entirely on what should be done.

Schmitt wonders: why is it any more reasonable to identify the will of the people with the majority than the minority? For instance, he wonders what we should say when the majority are in fact opposed to democracy, but a small democratic vanguard wants to overthrow the existing, say, monarchy and force people to be democratic. (Here, Schmitt is thinking of the French revolutionaries, who wanted to force France to be free.) Here, the minority goes against what the majority wants, but they might plausibly claim to enact the will of the people because they are trying to impose democracy. Or, if Schmitt were alive today, he might wonder whether the United States' and NATO's attempts to force democracy upon countries that don't want it counts as nevertheless acting on the "will of the people." Schmitt's point might be that sometimes the minority really can speak for the will of the people, but a safer interpretation is that he thinks "will of the people" is a political myth. Like every other system, democracy is a system in which some people rule over others. Talking of the will of the people is like talking about the divine right of kings. It's a useful story to generate compliance and acceptance, but it's not true.

Further, Schmitt worries that this understates the problem. The reality is that contemporary states never submit all or even most of their decisions to democratic rule. Democratic oversight is at best attenuated. Crises and problems occur, and decisions must be— and *will* be—made on the spot, without consulting the people or taking a vote. Schmitt claims that whenever a leader (or bureaucrat) makes a decision without actual majority approval, this means that democracy has been negated and we have, here, a kind of on-the-spot dictatorship. Further, in most states, the people who in fact hold power—for example, the president or prime minister—largely get to decide when the "exception" to the rules takes place, or when there is an emergency that grants them special powers.

Accordingly, Schmitt is skeptical that in a democracy the people are truly sovereign. If, say, a prime minister can unilaterally declare a public health emergency, close the borders, and force people to stay home in violation of their normal liberal freedoms, then that prime minister is sovereign, not the people.[14] It is not as though the people ahead of time consented to or accepted these rules. Instead, the true sovereign is that one who declares the exceptions.

Perhaps Schmitt's arguments are exaggerated—after all, most countries have some checks or institutional mechanisms to prevent exception-taking at will. But perhaps Schmitt's basic worry remains. In real democracy people have differential levels of power. The people do not rule as a unified group with one will. For any given decision, some impose their will upon others but then claim to speak for the people. At times, some leaders declare themselves exempt from previous rules and get away with it.

Nozick: The Tale of the Slave

Robert Nozick (1938–2002) was an American philosopher with an exceptionally broad range of expertise in an era when most academics hyper-specialize. He made major contributions to metaphysics, epistemology, and game theory. His most famous work, and the work that made him rise to prominence, was *Anarchy, State, and Utopia* (1974), which defends a libertarian conception of the state.

In *Anarchy, State, and Utopia*, Nozick ponders whether democracy is in effect a system of common *ownership* of the people by the people. Many liberal thinkers throughout history held that our rights over ourselves—such as freedom of conscience, speech, lifestyle choice, economic choice, and so on—can best be described and explained by the thought that each of us *owns* ourselves. You've probably seen versions of this in arguments for abortion or sexual freedom: "It's *my* body."

Nozick offers a serious of "hypothetical histories" in which he describes how a modern democratic state might arise. For instance, he imagines people selling shares of their rights over themselves or shares in their bodies to others, and then these shares being put into a kind of mutual fund that each person owns shares of. This hypothetical history is meant to shed light on how the state works: a modern democratic state, with its extensive regulatory and taxing powers, is functionally equivalent to a system in which every person has partial ownership rights over every other person. Since mutual ownership of one another is disturbing, a modern state is disturbing to that same extent.

One of Nozick's hypothetical histories challenges the claim that democracy is a form of freedom. It's worth quoting almost the whole thing:

> Consider the following sequence of cases, which we shall call the Tale of the Slave, and imagine it is about you.
>
> 1. There is a slave completely at the mercy of his brutal master's whims. He often is cruelly beaten, called out in the middle of the night, and so on.
> 2. The master is kindlier and beats the slave only for stated infractions of his rules (not fulfilling the work quota, and so on). He gives the slave some free time.
> 3. The master has a group of slaves, and he decides how things are to be allocated among them on nice grounds, taking into account their needs, merit, and so on.
> 4. The master allows his slaves four days on their own and requires them to work only three days a week on his land. The rest of the time is their own.
> 5. The master allows his slaves to go off and work in the city (or anywhere they wish) for wages. He requires only that they send back to him three-sevenths of their wages. He also retains the power to recall them to the plantation if some emergency threatens his land; and to raise or lower the three-sevenths amount required to be turned over to him. He further retains the right to restrict the slaves from participating in certain dangerous activities that threaten his financial return, for example, mountain climbing, cigarette smoking.
> 6. The master allows all of his 10,000 slaves, except you, to vote, and the joint decision is made by all of them. There is open discussion, and so forth, among them, and they have the power to determine to what uses to put whatever

percentage of your (and their) earnings they decide to take; what activities legitimately may be forbidden to you, and so on.

Let us pause in this sequence of cases to take stock. If the master contracts this transfer of power so that he cannot withdraw it, you have a change of master. You now have 10,000 masters instead of just one; rather you have one 10,000-headed master. Perhaps the 10,000 even will be kindlier than the benevolent master in case 2. Still, they are your master. However, still more can be done. A kindly single master (as in case 2) might allow his slave(s) to speak up and try to persuade him to make a certain decision. The 10,000-headed monster can do this also.

7. Though still not having the vote, you are at liberty (and are given the right) to enter into the discussions of the 10,000, to try to persuade them to adopt various policies and to treat you and themselves in a certain way. They then go off to vote to decide upon policies covering the vast range of their powers.

8. In appreciation of your useful contributions to discussion, the 10,000 allow you to vote if they are deadlocked; they commit themselves to this procedure. After the discussion you mark your vote on a slip of paper, and they go off and vote. In the eventuality that they divide evenly on some issue, 5,000 for and 5,000 against, they look at your ballot and count it in. This has never yet happened; they have never yet had occasion to open your ballot. (A single master also might commit himself to letting his slave decide any issue concerning him about which he, the master, was absolutely indifferent.)

9. They throw your vote in with theirs. If they are exactly tied your vote carries the issue. Otherwise, it makes no difference to the electoral outcome.

The question is: which transition from case 1 to case 9 made it no longer the tale of a slave?[15]

There's obviously a big difference between being a chattel slave on a plantation versus being a voting citizen in Canada. Nozick does not say otherwise.

Still, at the end of the story, many readers think the slave never quite stopped being a slave. Or, at least, quite a bit of the badness of slavery *remains* at the end of the story. (Remember, from the discussion of republicanism in chapter 8, that republicans argued that slavery is bad even if the master acts kindly and never imposes its will. But here we have a master than in fact imposes its will.) This is disturbing because by the end of the story, the situation very much resembles modern democracy.

Nozick's story suggests that being a member of rule-making body, especially a large one, does not give one much control. Each slave in the tale of the slave can legitimately claim that *everyone else makes all the decisions* and that *the decisions the body makes would have occurred without her input*. Even when democratic outcomes result from the equal input of all, we lack power. The collective rules us, and it's not much consolation that we are members of that collective.

Consider a realistic analogy: I went to Mardi Gras one year. At night, the streets were so congested that I could lift my feet to be carried along by the crowd. It took serious effort to move against the current. Everyone in the crowd had the same predicament. We were all equals. Our individual movements equally decided the collective movement of the crowd. Yet, we were each powerless. That's how Nozick sees democracy here.

Democracy is often equated with freedom: we choose for ourselves. But, upon inspection, this seems to be a fallacy of composition. In a liberal, free society, I choose for me, you choose for you, and so on. So, it seems tempting to conclude that we choosing for us is the same kind of thing. But, Nozick, Spooner, and others would say, it's not.

The Efficacy of a Single Vote

In a dictatorship, you have no say in how the country is governed. In a democracy, you get some say. Some philosophers claim that in a true or properly run democracy, you get an *equal* say—and real-world democracies are defective to the extent that they benefit some over others. (See the next two chapters.)

However, some of the skepticism about equating democracy with freedom concerns how small of a say this is. Rather than saying democracy gives everyone an equal slice of power, we might say it's giving them equal-sized crumbs.

Consider the difference between individual choices and democratic choices. If I choose to wear a Slayer T-shirt today, lo and behold, I wear that shirt. If I choose to go to church or stay away, lo and behold, I get my way. But when I vote, the same outcome occurs as if I didn't vote, and the same outcomes occurs regardless of whether I vote one way or another. To cast a vote seems like trying to stop—or cause—a tsunami with a bucket.

Starting after World War II, when political science started to become scientific, scholars began trying to determine how to model the power of an individual vote. Of course, the power of a vote varies depending on a wide range of conditions. For instance, the more people who can vote, the less an individual vote matters. A juror in a group of twelve angry people has more power than a voter in a district of two million. It also depends on how votes are counted. In proportional voting systems—where seats in parliament are allocated by the percentage of votes a party receives—votes have more power than in first-past-the-post voting systems. In the United States, thanks to the Electoral College, a voter for president in New Hampshire or Wyoming has more power than a voter in California or Texas.

Generally speaking, a vote does one of two things: it breaks a tie or does nothing. So, to calculate the power of a vote, we need to know what the probability is that it will break a tie.

There is significant debate among economists and political scientists over the precise way to calculate the probability that a vote will be decisive. For many decades, the standard practice was to model votes by asking, in effect, what the probability is that a weighted coin will land heads exactly 50 percent of the time.[16] On these "binomial" models, the idea is that if 55 percent of voters favor the Democrats and 45 percent the Republicans, and there are expected to be two million and one voters, then we ask what the chances are that a coin weighted 55 percent heads and 45 percent tails will come up heads exactly one million times and tails exactly one million times. (Binomial models are more sophisticated than this, as they have variables for other factors, but we can ignore those complexities here.) Binomial models imply that as the electorate becomes more biased toward one side—that is, as the other voters depart from being perfectly split between the two candidates—the chances that one's vote will break a time become vanishingly small very quickly.

However, many theorists now contend that binomial models are inadequate and must be false. They say that if the binomial models were correct, then we would expect to see most major elections have larger margins that we in fact find, and there would hardly ever be close elections.[17]

Over the past few decades, researchers have thus looked for alternatives. Perhaps the most popular alternative is the model defended by Aaron Edlin, Andrew Gelman, and Noah Kaplan. Their model uses state-level polling data to statistically estimate the chances that a vote would break a tie.

For instance, in the 2020 US presidential election between Donald Trump and Joe Biden, their model suggested, right before the election, that Republican or Democratic voters in Pennsylvania had a 1 in 8.8 million chance of breaking a tie. The estimates dropped from there. About eleven states had between 1 in 15 million to 1 in

99 million. They estimated voters in Texas had a 1 in 100 million chance. Voters in Illinois had a 1 in 680 million chance. Montana? 1 in 1.7 billion. Arkansas? 1 in 46 billion. Washington, DC? 1 in 240 trillion.[18] They would probably caution that their model works best for states with close contents. The model spits out somewhat arbitrary numbers for states with big majorities.[19]

Thus, even on this model, the typical voter's chances of deciding the presidential election are worse than their chances of winning, say, the Powerball lottery. Voters have better chances in smaller elections, but then the stakes are also lower. Still, one might wonder whether even the Edlin, Gelman, and Kaplan model overstates the power of a single vote because it omits some complications. First, if a major election is close, it might be decided by lawsuits rather than the single vote. Second, as the Caltech/MIT Voting Technology Project documents, counting errors, lost ballots, and the like make mean many votes do not count or are counted incorrectly.[20]

Similar remarks apply to the right to run for office, though there is no equivalent model for calculating any random person's odds of winning if they suddenly decided to run. For instance, there are over 1.7 million Americans for every seat in Congress. Even smaller, less important offices (such as town aldermen) tend at best to have ratios of 1 seat for every 2,000 citizens. If offices were distributed randomly, these would be bad odds. But, of course, they are not randomly distributed. Some people—such as celebrities or members of prominent political families—have high chances, while most have no chance at all. Most US congresspeople are millionaires or multi-millionaires.[21]

This remark brings us to our next set of concerns. How does democracy relate to the value of equality?

What We Should Learn

This chapter examined skeptical responses to the idea of identifying democracy with freedom. Hume claims that our relationship to government, democratic or otherwise, is not consensual. Many argue that as matter of fact, even in democracy, we always have some people bossing others around. Even in an ideal democracy with complete equality, they claim it's untrue that we each rule only ourselves, as Rousseau would argue. Instead, they claim that we are each bossed around by the group, and it's little consolation that each member of the group would say that same thing. If having a boss means you aren't fully free, then you don't fix the problem by making everyone equally everyone else's boss. You fix it by eliminating bosses.

10

For Equality

Democracy as the Public Expression of Equal Standing

The French Revolution (1789–1799) had many mottos. The one that everyone remembers, which later became France's national motto, is "Liberty, equality, and fraternity."

This motto acknowledges these are three distinct values. Liberty is not equality which is not community. All three seem important, so we might hope to realize them all. But it's an empirical question whether these values will support each together or conflict. When they conflict, it's a philosophical question which value should triumph.

Different approaches to political philosophy tend to favor one of these values over the other two. Or, because they favor one over the others, they often reinterpret the others to facilitate rendering them with their favored value.

For instance, liberal (and libertarian) philosophies value liberty over equality and fraternity. Liberals see situations as just when they result from free consent, and unjust otherwise. Communitarians and authoritarians value fraternity over liberty and equality. Their fundamental value axis is the collective good versus individual good; they tend to think societies work well when people work toward the social good but become corrupt when people favor their private good over the social. Egalitarians, including many socialists, see the fundamental value as equality. They think societies are good

Democracy. Jason Brennan, Oxford University Press. © Oxford University Press 2023.
DOI: 10.1093/oso/9780197558812.003.0010

when people are equal and regard inequality as evidence of or as constituting oppression or exploitation.[1]

Perhaps ironically, one of the first major appearances of the motto appears in a 1790 speech by Maximilien Robespierre (1758–1794) about how to organize the national guard, which under Robespierre became an army of conscripts.[2] It's doubly ironic because while on paper, Robespierre claimed to be a liberal committed to egalitarian direct democracy, in practice he was a tyrant and terrorist willing to force people to be (what he considered) free.

Over the past eight chapters, we have seen democracy defended (and criticized) for its relationship to many different values: stability and peace, virtue, wisdom, and freedom. In these final two chapters, we consider historically important arguments for and against democracy that concern its relationship to equality.

In the chapters on liberty, we saw two distinct ways of thinking about the value of democracy in terms of liberty. One way—the liberal way—holds that liberty consists of the right of the individual to choose for herself. Liberals tend to favor democracy because it tends to protect liberal freedom better than the alternatives. A second way, exemplified by Rousseau, identifies democracy *with* freedom; democracy keeps us free because we are the authors of the laws to which we are subject. Rousseau thought we could remain our own bosses in democracy.

With the relationship between democracy and equality, we see a similar divide. One could hold that democracy is good because it tends to produce egalitarian outcomes. Or one could hold that democracy instantiates equality because everyone has equal basic political standing. The first view says democracy *produces* equal results. The second says democracy just is equal.

Similarly, if one cares about equality, one could care about equality of outcomes or equality of rights and inputs. These are not the same. Granting everyone an equal vote does not guarantee the resulting laws produce equal outcomes or treat people equally. A democracy with equal voting rights could choose, say, inegalitarian tax policies, while a dictatorship or one-party communist state could choose to enforce income equality. Thus, an egalitarian might in principle oppose democratic equality because they want to ensure substantively equal outcomes. Historically, we have seen many authoritarians—such as Robespierre and Vladimir Lenin (1870–1924)—override or outlaw democracy *in the name of equality*.

Equality and the Rule of Law

This book focuses on the history of thought about democracy rather than the actual history of democracy. Still, sometimes to do the former, we must do the latter. One of the key concepts in egalitarian (and liberal) philosophy is the *rule of law*. But this concept developed less inside the minds of philosophers and more from actual legal practice over time. While some political ideas, such as the separation of powers, were developed by philosophers and later implemented by politicians,[3] the rule of law largely developed first and the philosophy came second.

Let's briefly consider European history after the collapse of the Roman empire. It's probably a mistake to refer to the next few centuries as "Dark Ages." As the economic historian George Grantham notes, going carefully through documents from those times

> yield[s] a far less catastrophic narrative of the early medieval transition than the one that scholars have constructed from late Roman and early medieval Christian polemics. In particular, the revisions indicate significant political, administrative, and economic continuity from the fourth through ninth century, sustained by a surprisingly literate political and administrative elite. The finding of widespread lay literacy is significant because the supposed illiteracy beyond the confines of ecclesiastical

establishments was long taken to be a structural determinant of early medieval autarchy. Intensive culling of that corpus further reveals persisting commercial connections between north and south Europe and between Europe and the near East. While the volume of trade contracted dramatically after 450 AD, the links were never severed.[4]

Nevertheless, there was significant economic contraction. The scope of economic trade declined. Economies tended to become concentrated around a central manor.

While there were smaller empires and kingdoms (such as the Merovingian kingdoms from the fifth through seventh century, or Carolingian empire of the ninth century), compared to the preceding Roman empire, there was a relative power vacuum. There was no strong authority that could maintain peace. During Roman times, war was mostly a phenomenon at the frontiers of the empire. Citizens inside the borders saw peace of and order. The early Middle Ages was a period of frequent conquest and raids.

Safety and protection was hard to find. As the historian Paul Vinogradoff argues, this helps explain why the feudal system emerged and why we see similar feudal systems elsewhere under similar conditions. Farmers needed protection and were willing to trade everything—including their previous freedoms under what had been Roman law—to get it:

Many peasants remained free, but most became serfs. A serf was bound to the land. He could not leave without buying his freedom, an unlikely occurrence in the Middle Ages. Life for a serf was not much better than the life of a slave. The only difference was that a serf could not be sold to another manor. Serfs would often have to work three or four days a week for the lord as rent. They would spend the rest of their week growing crops to feed their families.[5]

Why?

> The dangers of keeping outside the feudal nexus were self-evident: in a time of fierce struggles for bare existence it was necessary for everyone to look about for support, and the protection of the central authority in the State was, even at its best, not sufficient to provide for the needs of individuals.[6]

In theory, in feudalism all land—the primary means of production—is owned by a central king, who grants subordinate ownership to nobles in exchange for their fealty and agreement to fight on his behalf. They in turn grant portions to lesser peers, who in turn rule over unfree serfs or peasants. Serfs work the land for the lord in exchange for protection, though the lord could conscript them to fight if needed.

During the height of feudalism, most peasants saw the administration of justice as a private matter administered by their lord, who served as lawgiver, police administrator, and judge.[7] Many in the system had an oath of allegiance to those above and below them, but it would be a mistake to describe it as system of literal social contracts. After all, the oaths were usually not optional and the terms were preset. Still, a lord owed his serfs protection and to allow them to work on the land (he could not evict them), while serfs owed their lord fealty and work (they could not leave).

Over time, this system tended to evolve into absolute monarchies with strong central states. On its face, that might seem a step backward from the perspective of freedom and equality. But oddly, it was not. One reason is that as central governments became stronger, they were better at keeping the peace within their territory, which reduced the need for protection from the local lord, which reduced the need to abide by the lousy feudal bargain.

In Italy, there emerged strong city-states built around commerce. They developed laws protecting small merchants, business owners, and artisans. In the rest of Europe, larger cities started to emerge, often composed of similar artisans, merchants, and free workers—many of whom were escaped serfs who received the city's protection from jealous lords. Kings would often charter such cities and grant them direct protection as a means of keeping the power of nobles in check.

In many countries, there were often three competing systems of law—the Church, the local lord, and the king. For instance, Henry II of England (1154–1189) established circuit judges who went from town to town to hear cases. Disputants could often choose which court would take their case. These three systems competed for resources (court fees) and power. To win customers in a market for law, they had to offer better law and better decisions than the others.

Over time, what tended to emerge throughout Europe, though more so in some countries (say, England) than others (say, Russia), is what we now refer to as the rule of law.

Perhaps the central pillar of the rule of law is *due process* of law: police, courts, and other agencies must operate by written, public laws of the land.

Generally, a system institutes the rule of law to the extent it realizes the following principles:

1. Governments may not coerce individuals except in enforcement of a known law.
2. Laws should be public, known, certain, and clear.
3. Laws must apply equally to all, without privileging certain classes or individuals.
4. Laws must govern the governors too.
5. The creation of new general rules and the application of these rules should be kept separate.
6. There should be strict limits to the amount of discretion the administration has in administering the rules.
7. Rules must follow known, public procedures in order to be valid

Contrast the rule of law with the "rule of men." The "rule of men" is, roughly, a circumstance where some citizens presume a right to arbitrarily decides the fates of others. By contrast, under rule of law, no one is above the law, not even legislators themselves, indeed not even kings. No person has unopposed authority over others. Or at least, no one can claim a *right* to be unopposed in deciding the fates of others.

The idea of the rule of law presupposes a type of political equality, but it makes no essential reference to *democratic* equality. In principle, a democracy could run afoul of the rule of law—historically, many have—by capricious decision-making, no due process, and make-it-up-as-you-go procedures. In principle, a monarchy could implement the rule of law. In fact, the modern rule of law emerged at first in constitutional monarchies.

Nevertheless, as an empirical matter, if not a conceptual matter, democracy and the rule of law are connected. We tend to find them together or not at all. For instance, every year, the World Justice Project publishes a "Rule of Law Index" that ranks countries by how accountable government agents are under the law, whether the laws are public and fair, whether laws are enacted through public processes, and so on. It does not score countries higher simply for being democratic, though one of the sub-scores ("open government") does measure whether a country protects the liberal right of assembly. Every year, the top scoring countries overall, and on every sub-category, are stable and mature democracies, while non-democracies nearly always score low.[8] Other indices get similar results.

The connection is robust. Both the rule of law and democracy tend to make governments accountable to the governed. Democracies are most stable when constitutional culture imposes real limits on what they may do. Perhaps whatever social mechanism explains constitutionalism—the tendency to adhere to rather than ignore a constitution—tends to lead both to democracy and to the rule of law.

Democracy and Unequal Wealth

Rousseau, as we saw in chapter 8, believed that in the state of nature people are equal—but mostly solitary and incapable of language and reason. At times, Rousseau reads as if he regards civilization as a mistake, though that is probably not what he meant. Still, he holds that the invention of civil society, property, and government produced great evils.

Property creates income and wealth inequality. While everyone in the state of nature endured we now call extreme poverty, Rousseau contended they would not regard their poverty as such. People have limited capacities to think ahead. Having never seen wealth and never made comparisons, they could not understand their own deprivation.

According to Rousseau, governments and the division of labor create distinctions of class and rank. In the state of nature, everyone is equal. In every modern society, some people look down while others kneel, bow, or grovel.

Further, as we saw, Rousseau worried that every government other than direct democracy would ensure that the great mass of people are unfree. As we saw in chapter 8, he believed that electing one's representatives was incompatible with freedom. Instead, for Rousseau, to be free means to be autonomous, which means one must live only by laws one sets for oneself. (As a matter of etymology, "autonomy" literally comes from the Greek words for "self" and "law.")

Rousseau tended to think that people were by nature egalitarian and compassionate. He thought people were born with a natural desire to be equal and share equally.[9] However, society corrupts us into being selfish. It also corrupts us into accept subjugation out of necessity. As Bertram explains Rousseau's views:

> In an unequal society, human beings who need both the social
> good of recognition and such material goods as food, warmth,

etc. become enmeshed in social relations that are inimical both to their freedom and to their sense of self worth. Subordinates need superiors in order to have access to the means of life; superiors need subordinates to work for them and also to give them the recognition they crave. In such a structure there is a clear incentive for people to misrepresent their true beliefs and desires in order to attain their ends. Thus, even those who receive the apparent love and adulation of their inferiors cannot thereby find satisfaction for their *amour propre*. This trope of misrepresentation and frustration receives its clearest treatment in Rousseau's account of the figure of the European minister, towards the end of the *Discourse on Inequality*, a figure whose need to flatter others in order to secure his own wants leads to his alienation from his own self.

Many of the key ideas that animate modern left-wing philosophy find their roots—or at least modern roots—in Rousseau.

Rousseau argued that a properly designed direct democracy could create a situation in which all people are subject only to laws they set for themselves. How to make sense of this is of course a big puzzle, because in fact people disagree about what to do, have different values, have different ways of making trade-offs, disagree about the relevant facts, and so. Rousseau must claim that our *real* wills are not whatever we happen to want, but somehow correspond to a shared general will. As we saw, how exactly to interpret Rousseau here remains an ongoing dispute. One of the less extravagant readings holds that each of us has the capacity to think of ourselves as a citizen who cares about the shared and common interests of all. We can imagine ourselves as this citizen issuing laws, and then recognize that if we follow those laws, we follow only ourselves qua citizen. But it's puzzling why this would be seen as autonomous. "Your true self would will X, therefore if you are forced by law to do X you are still free" does not seem like a serious claim.

Rousseau wondered what background economic and social conditions were necessary for democracy to work properly. He was not the very first. For instance, Montesquieu's (1689–1755) *Spirit of the Laws* (1748) contains an entire book arguing that the climate determines people's attitudes, passions, and bearings, leading people in hot climates to be passionate and hot-headed, and people in cold climates to be stiff and aloof. Thus, Montesquieu claims, which kinds of governments work, which kinds of laws get passed, which kinds of laws are necessary, and how well government functions depends upon the climate. Good news: Montesquieu thought his own ancestors lived in the good laws Goldilocks climate zone. Further, while Montesquieu thought slavery was usually bad, he thought it acceptable for people who developed in climates conducive to indigence, laziness, and vice.

Rousseau's speculations here are less silly or evil. Rousseau instead wonders whether income and wealth inequality will corrupt democracy and prevent it from functioning properly. Though many socialists see Rousseau as an intellectual ancestor, Rousseau does not argue for socialism and even offers intellectual grounds to oppose it. Instead, he thinks it's best if each person owns sufficient property (including productive property) of his own so that he is not *dependent* upon others. Rousseau worried that when one person depends upon another—or even many others—this renders them controlled or at least controllable. (As we saw in chapter 8, Rousseau thought the division of labor always makes us partly dependent—after all, we need others to live—but at least if each person has substantial personal property, he is not dependent on anyone or any group in particular.)

Rousseau also thought that excesses in wealth could corrupt people by making them too self-concerned or impervious to the need for a shared community. In the end, he argued that democracy could work only if there were sufficiently equal degrees of wealth and income to prevent society from breaking off into class-based factions. Rousseau explicitly states that this requires not perfect inequality, but instead that "no citizen shall be rich enough to buy another and none so poor as to be forced to sell himself."[10]

Rousseau had a tempered view about inequality. In contemporary political philosophy, the question of what kind of external inequalities democracy can tolerate remains alive. Many political theorists and philosophers begin with the premise that democracy is good and just, but worry that for a democracy to be true or proper democracy, every citizen must have genuinely equal influence. However, they worry that all sorts of inequalities—in wealth, oratory skill, attractiveness, family connections, income, prestige, race, religion, and so on—can and do change the degree of influence people have. Obviously, a rich, attractive Kennedy with a Harvard MBA tends to have more effective power than a poor, uneducated, ugly nobody from nowhere.

Thus, many contemporary philosophers and political theorists argue for ever-increasing degrees of equality in all aspects of life, not just in formal political rights. This is especially true among deliberative democrats. Inequality easily threatens deliberative democracy's stringent principle. Some deliberative democrats say we must nevertheless observe the distinction between the personal and political; not all of life should be subservient to the democracy. Others go the other way and reject anything that interferes with perfect democratic functioning.

Rawls: The Social Bases of Self-Respect and the Fair Value of Political Liberty

John Rawls (1921–2002) was one of the leading political philosophers of the second half of the twentieth century. His followers and disciples often claim that political philosophy was stagnant until Rawls induced its "rebirth" with his 1971 magnum opus, *A Theory of Justice*.

In *A Theory of Justice,* Rawls wants to determine what principles of justice should govern the choice of a "basic structure" of society. The basic structure of a society consists of the fundamental rules of the game and institutions under which people live, such as government, money, marriage, property, and so on.

Rawls thinks a thought experiment called the "original position" can help us determine what the correct principles of justice are. We imagine that people are told to choose principles to govern a society they will inhabit. This society is closed, socially homogeneous, and autarkical. People enter only by birth and exit only by death. It has no relations with other countries and social identity is relatively uniform throughout. The people in the original position know general facts about economics, political science, sociology, such as how people behave in general, how markets work, or what governments can and cannot do.

Rawls imagines each person wants their own life to go as well as possible. Rawls also imagines that each person is under a veil of ignorance; they don't know anything specific about themselves, such as what race, religion, sex, or relative position in society they will occupy, nor do they know what percentage of people will occupy such categories. This means that when the parties choose principles with the hope of benefiting themselves, they thereby choose principles anyone and everyone can accept, principles that are good for all regardless of who they turn out to be.

It's a neat idea, though no one other than orthodox Rawlsians thinks it works. The problem is that the results of this thought experiment depend greatly on the particular parameters Rawls chooses. If we disagree about the best way to design the "original position," we'll disagree about what comes out of it or what the force of the thought experiment is.

For instance, Rawls stipulates that people are choosing for a closed autarkical society, but oddly, Rawls acts as though the results nevertheless apply to actual nation-states, which are not autarkical, closed, or homogeneous. Rawls stipulates that the parties in the original position do not care much about getting income above a level sufficient to have a satisfactory life. He stipulates that while parties can know general facts about the level of income and wealth inequality there will be in the society they choose, they are not allowed to know what percentage of people will fall into any group. These stipulations push the thought experiment to generate the results Rawls wants.

Rawls's second most famous book is called *Political Liberalism* (1993). While in *A Theory of Justice*, Rawls argues that ideally situated people would unanimously choose certain principles of justice, *Political Liberalism* instead claims that it unpacks the "fundamental political ideas viewed as implicit in the public political culture of a democratic society."[11] In *Political Liberalism*, Rawls says that the fundamental political problem is how to justify institutions to citizens despite their widespread reasonable disagreements about what is good. Surprisingly, Rawls argues that all reasonable people would, despite their private disagreements, more or less agree to live by the principles he articulated in the earlier book; indeed, for Rawlsians, being "reasonable" more or less reduces to being Rawlsian.

Rawls argues that the parties in the original position would choose two sets of principles of justice. The first principle of justice guarantees that each citizen will have an extensive set of liberties compatible with like liberties for all. The second principle governs inequalities in opportunity and in access to various goods. (The details of this second principle will not concern us here.)

In *A Theory of Justice*, Rawls argues that the parties would make the first principle lexically prior to the second. That is, whenever is a conflict between the two principles—for instance, if religious liberty and the kind of equality of opportunity Rawls endorses come into conflict—then liberty always wins. Rawls gradually weakened this commitment over his career as he became less liberal.

What interests us here are Rawls's views on democracy. Rawls's first principle of justice articulates the freedoms people are entitled to. More precisely, the liberty principle claims that all citizens are "entitled to a fully adequate scheme of equal basic liberties ... compatible with like liberties for all."[12]

"Basic liberty" is a technical term here. It means a liberty guaranteed by justice, which merits a high degree of protection, and which cannot easily be overridden by concerns for social stability, economic efficiency, economic fairness, or general welfare. While trade-offs among the basic liberties are permitted, trade-offs between the basic liberties and various other social goals generally are not, except perhaps in extreme cases. Note that Rawls thinks we have *other* liberties that are not basic. These are afforded lower levels of protection and can be traded off against other values. Suppose, for instance, that taxing Catholicism and taxing cigarettes would both promote various other goals of justice (as defined by Rawls's theory). Rawls would say that the latter is permissible but the former is not, because freedom of religion is a basic liberty but freedom to do recreational drugs is not.

The first principle of justice does not protect liberty *as such*. Rather, Rawls claims it protects an enumerated list of particular freedoms: liberty of conscience, freedom of thought, freedom of association, rights of due process and equal protection under the rule of law, freedom of occupation, a right to own a certain degree of personal property, the right to vote, and the right to hold office if elected.[13] It does not include much else. It excludes things others might think are basic rights. (For instance, libertarians and socialists both think the right to own productive property is basic, but Rawls does not.)

Rawls's first principle of justice gets us to democracy on its own. Everyone is afforded an equal right to vote and an equal right to run for office. Further, the later Rawls views these political liberties as *special*. As philosopher Steven Wall comments, for Rawls, "They, and they alone, must have their fair value guaranteed by the principles of justice."[14] Rawls says:

The liberties of both public and private autonomy are given side-by-side and unranked in the first principle of justice. These liberties are co-original for the further reason that both kinds of liberty are rooted in one or both of the two moral powers, respectively in the capacity for a sense of justice and the capacity for a conception of the good.

[W]e must take an important further step and treat the equal political liberties in a special way. This is done by including in the first principle of justice the guarantee that the political liberties, and only these liberties, are secured by what I have called their "fair value."

This guarantee means that the worth of the political liberties to all citizens, whatever their economic or social position, must be sufficiently equal in the sense that all have a fair opportunity to hold public office and to affect the outcomes of elections, and the like.

Rawls thinks that ensuring the fair value of our political liberties means that there should be public funding of campaigns, restrictions on campaign finance, and even (!) some press censorship to ensure freedom of the press doesn't undermine democracy. Further, Rawls thinks that income and other goods must be arranged to ensure that people can effectively exercise their political rights.

This is striking because it means that for Rawls, the political liberties are not merely basic rights, but the most highly protected rights. In comparison, Rawls thinks we have a right to freedom of speech, but there is no "guarantee" of the "fair value" of that speech. Society does not have to ensure you get a book deal or a speaking platform, or the money and time to write and express your thoughts. All we have to do is get out of your way and let you talk. We don't even have to listen to you. But society is supposed to positively support your exercise of your democratic rights.

That's Rawls's *conclusion*. Since we are interested in arguments here, the big question is *why* he thinks this. Why do some liberties—such as freedom of speech or to vote—get on the list of basic liberties, while others do not? In *A Theory of Justice*, Rawls offered his list without much argument, which earned him criticism from all sides. Later, he tried to advance a more substantive argument in favor of his list.

Rawls argues that something qualifies as a basic liberty just in case it bears the right relationship to the distinctive features of human moral personality, features Rawls calls our "two moral powers." These moral powers include both (1) a capacity for a sense of justice and (2) a capacity for a sense of the good life. To determine which liberties are basic requires that we "consider which liberties are essential social conditions for the adequate development and full exercise of the two powers of moral personality over a complete life."[15]

Rawls's theory of rights draws from two sets of ideas, one intuitive and one political. The intuitive idea concerns why human beings appear to have rights that certain animals or inanimate objects lack. Many believe this higher moral status results from our unique capacities for autonomous self-control, to develop meaningful lives centered on an idea of the good, and to understand and act on a concern for justice. Here, Rawls draws more from Kant. The political idea is that democracy presupposes a conception of citizens as free and equal participants in collective self-government.[16] Here, Rawls draws more from Rousseau. He wants to unlock, explain, and justify the ethos he thinks is implicit in a democratic culture. This ethos involves every citizen agreeing to see and treat every other citizen as a free and equal participant in self-government and a free and equal member of a cooperative venture for mutual gain.

For Rawls, then, a liberty qualifies as a basic liberty just in case it is an essential social condition for most people to adequately develop and fully exercise of the two moral powers. On its face, this seems like a strict test. To show that something is a basic liberty, we need to demonstrate that people cannot adequately develop their sense of the good life or their sense of justice without it. We also need to show that they cannot adequately exercise these moral powers without it—and we need to do so in a non-question-begging way. (After all, anyone who thinks that some liberty is basic might insist that of course lacking that liberty inhibits one from adequately exercising their two moral powers.)

Unfortunately, Rawls provides little guidance for how to interpret what it means to show a basic liberty is an "essential social condition" for most people to "adequately develop" or "fully exercise" their two moral powers. His most developed positive application of the test occurs in his discussion of freedom of conscience. Rawls argues that many of us are "not merely content" to accept whatever conception of the good life we happen to have; we "may also strive to appreciate *why* our beliefs are true."[17] Rawls then briefly discusses how a system of freedom of conscience helps us understand the grounds for our beliefs and our conceptions of the good, and thus helps us realize our conception of the good.

That might be right, but it leaves his argument incomplete and underdeveloped. Rawls is supposed to show us not only that *some* freedom of conscience is necessary for us to develop our two moral powers, but in particular, that *very extensive* freedom of conscience is necessary. However, instead of showing us that as he promised, he instead speculates a bit about why freedom of conscience would be helpful. His treatment of the political liberties is even more abbreviated.

The philosopher Steven Wall argues that Rawls has other grounds for treating democratic/political rights as special.[18] According to Wall, for Rawls, political rights are not special because they bear a special relationship to our two moral powers. Partly, they are special because they are instrumentally valuable for realizing good government:

The limited space of the public political forum, so to speak, allows the usefulness of the political liberties to be far more subject to citizens' social position and economic means than the usefulness of other basic liberties. Therefore, we add the requirement of fair value for the political liberties.

However, this is not enough. If equal, fair political liberties were valuable or special merely as a means to secure just legislation, then Rawls would have to reject democracy if some other form of government produced better legislation.

Instead, according to Wall, Rawls thinks equal democratic political rights merit special protection because they are necessary for us to have proper self-respect. Rawls's argument "begins with the plausible thought that political institutions established in a society bear importantly on the social component of self-respect. Some institutional arrangements do better than others in encouraging citizens to view one another as moral equals. . . . The public expression of . . . the fair value of political liberty is an affirmation of the equal status of all citizens."[19]

The philosopher Samuel Freeman, a leading scholar of Rawls, says:

> Rawls contends that the status required for self-respect in a well-ordered democratic society comes from having the status of equal citizenship, which in turn requires the equal basic liberties. It would not be rational for less advantaged persons to compromise this primary ground for their self-respect, by giving up the right to vote for example, for this would "have the effect of publicly establishing their inferiority." . . . This subordinate ranking would indeed be humiliating and destructive of self-esteem.[20]

Rawls and Freeman do not merely assert that democracy is one way of expressing the public equality of citizens. They think democracy is essential to express this equality. Rawls and Freeman (who concurs with Rawls) believe that it would be *irrational* for the relatively disadvantaged to give up the right to vote, even if that would massively improve their welfare, because this would be "humiliating," "destructive of self-esteem," and would *express* the idea that they are subordinate.

This, one of Rawls's arguments for democratic equality, is an instance of what is called a "semiotic" argument.[21] A semiotic argument holds that we should or should not do something, or that something is right or wrong, just or unjust, because of what the policy or action *expresses or symbolizes.* Semiotic arguments figure prominently in democratic theory, bioethics, theories of distributive justice, theories of punishment, and many other philosophical debates.[22] Semiotic arguments for democracy claim that imbuing everyone with equal fundamental power expresses, communicates, or symbolizes respect. Rawls thinks that to fail to give everyone equal voting rights expresses disrespect and creates a situation that undermines people's bases of self-respect. Rawls thinks that imbuing each citizen with the same fundamental political power rightly expresses the idea that each citizen has the same fundamental moral worth. Imbuing citizens with unequal power expresses the idea that citizens have unequal moral worth.

The later Rawls uses commitment to the "fair value of political liberty" to render his political theory more egalitarian than it otherwise would be. Taking a cue from Rousseau and perhaps his graduate students, Rawls became uncomfortable with these implications, so he later asserted ("argued" is too generous a word) that preserving the fair value of political liberty requires more equal incomes and wealth.

Rawls does not provide evidence for this empirical claim. He asserts that if there were too much income inequality, the rich could buy power. However, even if that were correct, one might wonder, even if Rawls did not, whether there are other ways to reduce the buying of powers. Philosopher Gerald Gaus (1952–2020) later took Rawls to task for this. He says that while many philosophers assume that "large inequalities of income and wealth undermine the value of 'the least advantaged' citizens' political liberties, this claim is in fact highly conjectural."[23] In fact, Gaus claims, if we examine things like degree of political pluralism, degree of participation, equality of the electoral process, and how high-functioning a government is, we see little clear statistical relationship between income inequality and these other traits. The relationship between wealth inequality and the fair value of political liberty is even weaker.

In the end, Gaus is somewhat flabbergasted by the later Rawls. Rawls says that whether a society should have robust markets and private ownership is merely an empirical matter, but Gaus notes that there has literally *never* been a society that respects liberal rights but lacks strong markets and protection of private property. Yet Rawls treats it the question of whether income/wealth inequality and democracy are compatible as if it could be settled from the armchair without data, when in fact it's an empirical question and the evidence does not support Rawls's conclusions.[24]

Christiano: The Public Expression of Equality

Above, we saw that Rawls offered multiple arguments for democratic equality. One of the arguments was developmental; he asserts (if not shows) that people cannot adequately develop their two moral powers without the guarantee of the fair value of the right to vote and run for office. But Rawls's strongest argument appears to be a *semiotic* argument. Non-democratic political structures publicly express the idea that some people are superior in judgment or standing than others, and thus will tend to undermine people's self-esteem. Democracy creates a system where everyone looks everyone else in the eye; non-democratic structures do the opposite.

Semiotic arguments for democracy are popular in contemporary democratic theory. For instance, Pablo Gilbert asserts that non-democratic political structures are bad because they insult citizens:

Being rendered a second-class citizen (which is normally the case in a nondemocratic regime) is arguably injurious to an individual's dignity, or a failure of due consideration. It is insulting to be told, or treated in a way that pragmatically implies, something like the following: "Our fundamental collective decisions are yours just as much as everyone else's, although you deserve fewer rights to participate in shaping them than some others." . . . Regardless of whether one actually takes offense, it is in fact an affront to one's dignity to be subject to a basic political structure within which one has less than equal rights of participation.[25]

Christopher Griffin says that a "denial of an equal share of power in the context of disagreement about the basic ground rules of social life is a public declaration of second-class citizenry."[26] David Estlund complains that epistocracy involves "invidious comparisons," as it relies upon the idea that some are more fit to rule than others.[27]

All such arguments rely on the idea that different political structures *say* different things, and what non-democracies say isn't nice. Some semiotic arguments, such as Rawls's, claim such expression produces bad effects. (For Rawls, the public expression of inequality will undermine citizens' self-esteem and esteem for others.) Others say that the expression itself is wrong apart from any downstream consequences. The value of democracy is like the value of painting, poem, or sculpture.

Philosopher Thomas Christiano produced one recent influential semiotic argument. Christiano claims that people have a variety of weighty interests that must be respected by states; these weighty interests ground many of our rights. (For instance, our weighty interest in living a life that is authentically ours is part of why we have freedom of lifestyle and conscience.) Christiano argues that some of these weighty interests are about the kinds of relationships we have with others. In particular, he asserts that we have a strong interest in being *equal* to others. But, Christiano says, it is not enough that the political system simply *treat us* as equals, say, by granting each of us equal liberal rights. Rather, it must treat us as equals in a way that *publicly expresses* our equality. Christiano argues that this requires the state to grant each of us equal rights of participation in government, and further, that the state must ensure we can effectively exercise those rights as equals.[28]

Indeed, Christiano even goes so far as to say that when a democracy decides, one must obey that decision, because failure to obey expresses the idea that one is *superior* to others. If I choose to disregard or refuse to obey a democratic law, Christiano says, "I am in effect saying that my judgment on these matters is better than [my fellow citizens']. . . . I am in effect treating myself like a god or the others like children."[29] By refusing to obey democratic law, I fail to treat their judgment as equal to mine.[30] By refusing to obey democratic laws, I would be "putting [my] judgment ahead of others . . . in effect expressing the superiority of [my] interests over others."[31] It is morally wrong to express such attitudes so therefore it is wrong to disobey democratic laws.[32]

The Demographic Objection to Epistocracy

Recall from chapter 7 that John Stuart Mill favored (nearly) universal enfranchisement, but not *equal* enfranchisement. He believed that democracy with equal voting would lead to a class-based political regime in which democracy fundamentally served the poor at others' expense. He also believed that we must balance several distinct goals, including (A) the educative value of participation; (B) the expressive function of enfranchisement; and (C) the quality of government decisions. For this reason, he advocated plural voting, in which (almost) everyone receives one vote, but those with better epistemic credentials receive multiple votes.

Mill was thus a kind of epistocrat. An epistocracy is any political system in which we retain the various features of representative government—such as constitutional restrictions, the separation of powers, bills of rights, frequent contested elections, liberal free speech, and so on—but in some way votes are allocated or weighed according to some measurable form of knowledge and competence. In fact, all existing *soi-disant* democratic governments are *partly* epistocratic, because they exclude children on the grounds that they are incompetent.

Empirical work on democratic knowledge is univocal: in most countries, most citizens know little about politics, some know less than nothing, but some know a great deal. Most democratic theorists throughout history argued that knowledge is vital for democracy. The people cannot govern themselves if most of them do not know how various policies or laws might work, do not know who is in charge or what those people have done, and cannot evaluate the probable outcomes of different polices or platforms. Indeed, the major justification for public education was to ensure the citizenry was competent and informed enough to self-govern.

However, recent democratic theorists offer a new objection to Mill's proposal. The problem, they claim, is that there are unfortunate *demographic* patterns in the distribution of knowledge. Perhaps unsurprisingly, political knowledge is correlated with privilege and thus anti-correlated with disadvantage.

Consider Michael X. Delli-Carpini and Scott Keeter's (1996) *What Americans Know about Politics and What It Matters*, one of the most famous studies on voter knowledge. They find clear patterns—patterns that persist today—on who has political knowledge and who does not: political knowledge is strongly positively correlated with having a college degree, but negatively correlated with having a high school diploma or less. It is positively correlated with being in the top half of income earners, but negatively correlated with being in the bottom half. It is strongly positively correlated with being in the top quarter of income earners, and strongly negatively correlated with being in the bottom quarter. It is positively correlated with living in the Western United States, and negatively correlated with living in the South. It is positively correlated with being between the ages of thirty-five and fifty-four, but negatively correlated with other ages. It is negatively correlated with being black or female.[33]

Accordingly, some democrats worry that if, as Mill suggests, we were to distribute voting power on the basis of knowledge, some demographic groups—such as middle-aged, college-educated white men—would get significantly more power than other groups—such as unemployed, uneducated black women. Call this the "demographic objection" to epistocracy. The worry is that any system that ends up empowering people this way will be unjust.

Really, there are two different ways of casting the worry:

1. *Unfairness*: The fact that epistocracy would lead to systematic overrepresentation of some groups and underrepresentation of others in the epistocratic electorate is unjust in itself, regardless of the policy consequences or outcomes it generates. Even if epistocracy produced more substantively just and effective policy outcomes, the fact that people of different demographic groups would have differential inputs renders the system unjust.

2. *The Bad Results Version*: Because epistocracy would lead to systematic overrepresentation of some groups and underrepresentation of others in the epistocratic electorate, it will likely produce substantively unjust outcomes, outcomes that tend to favor advantaged groups and fail to favor/disfavor disadvantaged groups. Even if citizens didn't *try* to vote in ways that favored their demographics over others', they might nevertheless inadvertently vote in such ways, perhaps because they do not know enough about how to promote the interests and goals of those who are different.

These two versions are distinct. The first one says that even if Mill is right and that plural voting generates substantively more just results, we should not have plural voting. On this view, it matters more that we decide things equally than that we make good or just decisions. This view prizes the *how* over the *what*. It's better to be stupid as equals than smart as unequals.

The second version instead holds that trying to apportion political power by political knowledge will *backfire*. If we create an electorate with voting power skewed toward demographic groups, then the resulting decisions will tend to of low quality because of this demographic skew. Perhaps people in those groups will vote for their interests at the expense of others. Or, perhaps even if they try to vote on behalf of all, their limited perspectives will cause them to vote poorly.[34]

What We Should Learn

Democracy instantiates a kind of equality that other systems lack. After all, what it is to be a democracy is to imbue each citizen (with "citizen" understood in a broad and inclusive way) with an equal fundamental share of power. Of course, in the real world, no democracy is fully equal, but democracies come closer to equality than do other systems.

But what is less obvious is *why* equality might matter. Previous chapters gave us possible answers why equality might be instrumentally valuable: perhaps it enhances stability, peace, virtue, good government, or freedom.

In this chapter, though, we saw that many theorists think democratic equality is constitutive of leading a fully human life or is an essential background condition for us to have proper esteem for ourselves and others. They claim that democracy is good not merely because of what it does, but because of what democratic laws express about our relative standing and value.

11

Against Equality

Is Democratic Equality an Illusion?

Democracies are by definition egalitarian in one way. What it means to be democratic is that by law and in actual practice, all citizens have equal fundamental political power. Further, in a real democracy, "citizen" must be construed widely. Countries that exclude significant portions of their permanent residents from voting or running from office are not true democracies. For instance, ancient Athens might have been democratic compared to other cities, but we wouldn't call a country democratic today if it had the same rules.

It's an open question whether any of the self-styled democratic governments today are truly equal or equal enough to quality as "democratic" by any particular theorist's definition. In all countries today, people have different levels of potential political influence even if by law they are equal. For this reason, some democratic theorists—especially deliberative democrats—advocate that we equalize almost everything outside politics. They believe inequalities outside politics will lead to inequality inside politics. If differential status, wealth, or education means we have differential effective power, they conclude that we need to eradicate differences in status, wealth, or education. Some regard this as reductio ad absurdum or an overextension of the democratic idea.

This helps illustrate why some people might be critical of democracy despite its conceptual connection to equality. One reason might be that de jure political equality has, in their view, unwelcome or unjust consequences. Over the past ten chapters, we have seen authors argue that political equality can produce instability,

Democracy. Jason Brennan, Oxford University Press. © Oxford University Press 2023.
DOI: 10.1093/oso/9780197558812.003.0011

mob behavior, moral or intellectual corruption, stupid decisions, or illiberalism.

This chapter focuses on why some authors have critiqued democracy from an egalitarian point of view. It's one thing to say that some people think other values sometimes trump equality. It's another—and more interesting—to see authors argue that democratic equality undermines, well, equality. Their worries include that equality of inputs can undermine equality of outputs, that the majority might tyrannize or abuse the minority, or even that, despite political equality, the minority can tyrannize and abuse the majority.

Tocqueville: Equality and Conformity

As we saw in chapters 2 and 4, Tocqueville was overall a fan of democracy. But he did not regard democracy as the font of all goodness, nor did he think all of democracy's flaws could be fixed with more democracy. Instead, he thought democracy had serious downsides.

Tocqueville claims that democracy produces a suffocating, close-minded political culture:

> At the present time the most absolute monarchs in Europe cannot prevent certain opinions hostile to their authority from circulating in secret through their dominions and even in their courts. It is not so in America; as long as the majority is still undecided, discussion is carried on; but as soon as its decision is irrevocably pronounced, everyone is silent, and the friends as well as the opponents of the measure unite in assenting to its propriety. The reason for this is perfectly clear: no monarch is so absolute as to combine all the powers of society in his own hands and to conquer all opposition, as a majority is able to do, which has the right both of making and of executing the laws.

The authority of a king is physical and controls the actions of men without subduing their will. But the majority possesses a power that is physical and moral at the same time, which acts upon the will as much as upon the actions and represses not only all contest, but all controversy.

I know of no country in which there is so little independence of mind and real freedom of discussion as in America. . . . In America the majority has enclosed thought within a formidable fence. A writer is free inside that area, but woe to the man who goes beyond it.[1]

This passage occurs in a chapter in which Tocqueville argues that the majority in a democracy has more absolute and pervasive power than even an absolute king. Tocqueville claims that democracy permits open discussion and debate only so long as the public remains undecided. But once the public takes a stand, it tolerates little dissent.

Further, Tocqueville claims democracies have greater ability to squash dissent than kings do, in part because the government is the people. A king might have his private opinions and wish to forbid disagreement, but even his own ministers will disagree with him, and the private people can say what they want in the bars or at parties.

But in democracy, the majority are or could be pretty much everywhere, at every meeting, at every coffee shop, at every office water cooler. If you contradict the received wisdom or challenge the majority, they might expose you, ridicule you, and destroy you.

In America the majority raises very formidable barriers to the liberty of opinion: within these barriers an author may write whatever he pleases, but he will repent it if he ever step beyond them. Not that he is exposed to the terrors of an auto-da-fe, but he is tormented by the slights and persecutions of daily obloquy. His political career is closed forever, since he has offended the only authority which is able to promote his success. Every sort of compensation, even that of celebrity, is refused to him. Before he published his opinions, he imagined that he held them in common with many others; but no sooner has he declared them openly than he is loudly censured by his overbearing opponents, whilst those who think without having the courage to speak, like him, abandon him in silence. He yields at length, oppressed by the daily efforts he has been making, and he subsides into silence, as if he was tormented by remorse for having spoken the truth.[2]

The idea that democracy has a narrow range of opinion might seem absurd to us today. In the United States, aren't Democrats and Republicans mortal ideological enemies with diametrically opposed views? Here, Tocqueville would laugh at how parochial this objection sounds. In reality, what we have is the narcissism of small differences and hypersensitivity to tiny details. The Republican and Democratic worldviews and ideologies are almost identical. The feud between them is less like that between pagans and Christians and more like that between among variations of Presbyterianism. Rivals brand each other as heretics and emphasize their differences, but outsiders see their differences are small.

According to Tocqueville, the majority tend to be self-righteous and secure in their own moral and intellectual authority. They think that challenging them is unacceptable because they have an inherent right to rule. They also believe democratic methods tend to ensure their decisions are correct. (As we saw in chapter 10, even today, some democratic theorists defend this view. Remember that Christiano claims that one must think oneself a god to disobey the majority.)

On this point, Tocqueville adds:

Several other circumstances concur in rendering the power of the majority in America not only preponderant, but irresistible. The moral authority of the majority is partly based upon the

notion that there is more intelligence and more wisdom in a great
number of men collected together than in a single individual,
and that the quantity of legislators is more important than their
quality. The theory of equality is in fact applied to the intellect
of man: and human pride is thus assailed in its last retreat by a
doctrine which the minority hesitate to admit, and in which they
very slowly concur. Like all other powers, and perhaps more than
all other powers, the authority of the many requires the sanction
of time; at first it enforces obedience by constraint, but its laws are
not respected until they have long been maintained.[3]

Tocqueville says that the old thinking was that the king had a divine
right to rule; the new thinking is that the people have something
like a divine right. The old thinking was that the king could do no
wrong; any apparent wrongdoing was actually the fault of his ministers. So too democrats claim that the people can do no wrong:

> The French, under the old monarchy, held it for a maxim (which
> is still a fundamental principle of the English Constitution) that
> the King could do no wrong; and if he did do wrong, the blame
> was imputed to his advisers. This notion was highly favor-
> able to habits of obedience, and it enabled the subject to com-
> plain of the law without ceasing to love and honor the lawgiver.
> The Americans entertain the same opinion with respect to the
> majority.[4]

The majority also exercises power everywhere. Its power is unchecked because it dominates and rules every major institution.
This means there can be no redress from the majority inside or outside government:

> When an individual or a party is wronged in the United States,
> to whom can he apply for redress? If to public opinion, public
> opinion constitutes the majority; if to the legislature, it represents

the majority, and implicitly obeys its injunctions; if to the executive power, it is appointed by the majority, and remains a passive tool in its hands; the public troops consist of the majority under arms; the jury is the majority invested with the right of hearing judicial cases; and in certain States even the judges are elected by the majority. However iniquitous or absurd the evil of which you complain may be, you must submit to it as well as you can.

In a democracy, the majority controls almost everything, and it believes itself to have the right to rule because it believes it expresses the will of the people. The view that "we speak for the people" is perhaps the very thing that seduces the majority into crushing opposing people. Tocqueville thus claims that what most alarms him about the United States is that the majority demands fidelity to its opinions.

Tocqueville claims that "The majority in the United States, takes over the business of supplying the individual with a quantity of ready-made opinions."[5] As we saw in chapter 5 and chapter 7, there is empirical evidence for this claim. People do not generally join or vote for a political party because they share the party's beliefs; rather they tend to share the party's beliefs because they joined it or voted for it. The causal arrow goes the wrong way.

Tocqueville claims that democracy tends to render politics inescapable, because it tends to ensure politics is everywhere. It tends to collapse the distinction between political activity, private activity, and civil society.

In free countries, where everyone is more or less called upon to give his opinion in the affairs of state; in democratic republics, where public life is incessantly commingled with domestic affairs, where the sovereign authority is accessible on every side, and where its attention can almost always be attracted by vociferation, more persons are to be met with who speculate upon its foibles and live at the cost of its passions than in absolute monarchies. Not because men are naturally worse in these States than elsewhere, but the temptation is stronger, and of easier access at the same time. The result is a far more extensive debasement of the characters of citizens.

So, Tocqueville claims, democracy is in this way inimical to freedom and to equality, because we are constantly badgered and pushed to conform.

Is Tocqueville correct? We might wonder how much his opinions here reflect not universal laws or tendencies of democracy, but perhaps particular tendencies he saw at a particular time in a particular culture. US history is characterized by periods of great religious and political furor and upheaval, followed by reactive periods of openness and tolerance. During a religious or political Great Awakening, people go out of their way to prove their moral worth through public expression. They seek out and crush opposition. In other times, people keep quiet. Some places and times have a thirst for new ideas; others do not.

As I write this sentence, in elite American society, there are certain views on diversity, sex, gender, and race that one is expected have. Active assent is expected. People who dissent from such views—for instance, "gender-critical radical feminists" who dispute whether transgender women are real women—are mobbed, harassed, disinvited, and deplatformed. (Not true, some of my colleagues say. Ohers say, yes, but rightly so!) I invoke this not because I necessarily dispute this orthodoxy. But there is orthodoxy and disputing it—indeed, even investigating it philosophically— hampers one's career.

Further, thanks in part to social media, political messaging is omnipresent. People signal their fidelity to their political tribe all over. Many proclaim that they simply cannot tolerate other political groups and their stupid, evil ideas. To preserve friendships or cordial work relations, we feel pressured to conform to prevailing political opinions.

Tocqueville's worry here is not simply that democracies could impede freedom of conscience. Rather, he worries it's a mistake to see democracy as truly equal. Democracy gives every individual an equal basic right to participate, vote, and run for office. In practice, this means the majority rules over minority factions. Equality on one end leads to massive inequality on other.

But it's worse than that. Sometimes formal equality of input does not even mean real equality on the front end. Tocqueville recounts a conversation with a person from Pennsylvania, which at the time was one of the most open, tolerant, and progressive states. He notes that in Pennsylvania, free blacks had the franchise, but hardly ever exercised it. According to Tocqueville, his Pennsylvanian interlocutor claims that blacks abstain from voting because they know that if they vote, they will be tormented and harassed. They might have formal equal political rights, but in actual practice, these rights mean little.

Democrats today are worried about problems like that. You would be hard-pressed to find a democratic theorist in the academy who would deny that blacks should be protected such that they feel safe voting. But Tocqueville claims the problem is even more pervasive. He thinks democracies tend to push around, abuse, and ultimately destroy ideological minorities.

Lenin: Equality of Outcomes, Not Inputs

Vladimir Lenin (1870–1924) was a political activist and agitator. He organized the Bolshevik October Revolution in Russia in 1917, and then installed himself as dictator (i.e., chairman of the Council of People's Commissars) until his death in 1924. In his early writings, Lenin identifies as a "Social Democrat," though he uses that label differently than we do today. He frequently extols workers' democracy in the abstract while criticizing existing democracies as tools of oppression. When given the chance to demonstrate his democratic bona fides over power and terror, Lenin chose power and terror.

During the Russian civil war, Lenin engaged in intentional hyperinflation, making money worthless because he regarded it as a bourgeois tool. He wanted to nationalize and collectivize farms. Though he failed to implement full land nationalization, he helped create a massive famine that claimed 5 million lives. He regarded these deaths as an opportunity; he used them as a pretext for seizing wealth from the Russian Orthodox Church. He created the Cheka (the first Soviet secret police) and left his heir, Stalin, a totalitarian police state. Lenin explicitly and knowingly relied on terror and terrorism to ensure conformity and get his way.

Here are some choice quotations:

> Introduce at once mass terror, execute and deport hundreds of prostitutes, drunken soldiers, ex-officers, etc. . . .
> It is the biggest mistake to think that the NEP [New Economic Policy] will put an end to the terror. We shall return to the terror, and to economic terror.[6]

These are not outliers. Lenin's letters and writings show a clear trend. He believed himself to be the founder of a future utopia. He believed he had the absolute right—as the representative of the proletariat—to do whatever anything it takes to achieve his vision. In chapter 10, we discussed how the rule of law institutes equality before the law by reducing the discretionary power of leaders and by making laws known and public. Lenin regarded the rule of law bourgeois invention that could impede his revolution.

Lenin is interesting for us here because he was an egalitarian but anti-democrat. He believed in creating a classless society in which government would wither away, but in fact created a totalitarian state in which government was everywhere. He thought the people should rule themselves and yet made himself dictator, all while torturing and killing the people who resisted his rule. He saw himself as the workers' champion but viewed peasants as enemies because they refused to relinquish their hard-won land.

Lenin's attitude toward the existing democratic states—such as the United States—was rather standard Marxism for the time. He said the United States was not a true democracy giving equal power to all people, but rather a state designed to further the interests of the bourgeoisie/capitalist class at workers' expense. Elected leaders tended to be rich and to represent the interests of capital over those of labor. Further, Lenin had little love for liberal rights. He thought the formal liberties the United States and other liberal countries enjoyed—such as freedom of speech, freedom to own property, freedom of lifestyle, and freedom of conscience—were of little value without a formal guarantee of economic equality. The liberal-democratic political system was a tool that enabled the capitalist exploitation of workers.

Marx had written that during his predicted communist revolution, the revolutionary workers would at first instantiate a dictatorship of the proletariat. What Marx intended by this cryptic phrase (as is most everything in Marx scholarship) is uncertain, but what Lenin understood it to mean is clearer. Lenin thought that eventually the revolution would dissolve the state, as the elimination of classes would eliminate the need for government to maintain order. But, Lenin thought, at first the state would need to focus power to eliminate threats and impediments to the worker's revolution. The state would have to destroy bourgeois property institutions and instead socialize economic production, with the central state making decisions and issuing instructions on behalf of the people. In Lenin's view, the dictatorship of the people required his own dictatorship—which is just fine because he is the agent of the people.

Lenin claimed that his own government was far more democratic than the United States', France's, or the United Kingdom's. His government did indeed have elected workers' councils and other deliberative apparatus, though they exercised little actual power, elections were hardly fair, and Lenin quickly outlawed and eliminated rival parties. Lenin was not under the illusion that the workers controlled his state through elections and deliberative forums. Rather, he saw his government as substantively democratic because it ruled on *behalf* of the people, even if it was authoritarian in form. In contrast, he saw the United States as democratic in form—in the letter of the law—but classist in substance.

Lenin is interesting from an intellectual standpoint because he seemed like a walking contradiction—an egalitarian dictator, an authoritarian who saw himself as a democrat. What explains this?

One of Lenin's big "innovations" in Marxist theory was his defense of a kind of intellectual elitism. Marx claimed that revolution was inevitable. Once capitalism reached a certain stage, its internal contradictions would induce its collapse. But Marx was rather silent about how exactly this would take place. Lenin wanted to fill in the details, plus respond to issues Marx did not anticipate.

For one, Marx's theory predicts that revolutions would occur first in the most industrialized and capitalistic countries. But Russia was hardly an industrial capitalist state. Here, Lenin argued that capitalist countries' empires exploited foreigners for the sake of their domestic workers. They could in effect bribe the workers with stolen goods to stop rebellion.[7]

More important, Lenin thought workers needed a nudge from an intellectual vanguard class. They would not spontaneously develop class consciousness and a thirst for revolution on their own. They needed some forward-thinkers—like Lenin!—to help them overcome their false consciousness and lack of class awareness.

In "What Is to Be Done?" (1902), Lenin argues:

> Social-Democracy represents the working class, not in its relation to a given group of employers alone, but in its relation to all classes of modern society and to the state as an organised political force. Hence, it follows that not only must Social-Democrats not confine themselves exclusively to the economic struggle, but that they must not allow the organisation of economic exposures to

become the predominant part of their activities. We must take up actively the political education of the working class and the development of its political consciousness.

"Everyone agrees" that it is necessary to develop the political consciousness of the working class. The question is, *how* that is to be done and what is required to do it.

The question arises, what should political education consist in? Can it be confined to the propaganda of working-class hostility to the autocracy? Of course not. It is not enough *to explain* to the workers that they are politically oppressed (any more than it is *to explain* to them that their interests are antagonistic to the interests of the employers). Agitation must be conducted with regard to every concrete example of *this* oppression (as we have begun to carry on agitation round concrete examples of economic oppression). Inasmuch as this oppression affects the most diverse classes of society, inasmuch as it manifests itself in the most varied spheres of life and activity—vocational, civic, personal, family, religious, scientific, etc., etc.—is it not evident that *we shall not be fulfilling our task* of developing the political consciousness of the workers if we do not *undertake* the organisation of the *political exposure* of the autocracy in *all its aspects?* In order to carry on agitation round concrete instances of oppression, these instances must be exposed (as it is necessary to expose factory abuses in order to carry on economic agitation).[8]

If we didn't know what Lenin later did, these passages might not be so disturbing. Already we see Lenin saying it is not enough to explain to workers how and why they are oppressed. They will need greater agitation than that.

Lenin concludes:

Let us return, however, to our theses. We said that a Social Democrat, if he really believes it necessary to develop comprehensively the political consciousness of the proletariat, must "go among all classes of the population." This gives rise to the questions: how is this to be done? have we enough forces to do this? is there a basis for such work among all the other classes? will this not mean a retreat, or lead to a retreat, from the class point of view? Let us deal with these questions.

We must "go among all classes of the population" as theoreticians, as propagandists, as agitators, and as organisers.[9]

In the 1902 essay, Lenin advocates Marxists creating a political party consisting of intellectuals and revolutionaries—ideally with representatives from a wide range of backgrounds. He worried that workers might fight battles over concrete goals, such as better wages and hours, but then stop fighting once they receive these. They were unlikely to spontaneously develop an understanding of their long-term interests or what it takes to end oppression. They would be satisfied and placated so long as the capitalists threw them a few crumbs and made things a little better.

One can see, then, how seductive this theory might be to Lenin's. Sure, he terrorized his subjects, but for their own long-term good. Sure, he stifled dissent, outlawed free speech, and mandated widespread propaganda, but that's OK, because he was correcting his subjects' false consciousness and purging them of alien ideas. He created an inegalitarian system because he thought this was necessary to create egalitarian outcomes. It was OK to curtail civil rights because liberal liberty isn't real liberty anyway.

Lenin opposed democracy on egalitarian grounds. He thought democracy would serve bourgeois rather than proletariat interests. As an intellectual elitist but economic egalitarian, he believed that the great mass of Russian people could not be trusted to vote in their true class interests. He regarded many as enemies or saboteurs of the revolution. He sometimes claimed that the state he created realized true democracy.

It's worth noting that some suspicion and ambivalence toward democracy (as we see it, as opposed to ideal democracy) remains among many Marxists today. For instance, consider these lines from the Marxist political scientist Adolphe Reed:

> We live under a regime now that is capable simultaneously of including black people and Latinos, even celebrating that inclusion as a fulfillment of democracy, while excluding poor people without a whimper of opposition. Of course, those most visible in the excluded class are disproportionately black and Latino, and that fact gives the lie to the celebration. Or does it really? From the standpoint of a neoliberal ideal of equality, in which classification by race, gender, sexual orientation or any other recognized ascriptive status (that is, status based on what one allegedly is rather than what one does) does not impose explicit, intrinsic or necessary limitations on one's participation and aspirations in the society, this celebration of inclusion of blacks, Latinos and others is warranted.
>
> But this notion of democracy is inadequate, since it doesn't begin to address the deep and deepening patterns of inequality and injustice embedded in the ostensibly "neutral" dynamics of American capitalism.[10]

Public Choice Economics: Rent Seeking and Minority Power

In the middle of the twentieth century, many economics textbooks followed a standard but misleading or confused format. First, they might explain how under certain somewhat ideal conditions of perfect rationality, perfect information, perfect competition, zero transaction costs, and zero externalities, markets could be expected to maximize welfare better than any alternative system of production and distribution. Second, though, they would rightly identify that in the real world, consumers are not perfectly rational or informed, competition is often imperfect, there are significant transaction costs, and there are often real externalities. As a result, in the real world, markets are expected not to produce ideally efficient outcomes, though they might still work better than other realistic methods of production and distribution.

So, economists would conclude, real-life markets suffer from what they call market failures. Note, however, that economists use the term "market failure" in a rather stringent way. A market failure occurs whenever the market is not perfectly efficient. Here, a situation is said to be efficient whenever it is impossible to improve the welfare of one person without reducing the welfare of another. This, a "market failure" so defined, does not necessarily mean the market is bad or disastrous. Market failures occur whenever a market is literally less than perfect. It'd be as though your professor used the word "failure" whenever a student scores under 100 on exams.

Economists would then say that when the market fails, a government could in principle identify and correct that failure through regulation, redistribution, taxes, or various other policies. For instance, if people pollute too much, in principle, we could calculate the social costs of pollution and tax polluters to make them bear those costs. This would reduce pollution and provide funding to correct its problems.

The problem with this way of thinking, though, is that economists were often asking what an *ideal* or *perfect* government would do in response to non-ideal, imperfect markets. Economist James Buchanan (1919–2013) won the Nobel Prize in Economics in 1986 in part for showing how silly this way of thinking is. It's one thing to assert that in principle a well-motivated, smart government bureaucracy could fix a market failure, if only every citizen automatically went along with whatever rule or regulation the government imposed. But, Buchanan said, we cannot assume that *real* government agents have either the desire or the knowledge to identify or solve such problems. We shouldn't presume that people will always comply with the law, either. We shouldn't assume that power will in fact be used for the noble purposes we intend.

Buchanan helped found a branch of economics referred to as "public choice economics." At base, public choice economics is about applying the tools of microeconomics, behavioral economics, and other subfields *consistently*. For instance, if we find people are mostly selfish, we should presume they remain mostly selfish even if they work at an NGO or a government. If we find that people have information problems in markets, we should presume they have similar information problems in politics. If we find that crowning someone CEO of Enron does not transform them into a moral saint, we should presume that crowning someone CEO of the Red Cross does not transform them either.

Public choice has produced many important insights into understanding how real-world governments, NGOs, and collective activities perform. For our purposes here, though, what matters is that public choice offers some worries about just how egalitarian democracy really is. While Tocqueville, John Stuart Mill, and other earlier democratic theorists realized that equal inputs could lead to the unequal outcomes through the tyranny of the majority, Buchanan and others analyzed how egalitarian democracy could also enable minority special interest groups to capture power and exploit the majority.

To illustrate, consider the phenomenon public choice theorists call "rent seeking." A rent seeker is anyone who uses a political process—as opposed to supplying a productive service—to obtain, extend, and preserve the flow of wealth and benefits to themselves. "Rent seeking" refers to when a person or group tries to rig the rules of the game to get a special advantage at the expense of others.

For example, the agricultural firm Archer Daniels Midland (ADM) lobbies for a large range of socially destructive tariffs, subsidies, and predatory regulations. As of 1995, nearly half of ADM's profits came from subsidized or protected products; for every $1 of profits ADM's corn sweetener products earned, consumers lost $10 from predatory subsidies and tariffs.[11] Or, consider that sugar costs twice as much in the United States as it does elsewhere in the world, costing Americans an extra $4 billion or so per year.[12] The reason is that sugar beet farmers, among others, in the United States successfully lobbied for protectionist quotas and tariffs, which artificially raise the price of foreign sugar in order to induce Americans to buy inefficiently produced but American-made sugar instead.

Why would Americans put up with this? If these rules hurt the majority for the benefit of the minority, why doesn't the majority stop it?

The answer is that the benefits of these bad policies are concentrated among the few, while the costs are spread among the many. For instance, there are about 10,000 farms represented by the American Sugarbeet Growers Association. $4 billion spread among them yields about $400,000 per farm, though of course the benefits are uneven. So, these farms have a strong incentive to spend time and money lobbying the US government for sugar tariffs or other protectionist policies. However, the costs of these bad policies are spread among the other 330 or so million Americans. Each of us pays/loses maybe $15 a year on these tariffs. Thus, for the rest of us, as individuals, it's not worth fighting the tariffs, or, frankly, even knowing about them. I work in Washington, DC, but going to my congressperson's office just once would cost me more in parking fees and time than I pay for the tariffs.

The mechanism here is not unequal amounts of money or power. While sure, some successful rent seekers are large and powerful corporations, others are small and weak. It's not as though sugar beet farmers are particularly powerful as a group or as individuals. Rather, what matters is *unequal capacity to benefit from government action.* Whenever a situation arises in which benefits can be concentrated among the few but the costs spread among the many, we can expect to see the few invest the time and resources into securing those benefits, while the many not only fail to resist or advocate for themselves, but do not even learn that they are being exploited.

Persistent Minorities and the Demographic
Objection to Democracy

One of the basic methodological principles in philosophy is that
if you offer an objection to another view, you are supposed to ask
whether that objection also applies to your own view. Hardly anyone sticks to this principle, though.

Consider the demographic objection to epistocracy from the
last chapter. This objection held that epistocracy—a system that
apportions political power according to knowledge—is bad because, as a matter of fact, knowledge is distributed unequally among
members of different demographic groups, and thus distributing
power according to knowledge will result in voting power being
skewed toward some demographic categories at the expense of
others. In the United States today, that would mean that white
voters have more votes than black voters.

However, the demographic objection to epistocracy also applies
to democracy as well, though in slightly different forms. Indeed,
one way to express the worry about majoritarianism is that in democracy, power skews to the majority even if every individual has
equal inputs.

Consider a hypothetical: imagine a society that is 90 percent
white and 10 percent black. Suppose there are no other relevant
demographic categories that affect how anyone thinks or acts. Now
suppose that everyone is a bit biased—they tend to know and care
about their own kinds of problems but not so much about others.
Here, if we grant everyone equal voting power—regardless of
whether we have direct or representative democracy—we would
expect the resulting policies to be skewed toward the interests of
whites over blacks. This was one of the main concerns the demographic objection to epistocracy expressed, yet it appears even in an
equal democracy.

The problem is that even if democracy equalizes inputs for each
person, it does not thereby mean equal outputs. If individuals form

and act as members of groups, equal inputs can be the very mechanism by which they produce unequal outputs.

Consider a more extreme version of this example. Suppose that all whites in this hypothetical society are extremely racist against all blacks. Suppose that despite this, there is a strong bill of rights protecting voting. All members of society have equal voting rights. Suppose the fair value of political liberty is guaranteed. In fact, everyone votes. Still, because whites so greatly outnumber blacks, we would expect the resulting policies to express white racism, and to actively target and harm blacks as much as the background constitution allows. Under these circumstances—where the majority whites want to hurt the minority blacks—rendering everyone a political equal could itself be the very mechanism that enables whites to harm blacks and render them unequal in other ways.

If this hypothetical seems too extreme to you, consider some real cases. In the Canada or the United States, how does the majority treat First Nations or Native Americans? Despite equal voting rights, the polities can get by largely ignoring the interests of small minorities.

Similar remarks apply to ideological minorities. For example, as Christiano says:

> This problem is the difficulty of persistent minorities. There is a persistent minority in a democratic society when that minority always loses in the voting. This is always a possibility in democracies because of the use of majority rule. If the society is divided into two or more highly unified voting blocks in which the members of each group votes in the same ways as all the other members of that group, then the group in the minority will find itself always on the losing end of the votes. . . . Though this problem is often connected with majority tyranny it is distinct from the problem of majority tyranny because it may be the case that the majority attempts to treat the minority well, in accordance with its conception of good treatment. It is just that the minority never

agrees with the majority on what constitutes proper treatment. Being a persistent minority can be highly oppressive even if the majority does not try to act oppressively. This can be understood with the help of the very ideas that underpin democracy. Persons have interests in being able to correct for the cognitive biases of others and to be able to make the world in such a way that it makes sense to them. These interests are set back for a persistent minority since they never get their way.[13]

Here, Christiano recognizes that while members of some groups can at least say that they will take turns between ruling and being rules, persistent ideological or demographic minorities might instead *never* rule. For them, political equality renders them unequal in one important respect.

Further, in most countries, voting turnout rates are not in fact equal among demographic groups. For instance, in countries with voluntary voting, the rich tend to vote at higher rates than the poor, while the old tend to vote at higher rates than the young. Accordingly, the actual voting electorate is skewed toward some groups rather than others. Even compulsory voting turns out not to fix this problem—as not everyone votes—though it reduces it.[14] Still, the previous worries remain. Even if we manage to ensure that all members of different demographic groups vote at identical rates, unequal sizes means unequal power. If this is a problem for epistocracy, it's also a problem for democracy.

Immigration versus Social Democracy

In the last chapter, we discussed how John Rawls wanted to provide a theoretical defense for the modern, democratic, liberal nation-state with a mixed economy. He argued that parties under the veil of ignorance in the "original position" would choose certain principles of justice, which in turn helps select the basic structure of a society. But, as we saw, Rawls helps himself to certain simplifying assumptions that severely reduce the justificatory power of his thought experiment. He imagines everyone lives in a largely uniform society in which everyone identifies as a member of that society, rather than a subsociety, tribe, or whatnot. He also imagines that the parties choose principles for an isolated, autarkical society.

Thus, his theory does not assess whether it is just, in the first place, to divide the world up into nation-states with discrete territories, or for those nations to exclude or inhibit people from other nations from moving to other nations, or for those nations to favor their own citizens over others in various ways. This reduces the power of his theory for assessing the justice of our actual world. Perhaps what Rawls should have done was imagine that parties in the original position know that dividing the world into nation-states (with various degrees of stringency is their borders) is merely one institutional possibility among many, and further, place them under a veil of ignorance such that they don't know which country or place they will be born into.

Rawls argues that *inside* a single state, the parties will choose to arrange inequalities in income such that this maximizes the welfare of the representative members of the least advantaged groups. Inequalities are allowed, but inequalities must work not only to everyone's benefit, but to the maximal benefit of the worst-off. Perhaps in a better-designed original position than Rawls's, inequalities across borders should be as least as disturbing. Oddly, Rawls is fine with some people being much richer than others, even when this disparity does not benefit the genuinely least advantaged, provided that we least advantaged live in foreign countries.[15]

Right now, the world is divided into nation-states. For the most part, people are stuck with their nation-state of birth. Even if they wanted to leave, other nation-states won't let them in. It is difficult to win the right to move to and work inside other countries for any serious length of time.

One of the major purported justifications for this practice is to protect democracy. Democracies, people say, function only when there is a clear demos. Who counts as inside and outside the voting public must be established by law. We need to know whom to count. People need to identify with a particular polity. Rawls himself was skeptical of the European Union for these reasons:

> It seems to me that much would be lost if the European union became a federal union like the United States. Here there is a common language of political discourse and a ready willingness to move from one state to another. Isn't there a conflict between a large free and open market comprising all of Europe and the individual nation-states, each with its separate political and social institutions, historical memories, and forms and traditions of social policy. Surely these are great value to the citizens of these countries and give meaning to their life. The large open market including all of Europe is the aim of the large banks and the capitalist business class whose main goal is simply larger profit.[16]

How does dividing the world into mostly closed-border nation-states affect world income and inequality? Here, we can do more than speculate, because economists have developed robust tools for studying such policies. Economists have published many peer-reviewed estimates of the deadweight losses from immigration restrictions, using the same well-established methods they use to calculate losses from other restrictions on international trade, by examining how existing internal and foreign immigration affects income, and so on. They generally estimate the deadweight loss of immigration restriction to be between 50 and 150 percent of current world product. The mean estimate in the literature is *100 percent of world product*.[17] In other words, immigration restrictions cut world production *in half*. These losses are spread among the many. First-world citizens of rich countries are poorer than they otherwise would be with more liberal immigration, but the citizens of poor countries are especially harmed.

One major economic study examined the effects of immigration to the United States on workers from forty-two poor countries. Workers' wages increased by factors of as low as 2.8 and as high as 15, with a median around 5. (The mean was higher than the median.) That is, the median low-skilled worker from a poor country who moves to the United States sees her real, cost-of-living-adjusted income go up by a factor of about 5.[18] The best estimate is that, under open borders, unskilled immigrants who move to developed countries would on average see their real (cost-of-living-adjusted) income increase by least 10,000 USD/year.[19]

In one recent paper, economist Glen Weyl examines how differing immigration policies affect both total welfare and global income inequality. He notes that the Gulf Cooperation Council Countries admit a far higher number of immigrants on a per capita (and often absolute) basis than what he calls the "fortress welfare states" of the Organization for Economic Cooperation and Development (OECD). Using this natural experiment, he then compares the effects of various policies: (A) heavy in-country redistribution and provision of various public goods; (B) monetary transfers from rich to poor countries; and (C) open immigration.

Weyl finds that even at current levels of immigration, and despite the massive restrictions that fortress welfare states impose, immigration already accounts for a larger reduction in global income inequality and already produces higher welfare gains for the world's poor than all the redistribution *inside* or *between* countries. That is, he claims that right now, even with mostly closed borders, immigration is already doing more to reduce poverty and promote economic equality than internal welfare states or foreign aid. Further, when Weyl estimates what would happen if there were either much more redistribution or much more immigration, he again shows that immigration would do far more (in some countries, ten times more) to increase the welfare of the poor and reduce income inequality than either form of redistribution.[20]

Note that poverty in Europe, Canada, the United States, and Japan is not like poverty in undeveloped nations. An American at the poverty line is about ten times richer—an order of magnitude better off—than the average person in Haiti. As I write, the US poverty line for a single adult living alone is $12,880. Adjusting for the cost of living in different countries, that still puts an American at poverty in the top 20 percent of income earners worldwide.[21] That estimate does not include the generous welfare benefits the American would receive that absolutely poor people in much poorer countries would not.

Whether modern social democracies and the system of nation-states can be rendered compatible with greatly liberalized immigration is an open question. I introduce the question here not to settle it but simply to introduce it. Some theorists think that the need to maintain stable and culturally coherent democracies trumps the goal of equalizing world income or enhancing the welfare of the world's poor, while others think the opposite.[22]

What We Should Learn

The same themes reappear again. We might think that democracy is an unusually egalitarian system. However, theorists object that in any realistic democracy, people have different levels of effective power. The system has inegalitarian inputs and inegalitarian outputs. Democracies might serve special interest groups or ignore the interests of minorities. Indeed, equalizing power could itself be a mechanism that guarantees unequal outcomes. Sometimes enfranchising everyone as equals is a way to ensure that entire groups of people are ignored or exploited. Perhaps egalitarianism also makes us conformists. Or so they claim.

This chapter ended by considering what should be a fundamental question that most theorists nevertheless ignore: who is in and who is out? When we ask whether a society should be democratic, we often take it for granted what counts as a society and where the borders should be drawn. However, drawing borders and creating a system of insiders and outsiders is itself something that can have radically inegalitarian outcomes and produce worldwide class divisions. Instead of asking whether Athens and Sparta should be democratic, we should ask whether Athens and Sparta should be distinct polities at all.

Notes

Chapter 1

1. "Constitution of the Union of Soviet Socialist Republics," 1936, https://www.marxists.org/reference/archive/stalin/works/1936/12/05.htm.
2. Economist Intelligence Unit 2020.
3. Azpuru and Hall 2017.
4. Bormeo 2016.
5. Nozick 1974, 48–51.
6. Singer 1975, 1–24.
7. One exception is Vallier 2017. However, even Vallier's work largely ignores empirical issues about what causes stability or instability in the real world, and instead focuses on trying to discuss how largely imaginary people could agree on policies despite disagreeing on fundamental issues. In contrast, earlier scholars writing about stability—such as Aristotle, Hamilton, or de Tocqueville, were more concerned about what causes real people to fight or lay down their arms.
8. Christiano 1990, 151.
9. Christiano 2006.
10. Kavka 1995, 2.
11. López-Guerra 2014, 2.
12. See Lisa Hill in Brennan and Hill 2014. This is one reason Hill favors compulsory voting (combined with certain ease-of-access laws); she thinks that underprivileged citizens face assurance problems in advocating for their shared interests, which compulsory voting would overcome.
13. E.g., Dryzek 2016; Collier, Hidalgo, and Maciuceanu 2006; Gallie 1956; Gray 1977.
14. Hume 2000.
15. Nozick 1981, 4.

Chapter 2

1. Rawls 1971, 3.
2. See Brennan 2020 for a review.

3. Aristotle 1996, 103.
4. Aristotle 1996, 71–72
5. Aristotle 1996, 62.
6. Aristotle 1996, 98–99.
7. Aristotle 1996, 103.
8. Aristotle 1996, 105.
9. Aristotle 1996, 107–108.
10. Mattingly 1958; Skinner 2000.
11. Gilbert 1965; Skinner 1981.
12. Machiavelli 1531.
13. Madison 1787.
14. Madison 1787.
15. Madison 1787.
16. Madison 1787.
17. Madison 1787.
18. Madison 1788.
19. Kant 1795.
20. Kant 1795.
21. Davis and Huttenback 1986 find this is precisely what happened. The benefits of imperialism were concentrated among the politically well-connected few.
22. Tocqueville 1968, 195, 200–202.
23. Tocqueville 1968, 315.
24. Rummel 1997; Moaz 1998; Oneal and Russett 1999; Weart 1998.
25. Farber and Gowa 1997; Gartzke 1998; Layne 1994.
26. Farber and Gowa 1997.
27. Ray 2003; Kinsella 2005; Pugh 2005.

Chapter 3

1. Plato 375 BC, 545d.
2. Plato 375 BC, 555d–555e.
3. Plato 375 BC, 556d.
4. Plato 375 BC, 560–566.
5. See Gaus 2003.
6. Hobbes 1994, I.xi.2.
7. Hobbes 1994, I.x.1.
8. Hobbes 1994, I.xiii.7.
9. Hobbes 1994, I.xiii.8.

10. Hobbes 1994, I.xv.5.
11. Here's his argument: a contract has force only if it can be enforced. The sovereign, by definition, has the final power and no one has power over it. So, there is no external force that can enforce a contract with the sovereign; if there were, that external force would be sovereign instead. Accordingly, the idea of a contract with a sovereign is incoherent.
12. E.g., see Acemoglu and Robinson 2012.
13. Hobbes 1845, *EW II*, 136.
14. Hobbes 1845, *EW IV*, 126, 141.
15. Hobbes 1845, *EW IV*, 141.
16. See Harris 2020.
17. Burke, 73
18. Burke 1790, 72.
19. Burke 1790, 73.
20. Burke 1790, 103–104.
21. Burke 1790, 78–79.
22. Burke 1790, 9.
23. Marx and Engels 1848.
24. Fine and Harris 1979.
25. Acemoglu and Robinson 2012.
26. Buchanan and Tullock 1962.
27. Haidt 2012; Westen et al. 2006.
28. Converse 1964; Barnes 1971; Inglehart and Klingemann 1976; Arian and Shamir 1983; Zaller 1992; McCann 1997; Goren 2005; Zechmeister 2006; Lewis-Beck et al. 2008; Achen and Bartels 2016; Kinder and Kalmoe 2017; Mason 2017; Mason 2018.
29. Kinder and Kalmoe 2017.
30. Mason 2018; Achen and Bartels 2016; Jardina 2019; Mason and Wronski 2018; Barber and Pope 2018; McCarty 2019.
31. Converse 1964; Barnes 1971; Inglehart and Klingemann 1976; Arian and Shamir 1983; Converse and Pierce 1986; Bartels 1986; Zaller 1992; McCann 1997; Goren 2005; Zechmeister 2006; Muddle 2007; Lewis-Beck et al. 2008; Achen and Bartels 2016; Kinder and Kalmoe 2017; Mason 2018.
32. Chong 2013; Citrin and Green 1990; Markus 1988, Miller 1999; Mutz and Mondak 1997; Ponza et al. 1988; Rhodebeck 1993; Sears and Funk 1990; Sears, Hensler, and Speer 1979; Sears and Lau 1983; Sears et al. 1980.
33. Feddersen, Gailmard, and Sandroni 2009.
34. Achen and Bartels 2016, 213–266; Campbell et al. 1960; Tajfel 1982; Green 1999; Gamm 1989.

35. Achen and Bartels 2016, 236–240.
36. Iyengar et al. 2012.
37. Iyengar and Westwood 2015.
38. Bishop 204.
39. Kaplan et al. 2020, 1.
40. Mutz 2006.
41. Schelling 1971.
42. See here for an account of historicity of this story: https://www.seattleti mes.com/nation-world/nation/a-republic-if-you-can-keep-it-did-ben-franklin-really-say-impeachment-days-favorite-quote/.
43. Mechkova et al. 2017, 162.
44. https://www.v-dem.net/pandem.html.
45. https://www.v-dem.net/pandem.html; Higgs 1987.

Chapter 4

1. John Rawls 1971, 325. Note that Rawls does not himself endorse this position.
2. See Hursthouse 2016.
3. Hursthouse 1999.
4. Aristotle 1996, 74.
5. Aristotle 1996, 74.
6. Kavka 1995, 2.
7. Aristotle 1996, 75.
8. Aristotle, 340 BC: 1.2.4–9,
9. Aristotle, 340 BC, 1.7.14.
10. Held 2006, 37.
11. Spinoza 1891a, chapter 16.
12. Spinoza 1891b, Pref IV, II/208/22–23, 28–29.
13. I take this point from Stephen Holmes 1995, 33–34.
14. Quoted by Holmes 1995, 34.
15. Quoted by Holmes 1995, 34.
16. Holmes 1995, 35.
17. See Brennan 2012a.
18. Mill 1861, 109–111.
19. Lopez-Guerra 2014; Brennan 2016.
20. Mill 1861, 32–33.
21. Mill 1861, 33.
22. Mill 1861, 34.

23. Mill 1861, 38.
24. Mill 1861, 34.
25. Mill 1861, 34.
26. Mill 1861, 104.
27. Mill 1861, 44.
28. Mill 1861, 35.
29. Mill 1861, 35–36.
30. Mill 1861, 46.
31. Dryzek et al. 2019.
32. Habermas 2001.
33. Fishkin 1993, 3.
34. I take this summary from Held 2006, 239.
35. Landemore 2012, 97.
36. Manin, Stein, and Mansbridge 1987, 354, 363.
37. Cohen 2006, 163.
38. Cohen 2006, 174.
39. Elster 1997, 12.
40. Gutmann and Thompson 1996, 9.
41. Ackerman and Fishkin 2005.
42. Landemore 2020.
43. Cohen 2009, 91–92. I ignore Cohen's proceduralism here, since pure proceduralism is controversial and may be seen as incompatible with the education argument.
44. Curato et al. 2017.
45. Mutz 2008.
46. Fishkin 1993.

Chapter 5

1. Hugh Thompson, at the time a warrant officer, was a helicopter pilot in the US-Vietnam war. He intervened to stop his fellow soldiers from killing civilians in the My Lai Massacre (1968), even ordering his gunners to fire upon other American soldiers if they kept killing civilians. He rescued a large number of civilians too.
2. Plato 375 BC, 550–575.
3. Plato 373 BC, 562a–563b.
4. Augustine 1988.
5. Liberal philosophers tend to reject perfectionism, but there are some important exceptions.

6. Miller 2021, 175.
7. Miller 2021, 175.
8. For a good discussion of these complexities, see Owen 2002.
9. Leiter 2014, 110
10. Nietzsche 1886, quoted here: http://www.thenietzschechannel.com/works-pub/bge/bge5.htm.
11. Nietzsche 1866.
12. Nietzsche 1895.
13. Leiter 2020.
14. Wall 2017.
15. Downs 1957.
16. Caplan 2007.
17. Lodge and Taber 2013, 169.
18. Huddy, Sears, and Levy 2013, 11.
19. Haidt 2010. Haidt is summarizing research (which he endorses) by Hugo Mercier and Dan Sperber.
20. Chong 2013, 111–112, citing Cohen 2003.
21. E.g., see Taber and Young 2013, 530; Lodge and Taber 2013, 149–169.
22. Kahan et al. 2013.
23. Lord, Ross, and Lepper 1979; Taber and Lodge 2006.
24. Nyhan and Reifler 2010.
25. Tajfel and Turner 1979; Tajfel 1981; Tajfel 1982; Cohen 2003; Mutz 2006; Iyengar et al. 2012; Kahan et al. 2013; Somin 2013; Iyengar and Westwood 2015.
26. Iyengar and Westwood 2015.
27. Mutz 2006.
28. Bishop 2014.
29. Talisse 2021.

Chapter 6

1. In the *Euthyphro*, the title character says that what makes things holy is that the gods like and approve of them. Socrates asks whether the Gods approve of what's holy *because* it is holy, or whether it is holy because they approve, as Euthyphro claims. If the latter, then it seems to make holiness an arbitrary thing. The gods happen to approve of, say, love, but had they at random and for no reason approved of rape and murder, then by Euthyphro's account, these things would be holy. But that seems untenable. So, the other alternative is that the gods approve of what is holy *because* it

is holy. But this means that holiness is not caused by the gods' approval, but instead that the gods simply recognize what is independently good or holy.

2. Aristotle 340, 96.

3. Ober 2009, 38–39, italics removed.

4. I take these last two criticisms from Somin 2009, 588.

5. Ober 2009, 118–167, discusses the myriad divisions of power and opportunities for participation which Athens presented to its eligible citizens.

6. Brennan 2011.

7. Gelman, Silver, and Edlin 2012; Edlin, Gelman, and Kaplan 2007; Edlin, Gelman, and Kaplan 2008; Barnett 2020.

8. Madison 1787.

9. Madison 1787.

10. Madison 1787.

11. Weiner 2012.

12. Ferguson 1782, 122.

13. Ball 2020.

14. Held 2006, 75–78.

15. The next few paragraphs are adapted from van der Vossen Brennan 2018.

16. Acemoglu and Robinson 2012, 372–373.

17. Somin 2013, 114; Page and Hong 2001, 163–186.

18. Thompson 2014; Brennan 2016.

19. Landemore 2012; Landemore 2020.

Chapter 7

1. Thaler and Sunstein 2021.

2. Brennan and Freiman 2022.

3. Plato, *Republic*, 488a–489a; http://www.perseus.tufts.edu/hopper/text?doc=Perseus%3Atext%3A1999.01.0168%3Abook%3D6%3Asection%3D489a.

4. Estlund 2008, 30.

5. See Brennan 2020.

6. To be more precise, he is willing to exclude adult citizens who cannot read, write, and perform basic arithmetic, though he thinks governments ought to provide education to help ensure every adult has these skills. Mill also thinks that people on public welfare should lose the franchise until they are no longer dependent.

7. Mill 1861, 103.

8. Mill 1861, 103.
9. Mill 1861, 103.
10. Mill 1861, 104.
11. Mill 1861, 109.
12. Caplan 2007, 206.
13. Hardin 2009, 60.
14. Somin 2013; Delli Carpini and Keeter 1996.
15. Somin 2013, 31.
16. https://www.ipsos-mori.com/researchpublications/researcharchive/ 3742/The-Perils-of-Perception-and-the-EU.aspx.
17. Somin 2013, 42.
18. Somin 2013, 92.
19. https://www.washingtonpost.com/outlook/people-dont-vote-for-want-they-want-they-vote-for-who-they-are/2018/08/30/fb5b7e44-abd7-11e8-8a0c-70b618c98d3c_story.html?utm_term=.b8109bf6cbb6.
20. Kinder and Kalmoe 2017. See also Mason 2018; Achen and Bartels 2016; Jardina 2019; Mason and Wronski 2018; Barber and Pope 2018; McCarty 2019.
21. Converse 1964; Barnes 1971; Inglehart and Klingemann 1976; Arian and Shamir 1983; Converse and Pierce 1986; Bartels 1986; Zaller 1992; McCann 1997; Goren 2005; Zechmeister 2006; Muddle 2007; Lewis-Beck et al. 2008; Achen and Bartels 2016; Kinder and Kalmoe 2017; Mason 2018.
22. Somin 2013; Achen and Bartels 2016; Simler and Hanson 2018; Mason 2018.
23. Achen and Bartels 2016, 213–266; Campbell et al. 1960; Tajfel 1982; Greene 1999; Gamm 1989.
24. Achen and Bartels 2016, 236–240.
25. Achen and Bartels 2016, 267–296; see also Lenz 2009; Lenz 2012.
26. Kinder and Kalmoe 2017; Mason 2017; Mason 2018.
27. Kahan 2016.

Chapter 8

1. Berlin 1997, 168.
2. Berlin 1997, 169.
3. Schmidtz and Brennan 2010.
4. Constant 1988.
5. Constant 1988, 311.
6. Constant 1988, 311.

7. Constant 1988, 311–312.
8. Raaflaub 2004, 242.
9. Raaflaub 2004, 276.
10. Raaflaub 2004, 276.
11. I put the "wrongful" qualifier in parentheses because some liberal thinkers say that of course some interference is permissible or even obligatory, but we wouldn't want to count that as an impediment to freedom. For instance, if I stop a mugger from mugging me, some people think it sounds absurd to say that I impeded the mugger's freedom to mug. Personally, I think it's confusing to moralize the definition of freedom this way. Instead, I think it's clearer to say that the freedom to mug and the absence of muggings are both forms of freedom, but the difference is that the former is a freedom people ought not to have while the latter is one they ought to have. Or, consider that constitutional restrictions on government indeed rightfully impose limits on the freedom of government leaders to do what they want as a means of rightfully ensuring that individual citizens have more freedom to do what they want.
12. Pettit 1996, 578, 581.
13. Marsilius 1980, 47–49.
14. Lovett 2018.
15. Lovett 2006.
16. Pettit 2012.
17. Brennan and Lomasky 2006.
18. Rousseau 1754.
19. Rousseau 1762.
20. Rousseau 1762.
21. Rousseau 1762.
22. Bertram 2017.
23. This section incorporates material from Brennan 2018.
24. E.g., Bolivia and Venezuela's political rights and civil rights scores have been declining gradually at the same rate for the past ten years.

Chapter 9

1. https://www.nandosperiperi.com/explore/news/nandos-serves-undemocratic-meals-to-stunned-customers.
2. Hume 1752.
3. Hume 1752.
4. Hume 1752.

5. Hume 1752.
6. Hume 1752.
7. Spooner 1780.
8. Spooner 1780.
9. Spooner 1780.
10. Spooner 1780.
11. Spooner 1780.
12. Spooner 1780.
13. Spooner 1780.
14. Schmitt 1986.
15. Nozick 1974, 290–291.
16. E.g., Brennan and Lomasky 1993.
17. Barnett 2020; Edlin, Gelman, and Kaplan 2007.
18. https://projects.economist.com/us-2020-forecast/president.
19. Edlin, Gelman, and Kaplan 2007.
20. https://electionlab.mit.edu/research#projects.
21. https://www.opensecrets.org/news/2020/04/majority-of-lawmakers-milli onaires/.

Chapter 10

1. I adapt these thoughts partly from Kling 2017. Kling discusses liberals and progressives in similar terms. However, the communitarian description I give here is mine. I omit his discussion of conservatives.
2. https://www.persee.fr/doc/arcpa_0000-0000_1885_num_21_1_9309 _t1_0238_0000_8, article 4. Robespierre proposes that the army carry signs, much like the Romans, that say, "The people of France," plus another saying "Liberty or Death." He also suggests that the army wear blue, red, and white on their uniforms, with "liberty, equality, and fraternity" written underneath.
3. Montesquieu described England as enjoying the kind of mixed polity with separation of powers he favored, but most scholars agree that his depiction of the politics of England was factually incorrect.
4. Grantham 2008, 3.
5. Vinogradoff 1924.
6. Vinogradoff 1924.
7. Danford 2000, 26–27.
8. World Justice Project 2020.
9. Bertram 2017.

10. Rousseau 1762.
11. Rawls 1996, 223.
12. Rawls 2001, 42.
13. Rawls, 1996; Freeman 2007, 46.
14. Wall 2006, 245.
15. Rawls 1996, 293.
16. Freeman 2007, 54.
17. Rawls 1996, 313.
18. Wall 2006.
19. Wall 2006, 257–258.
20. Freeman 2007, 76.
21. Brennan 2012b; Brennan 2016; Brennan and Jaworski 2016.
22. Crummett 2019.
23. Gaus 2010, 517.
24. Ibid.
25. Gilbert 2012, 13.
26. Griffin 2003, 120.
27. Estlund 2007, 37.
28. Christiano 2008.
29. Christiano 2008, 98.
30. Christiano 2008, 99.
31. Christiano 2008, 99.
32. Christiano 2008, 287.
33. Althaus 2003, 16; Delli Carpini and Keeter 1996, 135–177. E.g., less than 40 percent of all blacks can identify which political party was more conservative, but the majority of whites can. (Delli Carpini and Keeter 1996, 166.) On the 1988 survey, high-income older men get average scores that are nearly three times as high as the average score of low-income black women (Delli Carpini and Keeter 1996, 162). See also Delli Carpini and Keeter 1991; Neuman 1986; Palfrey and Poole 1987; Althaus 1998.
34. Estlund 2008.

Chapter 11

1. Tocqueville 1968, quotation taken from here: https://xroads.virginia.edu/ ~Hyper/DETOC/1_ch15.html.
2. Ibid.
3. Tocqueville 1968.
4. Tocqueville 1968.

5. Tocqueville 1968.

6. Amis 2003, 33.

7. Here, it's worth noting the contrast to Adam Smith and mainstream economics. Adam Smith's *Wealth of Nations* argued, based on rigorous data, that imperialism was bad for most citizens of the conquering countries. They paid more in taxes and other costs than they received in appropriated goods from the empire. For Smith, imperialism is explained by concentrated benefits and diffused costs. The benefits of empire are concentrated among the politically well-connected few, while the costs are spread among the many citizens. In fact, our best data indicates that Smith was right. (See, e.g., *Mammon and Empire*.) While Smith argued that imperialism led to economic loss, Lenin regarded imperialism as a source of riches. Similar remarks apply to slavery. Classical and neoclassical economists argued slavery was inefficient, but many Marxists today seem to think that slavery explains why the West, or at least the United States, became rich. So, to summarize, Smith and liberal economists believed imperialism and slavery are not only evil, but they don't *work*; Lenin thought they were evil but worked.

8. Lenin 1902.

9. Lenin 1902.

10. Reed 2009.

11. Bovard 1995, 1.

12. http://www.aei.org/publication/u-s-sugar-policy-cost-american-consum ers-almost-4-billion-last-year/.

13. Christiano 2006.

14. Delli-Carpini and Keeter 1996; Hill 2002; Somin 2013; Brennan and Hill 2014.

15. Rawls's official explanation for this seems to be that *inside* a country, everyone is a member of the same system of cooperation and coercion. But this fails as an argument for at least two reasons. One is that this simply begs the question. It takes closed-to-immigration nation-states for granted. Insofar as the web of cooperation tends to be tighter inside a nation-state than between them, this is *because* the existence of national borders and national governments makes it so. But Rawls is supposed to be asking about whether this institutional arrangement is just in the first place. Second, it's factually mistaken. In fact, nations coerce members of other nations (by restricting their entry and trade) and in fact the web of cooperation upon which each of us depends extends across many nations. If you're an American, your personal welfare depends greatly upon

production from people in other countries, and everything you own results partly from the input of foreigners.

16. Rawls and Van Parijs 2003.
17. Clemens 2011, 85.
18. Clemens, Montenegro, and Pritchett 2009.
19. Clemens, Montenegro, and Pritchett 2009.
20. Weyl 2018.
21. Calculations according to https://howrichami.givingwhatwecan.org/how-rich-am-i, which uses data from the World Bank and here: https://web.archive.org/web/20160518000924/https:/www.piie.com/sites/default/files/publications/wp/wp15-7.pdf.
22. See Van der Vossen and Brennan 2018 for a review and discussion.

Works Cited

Acemoglu, Daron, and James Robinson. 2012. *Why Nations Fail*. New York: Crown Business.

Achen, Christopher, and Larry Bartels. 2002. "Blind Retrospection: Electoral Responses to Draught, Flue, and Shark Attacks." Prepared for presentation at the annual meeting of the American Political Science Association, Boston.

Achen, Christopher, and Larry Bartels. 2016 *Democratic Theory for Realists*. Princeton, NJ: Princeton University Press.

Ackerman, Bruce, and James Fishkin. 2005. *Deliberation Day*. New Haven, CT: Yale University Press.

Althaus, Scott. 1998. "Information Effects in Collective Preferences." *American Political Science Review* 92: 545–558.

Althaus, Scott. 2003. *Collective Preferences in Democratic Politics*. New York: Cambridge University Press.

Amis, Martin. 2003. *Koba the Dread*. New York: Vintage International.

Arian, Asher, and Michal Schamir. 1983. "The Primarily Political Functions of the Left-Right Continuum." *Comparative Politics* 15: 139–158.

Aristotle. 340 BC. *Nicomachean Ethics*. http://www.perseus.tufts.edu/hopper/text?doc=Perseus:text:1999.01.0054.

Aristotle. 1996 [350 BC]. *The Politics and the Constitution of Athens*. 2nd ed. Translated by Stephen Everson. New York: Cambridge University Press.

Augustine. 1988 [426]. *The City of God against the Pagans*. Edited and translated by R. W. Dyson. Cambridge: Cambridge University Press.

Azpuru, Dinorah, and Michael Hall. 2017. "Yes, Our 'Flawed' Democracy Just Got Downgraded. Here's Why," *Washington Post*, February 23. https://www.washingtonpost.com/news/monkey-cage/wp/2017/02/23/yes-our-flawed-democracy-just-got-downgraded-heres-why/.

Ball, Terence. 2020. "James Mill." In *Stanford Encyclopedia of Philosophy*, edited by Edward N. Zalta. https://plato.stanford.edu/entries/james-mill/.

Barber, Michael, and Jeremy Pope. 2018. "Does Party Trump Ideology?" *American Political Science Review* 113: 38–54.

Barnes, Samuel H. 1971. "Left, Right, and the Italian Voter." *Comparative Political Studies* 4: 157–175.

Barnett, Zach. 2020. "Why You Should Vote to Change the Outcome." *Philosophy & Public Affairs* 48: 422–446.

Bartels, Larry. 1986. "Issue Voting under Uncertainty: An Empirical Test." *American Journal of Political Science* 30: 709–728.

Berlin, Isaiah. 1997. "Two Concepts of Liberty." In Isaiah Berlin, *The Proper Study of Mankind*, edited by Henry Hardy, Roger Hausheer, and Noel Annan, 191–242. New York: Farrar, Straus & Giroux.

Bertram, Christopher. 2017. "Jean-Jacques Rousseau." In *Stanford Encyclopedia of Philosophy*, edited by Edward N. Zalta. https://plato.stanford.edu/entries/rousseau/.

Bishop, Bill. 2014. *The Big Sort*. New York: Mariner.

Bormeo, Nancy. 2016. "On Democratic Backsliding." *Journal of Democracy* 27: 5–19.

Bovard, James. 1995. *Archer Daniels Midland: A Case Study in Corporate Welfare*. Policy Analysis 241. Washington, DC: Cato Institute.

Brennan, Geoffrey, and Loren Lomasky. 1993. *Democracy and Decision*. Cambridge: Cambridge University Press.

Brennan, Geoffrey, and Loren Lomasky. 2006. "Against Reviving Republicanism." *Politics, Philosophy, and Economics* 5: 221–252.

Brennan, Jason. 2011. "Condorcet's Jury Theorem and the Optimum Number of Voters." *Politics* 31: 55–62.

Brennan, Jason. 2012a. "For-Profit Business as Civic Virtue." *Journal of Business Ethics* 106: 313–324.

Brennan, Jason. 2012b. "Political Liberty: Who Needs It?" *Social Philosophy and Policy* 29: 1–27.

Brennan, Jason. 2016. *Against Democracy*. Princeton, NJ: Princeton University Press.

Brennan, Jason. 2018. "Democracy and Freedom." In *The Oxford Handbook of Freedom*, edited by David Schmidtz and Carmen Pavel, 335–349. New York: Oxford University Press.

Brennan, Jason. 2020. *Why It's OK to Want to Be Rich*. New York: Routledge Press.

Brennan, Jason, and Christopher Freiman. 2022. "Why Paternalists Must Endorse Epistocracy." *Journal of Ethics and Social Philosophy* 21. https://doi.org/10.26556/jesp.v21i3.926.

Brennan, Jason, and Lisa Hill. 2014. *Compulsory Voting: For and Against*. New York: Cambridge University Press.

Brennan, Jason, and Peter Jaworski. 2016. *Markets without Limits*. New York: Routledge Press.

Buchanan, James, and Gordon Tullock. 1962. *The Calculus of Consent*. Ann Arbor: University of Michigan Press.

Burke, Edmund. 1790. *Reflections on the Revolution in France*. https://socialsciences.mcmaster.ca/econ/ugcm/3ll3/burke/revfrance.pdf.

Campbell, Angus, Converse, Philip E., Miller, Warren E., and Donald E. Stokes. 1960. *The American Voter*. New York: John Wiley.

Caplan, Bryan. 2007. *The Myth of the Rational Voter*. Princeton, NJ: Princeton University Press.

Chong, Dennis. 2013. "Degrees of Rationality in Politics." In *The Oxford Handbook of Political Psychology*, edited by David O. Sears and Jack S. Levy, 96–129. New York: Oxford University Press.

Christiano, Thomas. 1990. "Freedom, Consensus, and Equality in Collective Decision-Making." *Ethics* 101: 151–181.

Christiano, Thomas. 2006. "Democracy." In *Stanford Encyclopedia of Philosophy*, edited by Edward N. Zalta. https://plato.stanford.edu/entries/democracy.

Christiano, Thomas. 2008. *The Constitution of Equality*. New York: Oxford University Press.

Citrin, Jack, and Green, Donald. 1990. "The Self-Interest Motive in American Public Opinion." *Research in Micropolitics* 3: 1–28.

Clemens, Michael. 2011. "Economics and Emigration: Trillion-Dollar Bills on the Sidewalk?" *Journal of Economic Perspectives* 23: 83–106.

Clemens, M. A., C. E. Montenegro, and L. Pritchett. 2009. *The Place Premium: Wage Differences for Identical Workers across the US Border*. The World Bank.

Cohen, Geoffrey. 2003. "Party over Policy: The Dominating Impact of Group Influence on Political Beliefs." *Journal of Personality and Social Psychology* 85: 808–822.

Cohen, Joshua. 2006. "Deliberation and Democratic Legitimacy." In *Contemporary Political Philosophy*, edited by Robert Goodin and Philip Pettit, 159–170. Boston: Wiley-Blackwell.

Cohen, Joshua. 2009. "Deliberation and Democratic Legitimacy." In *Democracy*, edited by David Estlund, 87–106. Malden, MA: Blackwell.

Collier, David, Fernando Daniel Hidalgo, and Andra Olivia Maciuceanu. 2006. "Essentially Contested Concepts." *Journal of Political Ideologies* 11: 211–246.

Constant, Benjamin. 1819. "The Liberty of the Ancients Compared with That of the Moderns." https://oll.libertyfund.org/title/constant-the-liberty-of-ancients-compared-with-that-of-moderns-1819#preview.

Constant, Benjamin. 1988. "The Liberty of the Ancients Compared with That of the Moderns." In *Constant: Political Writings*, edited by Biancamaria Fontana, 309–328. New York: Cambridge University Press.

Converse, Philip. 1964. "The Nature of Belief Systems in Mass Publics." In *Ideology and Discontent*, edited by D. E. Apter, 206–261. London: Free Press of Glencoe.

Converse, Philip. 1990. "Popular Representation and the Distribution of Information." In *Information and Democratic Processes*, edited by John A. Ferejohn and James H. Kuklinski, 369–388. Urbana: University of Illinois Press.

Converse, Philip, and Pierce, Richard. 1986. *Political Representation in France.* Cambridge MA: Harvard University Press.

Crummett, Dustin. 2019. "Expression and Indication in Ethics and Political Philosophy." *Res Publica* 25: 387–406.

Curato, Nicole, Dryzek, John S., Ercan, Selen A., Hendriks, Carolyn M., and Simon Niemeyer. 2017. "Twelve Key Findings in Deliberative Democracy Research." *Daedalus* 146: 28–38.

Danford, John W. 2000. *Roots of Freedom.* Wilmington, DE: ISI Press.

Davis, Lance E., and Robert A. Huttenback. 1986. *Mammon and Empire.* New York: Cambridge University Press.

Delli Carpini, Michael X., and Scott Keeter. 1991. "Stability and Change in the U.S. Public's Knowledge of Politics." *Public Opinion Quarterly* 55 (1991): 583–612.

Delli Carpini, Michael X. and Scott Keeter. 1996. *What Americans Know about Politics and Why It Matters.* New Haven, CT: Yale University Press.

Downs, Anthony. 1957. *An Economic Theory of Democracy.* New York: Harper.

Dryzek, John. 2016. "Can There Be a Right to an Essential Contested Concept? The Case of Democracy." *Journal of Politics* 78: 357–367.

Dryzek, J. S., A. Bächtiger, S. Chambers, J. Cohen, J. N. Druckman, A. Felicetti, J. S. Fishkin, D. M. Farrell, A. Fung, A. Gutmann, and H. Landemore. 2019. "The Crisis of Democracy and the Science of Deliberation." *Science* 363: 1144–1146.

Economist Intelligence Unit. 2020. "Democracy Index 2020: In Sickness and in Health." https://www.eiu.com/n/campaigns/democracy-index-2020.

Edlin, Aaron, Andrew Gelman, and Noah Kaplan. 2007. "Voting as a Rational choice: Why and How People Vote to Improve the Well-Being of Others." *Rationality and Society* 19: 293–314.

Edlin, Aaron, Andrew Gelman, and Noah Kaplan. 2008. "Vote for Charity's Sake." *The Economists' Voice* 5.

Elster, Jon. 1997. "The Market and the Forum." In *Deliberative Democracy*, edited by James Bohman and William Rehg, 3–34. Cambridge, MA: MIT Press.

Estlund, David. 2008. *Democratic Authority.* Princeton, NJ: Princeton University Press.

Faber, Henry S., and Joanna Gowa. 1997. "Common Interests or Common Polities? Reinterpreting the Democratic Peace." *Journal of Politics* 59: 393–417.

Feddersen, Timothy, Sean Gailmard, and Alvaro Sandroni. 2009. "A Bias toward Unselfishness in Large Elections: Theory and Experimental Evidence." *American Political Science Review* 103: 175–192.

Ferguson, Adam. 1782. *An Essay on the History of Civil Society.* London: T. Cadell. https://oll.libertyfund.org/title/ferguson-an-essay-on-the-history-of-civil-society.

Fine, Ben, and Laurence Harris. 1979. *Rereading Capital.* New York: Macmillan.

Fishkin, James. 1993. *Democracy and Deliberation*. New Haven, CT: Yale University Press.

Freeman, Samuel. 2007. *Rawls*. New York: Routledge Press.

Gallie, W. B. 1956. "Essentially Contested Concepts." *Proceedings of the Aristotelian Society* 56: 167–198.

Gamm, Gerald H. 1989. *The Making of New Deal Democrats: Voting Behavior and Realignment in Boston, 1920–1940*. Chicago: University of Chicago Press.

Gartzke, Erik. 1998. "Kant We All Just Get Along?" *American Journal of Political Science* 42: 1–27.

Gaus, Gerald. 2003. *Contemporary Theories of Liberalism*. Thousand Oaks, CA: Sage.

Gaus, Gerald. 2010. *The Order of Public Reason*. New York: Oxford University Press.

Gelman, A., N. Silver, and A. Edlin. 2012. "What Is the Probability Your Vote Will Make a Difference?" *Economic Inquiry* 50: 321–326.

Gilbert, F. 1965. *Machiavelli and Guicciardini*. Princeton, NJ: Princeton University Press.

Gilbert, Pablo. 2012. "Is There a Human Right to Democracy? A Response to Cohen." *Revista latinoamericana de filosofía política* 1: 1–37.

Goren, Paul. 2005. "Party Identification and Core Political Values." *American Journal of Political Science* 49: 882–897.

Grantham, George. 2008. "The Prehistoric Origins of European Economic Integration." Montreal: Departmental Working Papers, McGill Economics Department.

Gray, John. 1977. "On the Contestability of Social and Political Concepts." *Political Theory* 5: 331–349.

Greene, Steven. 1999. "Understanding Party Identification: A Social Identity Approach." *Political Psychology* 20: 393–403.

Griffin, Christopher. 2003. "Democracy as a Non-Instrumentally Just Procedure." *Journal of Political Philosophy* 11: 111–121.

Gutmann, Amy, and Dennis Thompson. 1996. *Democracy and Disagreement*. Cambridge: Cambridge University Press.

Habermas, Jürgen. 2001. *Moral Consciousness and Communicative Action*. Cambridge, MA: MIT Press.

Haidt, Jonathan. 2010. "The New Science of Morality." *Edge*. http://www.edge.org/3rd_culture/morality10/morality.haidt.html.

Haidt, Jonathan. 2012. *The Righteous Mind*. New York: Pantheon.

Hardin, Russell. 2009. *How Do You Know?: The Economics of Ordinary Knowledge*. Princeton, NJ: Princeton University Press.

Harris, Ian. 2020. "Edmund Burke." In *Stanford Encyclopedia of Philosophy*, edited by Edward N. Zalta. https://plato.stanford.edu/entries/burke/.

Held, David. 2006. *Models of Democracy*. Stanford, CA: Stanford University Press.

Higgs, Robert. 1987. *Crisis and Leviathan*. New York: Oxford University Press.

Hill, Lisa. 2002. "On the Reasonableness of Compelling Citizens to 'Vote': The Australian Case." *Political Studies* 50: 80–101.

Hobbes, Thomas. 1845. *The English Works of Thomas Hobbes*. Edited by William Molesworth. http://onlinebooks.library.upenn.edu/webbin/metab ook?id=hobbesworks.

Hobbes, Thomas. 1994 [1688]. *Leviathan*. Edited by Edward Curly. Indianapolis: Hackett.

Holmes, Stephen. 1995. "Tocqueville and Democracy." In *The Idea of Democracy*, edited by David Copp, Jean Hampton, and John Roemer, 33–34. New York: Cambridge University Press.

Huddy, Leonie, David Sears, and Jack S. Levy. 2013. "Introduction." In *The Oxford Handbook of Political Psychology*, edited by Leonie Huddy, David Sears, and Jack S. Levy, 1–21. 2nd ed. New York: Oxford University Press.

Hume, David. 1752. "Of the Original Contract." https://teachingamericanhist ory.org/document/of-the-original-contract/.

Hume, David. 2000 [1740]. *A Treatise on Human Nature: An Attempt to Introduce the Experimental Method of Reasoning into Moral Subjects*. Edited by David Norton and Mary Norton. New York: Oxford University Press.

Hursthouse, Rosalind. 1999. *On Virtue Ethics*. New York: Oxford University Press.

Hursthouse, Rosalind. 2016. "Virtue Ethics." In *Stanford Encyclopedia of Philosophy*, edited by Edward N. Zalta. https://plato.stanford.edu/entries/ ethics-virtue/.

Inglehart, Ronald, and Hans Klingemann. 1976. "Party Identification, Ideological Preference, and the Left-Right Dimension among Western Mass Publics." In *Party Identification and Beyond*, edited by Ian Budge, Ivor Crewe, and Dennis Fairlie, 599–621. London: Wiley.

Iyengar, Shanto, Guarav Sood, and Yphtach Lelkes. 2012. "Affect, Not Ideology: A Social Identity Perspective on Polarization." *Public Opinion Quarterly* 76: 405–431.

Iyengar, Shanto, and Sean J. Westwood. 2015. "Fear and Loathing across Party Lines: New Evidence on Group Polarization." *American Journal of Political Science* 59: 690–707.

Jardina, Ashley. 2019. *White Identity Politics*. New York: Cambridge University Press.

Kahan, Dan. 2016. "The Politically Motivated Reasoning Paradigm, Part 1: What Political Motivated Reasoning Is and How to Measure It." In *Emerging Trends in the Social and Behavioral Sciences: An Interdisciplinary, Searchable, and Linkable Resource*. https://onlinelibrary.wiley.com/doi/abs/10.1002/ 9781118900772.etrds0417.

Kahan, Dan, Ellen Peters, Erica Cantrell Dawson, and Paul Slovic. 2013. "Motivated Numeracy and Enlightened Self-Government." *Behavioral Public Policy* 1: 54–86.

Kant, Immanuel. 1795. "Perpetual Peace: A Philosophical Sketch." https://www.mtholyoke.edu/acad/intrel/kant/kant1.htm.

Kaplan, Ethan, J. Spenkuch, and Rebecca Sullivan. 2020. *Partisan Spatial Sorting in the United States: A Theoretical and Empirical Overview.* Working Paper, University of Maryland. http://econweb.umd.edu/~kaplan/big_sort_APSA.pdf.

Kavka, Gregory. 1995. "Why Even Morally Perfect People Would Need Government." *Social Philosophy and Policy* 12: 1–18.

Kinder, Donald, and Nathan Kalmoe. 2017. *Neither Liberal nor Conservative: Ideological Innocence in the American Public.* Chicago: University of Chicago Press.

Kinsella, David. 2005. "No Rest for the Democratic Peace." *American Political Science Review* 99: 453–457.

Kling, Arnold. 2017. *The Three Languages of Politics.* Washington, DC: Cato Institute.

Landemore, Hélène. 2012. *Democratic Reason.* Princeton, NJ: Princeton University Press.

Landemore, Hélène. 2020. *Open Democracy.* Princeton, NJ: Princeton University Press.

Layne, Christopher. 1994. "Kant or Cant: The Myth of the Democratic Peace." *International Security* 19: 5–49.

Leiter, Brian. 2014. *Nietzsche on Morality.* New York: Routledge.

Leiter, Brian. 2020. "Nietzsche." In *Stanford Encyclopedia of Philosophy,* edited by Edward N. Zalta. https://plato.stanford.edu/entries/nietzsche-moral-political/.

Lenin, Vladimir. 1902. *What Is to Be Done?* https://www.marxists.org/archive/lenin/works/1901/.

Lenz, Gabriel S. 2009. "Learning and Opinion Change, Not Priming: Reconsidering the Priming Hypothesis." *American Journal of Political Science* 53: 821–837.

Lenz, Gabriel S. 2012. *Follow the Leader? How Voters Respond to Politician's Policies and Performance.* Chicago: University of Chicago Press.

Lenz, Gabriel, and Chappell Lawson. 2008. "Looking the Part: Television Leads Less Informed Citizens to Vote Based on Candidates' Appearance." Unpublished manuscript, Department of Political Science, Massachusetts Institute of Technology, Cambridge, MA.

Lewis-Beck, Michael, William Jacoby, Helmut Norpoth, and Herbert Weisberg. 2008. *The American Voter Revisited.* Ann Arbor: University of Michigan Press.

Lodge, Milton, and Charles Taber. 2013. *The Rationalizing Voter*. New York: Cambridge University Press.

Lopez-Guerra, Claudio. 2014. *Democracy and Disenfranchisement*. Oxford: Oxford University Press.

Lord, Charles, Lee Ross, and Mark R. Lepper. 1979. "Biased Assimilation and Attitude Polarization: The Effects of Prior Theories on Subsequently Considered Evidence." *Journal of Personality and Social Psychology* 37: 2098–2109.

Lovett, Frank. 2022. "Republicanism." In *Stanford Encyclopedia of Philosophy*, edited by Edward N. Zalta. https://plato.stanford.edu/entries/republicanism/.

Machiavelli, Niccolò. 1531. *Discourses on the First Decade of Titus Livius*. https://www.gutenberg.org/files/10827/10827-h/10827-h.htm.

Madison, James. 1787a. "Federalist Paper 10." https://guides.loc.gov/federalist-papers/text-1-10.

Madison, James. 1787b. "Federalist Paper 14." https://avalon.law.yale.edu/18th_century/fed14.asp.

Madison, James. 1788. "Federalist Paper 51." https://avalon.law.yale.edu/18th_century/fed51.asp.

Manin, Bernard, Elly Stein, and Jane Mansbridge. 1987. "On Legitimacy and Political Deliberation." *Political Theory* 15: 333–368.

Markus, Gregory. "The Impact of Personal and National Economic Conditions on the Presidential Vote: A Pooled Cross-Sectional Analysis." *American Journal of Political Science* 32 (1988): 137–154.

Marsilius of Padua. 1980 [1324]. *Defensor Pacis*. Translated and edited by Alan Gewirth. Toronto: University of Toronto Press.

Marx, Karl, and Friedrich Engels. 1848. "Manifesto of the Communist Party." https://www.marxists.org/archive/marx/works/1848/communist-manifesto/ch01.htm.

Mason, Lilliana. 2017. *Uncivil Agreement: How Politics Became Our Identity*. Chicago: University of Chicago Press.

Mason, Lilliana. 2018. "Ideologues without Issues: The Polarizing Consequences of Ideological Identities." *Public Opinion Quarterly* 82: 280–301.

Mason, Lilliana, and Julia Wronski. 2018. "One Tribe to Bind Them All." *Political Psychology* 39: 257–277.

Mattingly, Garrett. 1958. "The Prince: Political Science or Political Satire?" *American Scholar* 27: 482–491.

McCann, James A. 1997. "Electoral Choices and Core Value Change: The 1992 Presidential Campaign." *American Journal of Political Science* 41: 564–583.

McCarty, Nolan. 2019. *Polarization: What Everyone Needs to Know*. New York: Oxford University Press.

Mechkova, Valeriya, Anna Lührmann, and Staffan I. Lindberg. 2017. "How Much Democratic Backsliding?" *Journal of Democracy* 28: 162–169.

Mill, John Stuart. 1861. *Considerations on Representative Government*. https://socialsciences.mcmaster.ca/econ/ugcm/3ll3/mill/repgovt.pdf.

Miller, Dale. 1999. "The Norm of Self-Interest." *American Psychologist* 54: 1053–1060.

Miller, Paul. 2021. "Augustinian Liberalism." In *Augustine in a Time of Crisis: Politics and Religion Contested*, edited by Boleslaw Kabala, Ashleen Menchaca-Bagnulo, and Nathan Pinkoski, 167–186. New York: Palgrave Macmillan.

Moaz, Zeev. 1998. "Realist and Cultural Critiques of the Democratic Peace." *International Interactions* 24: 3–89.

Muddle, Case. 2007. "The Single-Issue Party Thesis: Extreme Right Parties and the Immigration Issue." *West European Politics* 22: 182–197.

Mutz, Diana. 2006. *Hearing the Other Side*. Cambridge: Cambridge University Press.

Mutz, Diana. 2008. "Is Deliberative Democracy a Falsifiable Theory?" *Annual Review of Political Science* 11: 521–538.

Mutz, Diana, and Jeffrey Mondak. 1997. "Dimensions of Sociotropic Behavior: Group-Based Judgments of Fairness and Well-Being." *American Journal of Political Science* 41: 284–308.

Neuman, W. Russell. 1986. *The Paradox of Mass Politics*. Cambridge, MA: Harvard University Press.

Nietzsche, Friedrich. 1886. *Beyond Good and Evil*. https://www.gutenberg.org/files/4363/4363-h/4363-h.htm.

Nietzsche, Friedrich. 1895. *Twilight of the Idols*. https://www.handprint.com/SC/NIE/GotDamer.html.

Nozick, Robert. 1974. *Anarchy, State, and Utopia*. New York: Basic Books.

Nozick, Robert. 1981. *Philosophical Explorations*. Cambridge, MA: Harvard University Press.

Nyhan, Brendan, and Jason Reifler. 2010. "When Corrections Fail: The Persistence of Political Misperceptions." *Political Behavior* 32: 303–330.

Ober, Josiah. 2009. *Democracy and Knowledge: Innovation and Learning in Classical Athens*. Princeton, NJ: Princeton University Press.

Oneal, John, and Bruce Russett. 1999. "Assessing the Liberal Peace with Alternative Specifications: Trade Still Reduces Conflict." *Journal of Peace Research* 36: 423–442.

Owen, David. 2002. "Equality, Democracy, and Self-Respect: Reflections on Nietzsche's Agonal Perfectionism." *Journal of Nietzsche Studies* 24: 113–131.

Palfrey, Thomas, and Keith Poole. 1987. "The Relationship between Information, Ideology, and Voting Behavior." *American Journal of Political Science* 31: 510–530.

Page, Scott, and Lu Hong. 2001. "Problem Solving by Heterogeneous Agents." *Journal of Economic Theory* 97: 123–163.

Pettit, Philip. 1996. "Freedom as Antipower." *Ethics* 106: 576–604.

Pettit, Philip. 2012. *On the People's Terms*. New York: Cambridge University Press.

Plato. 375 BC. *The Republic*. http://www.perseus.tufts.edu/hopper/text?doc= Perseus%3Atext%3A1999.01.0168%3Abook%3D8.

Ponza, Michael, Greg Duncan, Mary Corcoran, and Fred Groskind. 1988. "'The Guns of Autumn? Age Differences in Support for Income Transfers to the Young and Old." *Public Opinion Quarterly* 52: 441–466.

Pugh, Michael. 2005. "The Political Economy of Peacebuilding." *International Journal of Peace Studies* 10: 23–42.

Raaflaub, Kurt. 2004. *The Discovery of Freedom in Ancient Greece*. Chicago: University of Chicago Press.

Rawls, John. 1971. *A Theory of Justice*. Cambridge, MA: Harvard University Press.

Rawls, John. 1996. *Political Liberalism*. New York: Columbia University Press.

Rawls, John. 2001. *Justice as Fairness: A Restatement*. Cambridge, MA: Harvard University Press.

Rawls, John, and Philippe Van Parijs. 2003. "Three Letters on the Law of Peoples and the European Union." *Revue de philosophie économique* 7: 7–20.

Ray, James Less. 2003. "A Lakatosian View of the Democratic Peace Research Program." In *Progress in International Relations Theory: Assessing the Field*, edited by Colin Elman and Miriam Elman, 205–243. Cambridge, MA: MIT Press.

Reed, Adolphe, Jr. 2009. *Left Business Observer* 121. https://www.leftbusinesso bserver.com/Antiracism.html.

Rhodebeck, Laurie. 1993. "The Politics of Greed? Political Preferences among the Elderly." *Journal of Politics* 55: 342–364.

Rousseau, Jean Jacques. 1754. *Discourse on the Origins of Inequality*. https://www.marxists.org/reference/subject/economics/rousseau/inequality/ch02.htm.

Rousseau, Jean Jacques. 1762. *The Social Contract*. https://sourcebooks.ford ham.edu/mod/rousseau-contract2.asp.

Rummel, R. J. 1997. *Power Kills*. New Brunswick, NJ: Transaction Publishers.

Schelling, Thomas. 1971. "Dynamic Models of Segregation." *Journal of Mathematical Sociology* 1: 143–186.

Schmidtz, David, and Jason Brennan. 2010. *A Brief History of Liberty*. Oxford: Wiley-Blackwell.

Schmitt, Carl. 1986. *Political Theology*. Cambridge, MA: MIT Press.

Sears, David O., and Carolyn L. Funk. 1990. "Self-Interest in Americans' Political Opinions." In *Beyond Self-Interest*, edited by Jane Mansbridge, 147–170. Chicago: University of Chicago Press.

Sears, David, Carl Hensler, and Leslie Speer. 1979. "Whites' Opposition to 'Busing': Self-Interest or Symbolic Politics?" *American Political Science Review* 73: 369–384.

Sears, David, and Richard Lau. 1983. "Inducing Apparently Self-Interested Political Preferences." *American Journal of Political Science* 27: 223–252.

Sears, David, Richard Lau, Tom Tyler, and Harris Allen. 1980. "Self-Interest vs. Symbolic Politics in Policy Attitudes and Presidential Voting." *American Political Science Review* 74: 670–684.

Simler, Kevin, and Robin Hanson. 2018. *The Elephant in the Brain*. New York: Oxford University Press.

Singer, Peter. 1975. *Animal Liberation*. New York: HarperCollins.

Skinner, Quentin. 1981. *Machiavelli*. New York: Oxford University Press.

Skinner, Quentin. 2000. *Machiavelli: A Very Short Introduction*. New York: Oxford University Press.

Somin, Ilya. 2009. "Review of *Democracy and Knowledge*." *Ethics* 119: 585–590.

Somin, Ilya. 2013. *Democracy and Political Ignorance*. Stanford, CA: Stanford University Press.

Spinoza, Benedict. 1891a [1670]. *Tractatus-Theologico-Politicus*. Edited by R. H. M. Elwes. https://oll.libertyfund.org/title/elwes-the-chief-works-of-benedict-de-spinoza-vol-1.

Spinoza, Benedict. 1891b [1677]. *Ethics*. http://www.gutenberg.org/files/3800/3800-h/3800-h.htm.

Spooner, Lysander. 1870. "No Treason: The Constitution of No Authority." https://oll.libertyfund.org/title/spooner-no-treason-no-vi-the-constitution-of-no-authority-1870.

Taber, Charles, and Milton R. Lodge. 2006. "Motivated Skepticism in the Evaluation of Political Beliefs." *American Journal of Political Science* 50: 755–769.

Taber, Charles, and Everett Young. 2013. "Political Information Processing." In *The Oxford Handbook of Political Psychology*, edited by Leonie Huddy, David Sears, and Jack S. Levy, 525–558. 2nd ed. New York: Oxford University Press.

Tajfel, Henry. 1981. *Human Groups and Social Categories*. New York: Cambridge University Press.

Tajfel, Henry. 1982. "Social Psychology of Intergroup Relations." *Annual Review of Psychology* 33: 1–39.

Tajfel, Henry, and J. C. Turner. 1979. "An Integrative Theory of Intergroup Conflict." In *The Social Psychology of Intergroup Relations*, edited by W. G. Austin and S. Worchel, 94–109. Monterey, CA: Brooks-Cole.

Talisse, Robert. 2021. *Sustaining Democracy*. New York: Oxford University Press.

Thaler, Richard, and Cass Sunstein. 2021. *Nudge (The Final Edition)*. New York: Penguin Books.

Thompson, Abigail. 2014. "Does Diversity Trump Ability?" *Notices of the AMS* 69: 1024–1103.

Tocqueville, Alexis de. 1968 [1835]. *Democracy in America.* 2 Vols. London: Fontana.

Vallier, Kevin. 2017. "Three Concepts of Political Stability." *Social Philosophy and Policy* 34: 232–259.

van der Vossen, Bas, and Jason Brennan. 2018. *In Defense of Openness.* New York: Oxford University Press.

Vinogradoff, Paul. 1924. "Feudalism." Originally published in *Cambridge Medieval History*, 3:458–484. http://socserv.mcmaster.ca/econ/ugcm/3ll3/vinogradoff/feudal.

Wall, Steven. 2006. "Rawls and the Status of Political Liberty." *Pacific Philosophical Quarterly* 87: 245–269.

Wall, Steven. 2017. "Perfectionism in Moral and Political Philosophy." In *Stanford Encyclopedia of Philosophy*, edited by Edward N. Zalta. https://plato.stanford.edu/entries/perfectionism-moral/.

Weart, Spencer. 1998. *Never at War: Why Democracies Will Not Fight Each Other.* New Haven, CT: Yale University Press.

Weiner, Greg. 2012. *Madison's Metronome.* Lawrence: University Press of Kansas.

Westen, Drew, Pavel S. Blagov, Keith Harenski, Clint Kilts, and Stephan Hamann. 2006. "The Neural Basis of Motivated Reasoning: An fMRI Study of Emotional Constraints on Political Judgment during the U.S. Presidential Election of 2004." *Journal of Cognitive Neuroscience* 18: 1947–1958.

Weyl, E. Glen. 2018. "The Openness-Equality Trade-off in Global Redistribution." *Economic Journal* 128: F1–F36.

World Justice Project. 2020. *WJP Rule of Law Index.* https://worldjusticeproject.org/rule-of-law-index/factors/2020/Constraints%20on%20Government%20Powers/.

Zaller, John. 1992. *The Nature and Origins of Mass Opinion.* New York: Cambridge University Press.

Zechmeister, Elizabeth. 2006. "What's Left and Who's Right? A Q-method Study of Individual and Contextual Influences on the Meaning of Ideological Labels." *Political Behavior* 28: 151–173.

Index